DATE	ISSUED TO
MAR 2 3 1999	

© DEMCO 32-2125

Medicine Women

Also by

CATHY LUCHETTI

Women of the West
(with Carol Olwell)

Home on the Range
A Culinary History of the American West

Under God's Spell
Frontier Evangelists, 1772–1915

"I Do!"
Courtship, Love and Marriage on the American Frontier

Medicine Women

The Story of
Early-American Women Doctors

CATHY LUCHETTI

Crown Publishers, Inc./NEW YORK

Published by Crown Publishers, Inc., 201 East 50th Street, New York, New York 10022.
Member of the Crown Publishing Group.

Random House, Inc. New York, Toronto, London, Sydney, Auckland
www.randomhouse.com

Crown is a trademark of Crown Publishers, Inc.

Printed in the United States of America

DESIGN BY LYNNE AMFT

Library of Congress Cataloging-in-Publication Data
Luchetti, Cathy
Medicine women : the story of early-American women doctors / by
Cathy Luchetti. — 1st ed.
1. Women in medicine—United States—History.
2. Women physicians—United States—History. I. Title.
R692.L83   1998
610'.82'0973—dc21   97-53120
CIP

ISBN 0-517-59848-5

10 9 8 7 6 5 4 3 2 1

First Edition

To my parents, Coralee and Myles,

and to Peter

Acknowledgments

Goodness, I hope if heaven is crowded,
that all the rest of humanity will be cast out to make
room for the doctors.

— AGNES REID, 1874

HIS BOOK WAS WRITTEN AS A CHRONICLE OF THE CHALLENGES FACED BY women who served in the field of medicine from 1849 until the middle years of the twentieth century, mostly in rural parts of the United States. The unfolding of their stories provides personal accounts not only of care and skill and professional success, but also of the terrible obstacles and deep personal sacrifice demanded of most—of their unsung dedication to the art of healing, their thirst for knowledge, and, in the case of many, their burning dedication to the advancement of women's rights.

Written less as a scholarly treatise than a gathering of individual stories, this comment on the primary accounts of women practitioners describes the development of medicine and of women's role in it, and captures the essence of the everyday in nineteenth-century life.

These stories exist today thanks to the efforts of historians, archivists, and recordkeepers of this important past. Accounts included in this book result from the archival and research efforts of many. My thanks to Ellie Arguimbau, archivist of the Montana Historical Society, for pursuing information about Dr. Mary Babcock Moore; Elizabeth Jacox, of the Idaho State Historical Society, for a very helpful database search and for additional information on women physicians in Idaho; Barbara Papik, of the Lommen Health Sciences Library of the University of South Dakota, who provided helpful materials about Dr. Jenny Murphy of Yankton, in collaboration with the Yankton Public Library and the South Dakota State Historical Society; and the cooperative staff of the Archives and Special Collections on Women in Medicine at the Hahnemann University School of Medicine in Philadelphia.

Photographs were helpfully provided by many. Thanks to Lisa Backman, of the Western History Room in Denver; Kathryn M. Totten, of the University of Nevada; Tom Shelton, of the Institute of Texan Cultures; Rebecca Lintaz, Assistant Director of the Colorado Historical Society; Cynthia Monro, of the Nebraska State Historical Society; Richard Engman, of the University of Washington Libraries; the late Katherine Wyatt, of the Nebraska State Historical Society; and particularly to the Minnesota Historical Society, for its outstanding research efforts and ability to find just the right photograph. And I appreciate the efforts of Dr. William M. Straight of Miami, Florida, for his help in obtaining photographs and information about Dr. Anna Darrow and for sending a copy of his article on Sister Darrow.

Initial research by Erin Williams provided an organized and thorough groundwork for this book; special thanks also to Jacki Whitford for providing an amazing supply of books, articles, and papers of great interest and use, including a timeline of American women in medicine. My appreciation to Sheila Cogan and Judy Edelhoff of the National Archives for facilitating research time in Washington and for their hospitality. Special thanks to my original Crown editor, Peter Ginna.

Contents

❧❧❧

PART FIVE

TOOLS OF THE TRADE

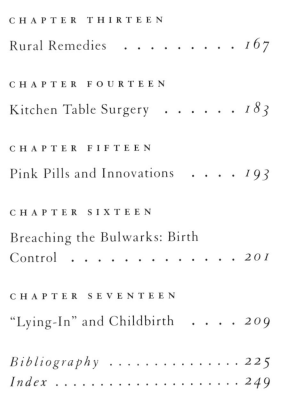

Medicine Women

Utah midwifery class.

LDS Archives

Introduction

✎✎✎✎

All interest in disease and death is only another
expression of interest in life.

— THOMAS MANN

HE STORY OF WOMEN IN MEDICINE BEGINS WITH THEIR POWERFUL ascendancy as healers and midwives in the early years of the American colonies. Gradually, however, they were eclipsed by men, whose entrance into the medical ranks brought new standards of exclusionary professionalism. All-male medical schools, state medical boards, and licensing forced healing women into the categories of midwife or nurse, far from a position of community respect.

Women retaliated by forming their own colleges, studying independently, and eventually forcing their way into competition in regular medical institutions—a story of high drama. Their "encroachment" into a field that had once been theirs is nothing short of miraculous, and is told poignantly in the writings of many female medical pioneers, including Elizabeth Blackwell and Harriot Hunt. The circuitous path from midwifery to medical training and then back, in many cases, to the handling of "women's issues" adds an ironic dimension to years of female accomplishment. Yet without this window provided by obstetrics and gynecology, many women

Caterina Flores
de Guerrero,
midwife in the
San Jose Mission
area from 1875
until her death
in 1940.

*University of
Texas, Institute
of Texan
Cultures, San
Antonio,
courtesy of Julian
C. Mungia*

would have been denied careers in medicine.

Women doctors had a twin burden of prejudice to overcome: first, society's Victorian grudge against any woman who wished to snap the bonds of domesticity and become *any* kind of professional, and then the basic distrust by rural populations of professionalism in general and medicine specifically.

The idea of medicine as a dominant, scientific enterprise reigns almost sacred in Western society. Yet on the frontier, women doctors not only had to find their place in medicine, but they had to help find a place *for* medicine. In the unsettled West, where Jacksonian ideals of rugged individualism were firmly embraced, professional skills inspired little reverence, and the hierarchical doctor-patient relationship could not be assumed unless the physician had achieved, through heroic action, a reputation for trustworthiness. Pioneers were as likely to self-diagnose as self-medicate, and to do so with a particular kind of jaunty satisfaction. Why go to a professional, *and pay,* when coal tar oil might work just as well?

Women physicians also had to contend with one of the Victorian world's most pervasive phenomenons—the infantilization of women by the medical profession. Not only were women judged incapable of wielding a surgical knife, but they were seen as prone to a litany of "female complaints," including the vapors, fainting fits, the change of life, ennui, or simple madness. In a Victorian society that prescribed clitoridectomies for excess passion and magnetic girdles for excess poundage, how could women physicians respond?

They had to win the confidence of their female patients before launching into feminist encouragement, advocating fresh air, exercise, and uncorseted clothing. The relationship between physician and patient could hover between female competition or one of feminine support.

Understanding the stories of these medical pioneers—their motivations, the hardships they faced, their emotional losses, their conflicts, and their loves—assigns a human face to otherwise dry statistics. Too often history is made into a lifeless procession of facts marching off toward a sweeping generality. Instead, these pioneer medicine women deserve to be known through the medium of their own lives. How did they get through school and set up offices? What inspired them? What were their sacrifices? More important than events is an understanding of the thoughts that caused the events. When people of the past speak for themselves, we can glimpse our history in a way that respects its participants, a way that is relevant to them, that affords them dignity.

Intent is the key to historical significance. And the intent of the early female American doctor comes to life through her writings—books, treatises, medical reports, journal entries, and magazine articles, some of which have been incorporated into the text of this book. Knowing *why* she chose medicine, *how* she went about achieving a degree, and *who* she had to become during the process are the building blocks of understanding—keys to the heart of the rural frontier doctor.

> *For history, the object to be discovered is not the mere event, but the thought expressed in it.*
>
> R. G. COLLINGWOOD

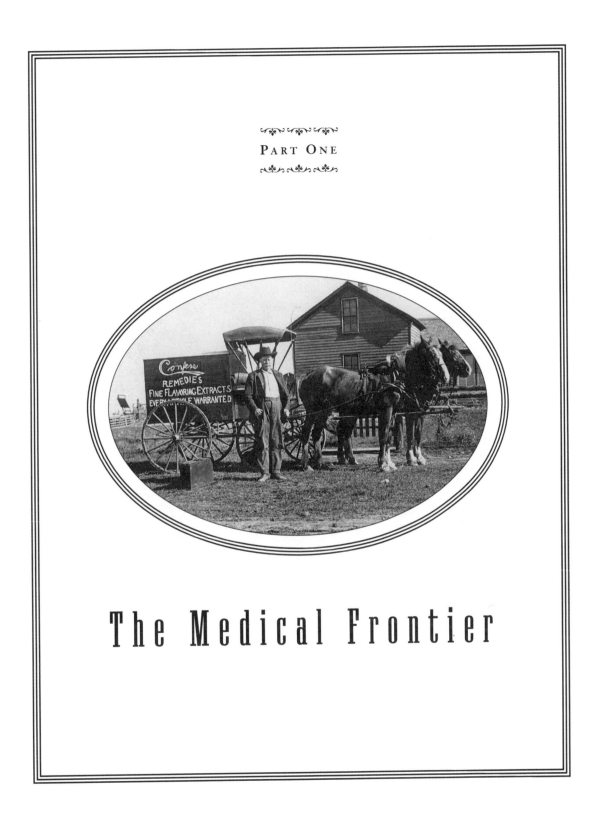

PART ONE

The Medical Frontier

Visiting an Indian reservation.

National Library of Medicine

Frontier Medicine

From Midwives to M.D.'s

Women physicians represent not only a profession,

but a cause.

—DR. HENRY HARTSHORNE

N THE FLUX AND FOLLY OF AMERICA'S FRONTIER YEARS, MEDICAL FORtunes rose and fell, bringing a motley assortment of healers, charlatans, midwives, and doctors into sudden vogue or quick obscurity. Loosed from precedent, free to scramble through the twists and turns of nineteenth-century society, medicine was a rambunctious and unpredictable arena where the unschooled were healed by the unlicensed; where "granny" women dispensed medicine and preached health homilies as they removed arrowheads, deftly spun about breech babies *in utero,* and dosed ailing women for "female complaints"; where doctors were sometimes more interested in finding their fortunes amid the opportunities of the frontier than in healing and helping.

The nineteenth century at its beginning was awash in "irregulars," or quacks. Any man who worked with his hands and carried tools in a leather bag could set up a practice, dispensing pills and potions, binding bones, and profiting from the sales of homemade nostrums. Not unusual was the case of Old Doc Gillespie of Oelrichs, South Dakota, who, "besides being something of a quack doctor, started an evening singing school, open to the public," according to a resident of the town. When pressed for a diagnosis, these rough-hewn practitioners might compare the digestive system to a stovepipe, to be cleaned out frequently with harsh purgatives. It was the heyday of empirics, bonesetters, herbalists, folk practitioners, and advocates of galvanism, not to mention the legions of phrenologists who predicted character by head size and shape and designed bizarre, restrictive headgear to correct vagaries of skull design. Doctors doubled as dentists, while nannies, female assistants, and even wet nurses were viewed as fringe practitioners. On the frontier, doctors were plentiful and veterinarians scarce, and even the best-trained physician, male or female, often had to prove his or her skills by healing horses first and people next, depending upon how the horse did.

⁓

According to one survey, between 1790 and 1840 only 27 percent of the practicing male physicians in the country had graduated from a medical college. Yet despite such scant training, few had any compunction about operating. Surgery was seen as the realm of any person with a steady hand and unclouded mind, a feat capable of performance by "any man, unless . . . an idiot or an absolute fool"— at least to the mind of A. G. Goodlett, the author of the 1838 volume *Family Physician.*

Medical shingles were hung based on the barest qualifications—that the practitioners were white and male seemed recommendation enough. Although, according to German traveler Gottfried Duden, "the inhabitants of all the states are capable enough of recognizing within a short time the great difference when a man has been trained," medicine welcomed anyone who could dress a wound and figure out how to take a pulse. As Duden noted:

A man will soon establish himself in places where the population is not too spars, and no quack can compete with him. As I have already said in detail, Where there is no competent doctor, people try to help themselves as well as is possible. If one trusts a quack, a midwife, or some other person in the neighborhood more than himself, he consults this person in times of trouble. Often the advice received is worse than his own opinion.

Early medicine was without notable financial reward and carried only modest prestige. Doctoring was generally pursued as an afterthought—an adjunct to farming or running a store. In this lack of organization and standards confusion reigned, aggravated by ruthless competition, general ill will between practitioners, and profound dissension among the many branches of nineteenth-century medicine. Historian Moses Strong notes that while still a territory, Wisconsin in 1847 found itself "invaded by a tribe of interlopers, who, without license [or] lancets, under the various names of homeopaths, hydropaths, animal magnetizers, phreno-magnetizers,

Early remedies.

Murphy Library, University of Wisconsin, La Crosse

endocrine doctors and poudrette doctors undertake to cure our diseases without any regular system ... and bleeding our pockets more than our veins." Allopaths decried homeopaths, and both scorned the "primitive" applications of herbalists. Thompsonians sold health plan shares in vegetable remedies—a movement so popular that, at its height, the movement claimed four million followers out of a total national population of seventeen million. The founder of this movement, Dr. John Thompson, touted, among other things, a foot soak in soup as the road to a rapid recovery.

Steam doctors and hydropaths were usually held in low medical regard despite a popular appeal based on lower prices and greater availability. Galvanism, or electricity as a treatment, was enthusiastically revived in the late 1800s with the use of such devices as "galvanic soles" to charge the feet; its earnest lay practitioners believed electrical devices would shock the system into startled vigor. Canada's first licensed doctor, Jenny Trout, founded the Electro-Therapeutic Institute in Toronto to minister to patients with neuralgia, painful joints, or paralysis. Dr. Scott's Electric Corset was a popular device that would "flood the vital organs" with "steel magnetoids"—curative entities apparently beyond definition. Its inventor insisted that ladies plagued with "any bodily ailment" at all—particularly hefty ones who hoped to trim their bulk—should fit into the corsets without delay. Ahead lay a future of "astonishing" corset cures that would "invigorate every part of the system."

For many, self-medication proved logical and economical. The trade in nostrums and patent medicines flourished, whether through mail order, from the satchel of a traveling vendor, or direct from the garden. Nostrum sales became a second income for many and were easily sustained as long as goose grease, weasel skins, and pumpkin-seed tea, among many, could be found. The husband of Dr. Esther Hawks, Dr. Milton Hawks, added to the family income by inventing a "relaxant" out of rum or other diluted alcohol, bitters, and pulverized lobelia seed, mixed and "settled" for fourteen days, after which it was shaken regularly and then blended with sugar water. The elixir was sold directly to federal troops during the Civil War as well as through agents.

Potions such as Dr. Schoop's Cough Remedy, advertised to readers of the *Wahpeton Times* of Wahpeton, North Dakota, in 1911, were guaranteed as "safe yet certain" elixirs, "unlike any others," according to their manufacturers: "Its taste will be entirely new.... No opium, chloroform, or any other stupefying ingredients are used. Only the tender leaves of a harmless, lung-healing mountainous shrub." In addition to the salubrious syrup, Schoop's "health coffee"—available for purchase just about everywhere—was nutritionally replete with "pure, healthful toasted grains, malt, nuts, etc. ... so cleverly blended as to give a wonderfully true coffee taste, color and flavor. You actually get 100 full cups from a 25-cent 1-lb. package, made in a minute. And besides, there is not a grain of real coffee in it."

Not unusual was the marketing of eye

stones—small white objects to be inserted under the upper eyelid to cure eye distress—or the prescribing of hot horse manure for sore feet. As late as 1824 consumptive patients were instructed to soak their feet daily in dung to "restore the equilibrium of the system."

These treatments and more were sought so eagerly because of the sheer amount of disease and suffering people faced daily. The means by which disease was transmitted were as yet largely unknown; malnutrition was common among the less well off; people were often ignorant of basic hygiene, including maternal and infant hygiene. A new mother might lie for a week in blankets caked and stained with blood, with nothing but her face and hands washed. "It was thought certain death to change the underclothes under a week," wrote one English woman, who remembered that the bedclothes were "stiff and stained, and the stench under the covers abominable." What was worse, some midwives ordered women to keep their babies under these dirty cloths—it is a wonder any child survived at all. Weaning mothers put plasters on their breasts, which often proved irritating, causing painful inflammation and suffering.

But with time and the new knowledge it brought, medical science improved. Anesthesia and antisepsis came to be used in hospitals, and an array of precise new instruments were invented. Meanwhile, medical examining boards and four-year medical schools gradually raised the caliber of physicians in practice. To block abuses by the untrained and by charlatans, doctors were increasingly required to

be licensed; this promoted both quality and the ability to exclude. In the 1800s, wealthy, landowning medical practitioners with diplomas (although a brief apprenticeship and an equally brief course of lectures at a medical school was usually all that was necessary to qualify an applicant for a medical degree) were often able to use their political connections to have legislation passed prohibiting the practice of medicine without a license and making it impossible to obtain a license without a diploma.

Frontier physicians, however, were often a different breed of doctor than their more cliquish urban counterparts. While many conscientious medical men practiced on the frontier and flourished there, some pioneer M.D.'s were prosperous dandies whose medical accoutrements were, like as not, a plug hat, a Prince Albert coat, and a silver-headed cane—men who found medicine a passport to adventure. Western medical practice was for them not the hardworking servitude dictated by the Hippocratic Oath, but a quest to strike it rich on the new, western frontier. Author Robert Karolevitz in *Doctors of the Old West* cites a letter written by Dr. Thomas M. Logan to a fellow physician in the East in 1850, in which he describes the lives of physicians in California. Logan had seen "M.D.'s driving ox teams . . . laboring in our streets . . . serving at barrooms, monte tables, boarding house[es] etc., and digging and delving among the rocks and stones." Many placed fortune first, and resumed their medical practice only when money was short, as a last resort. In expansionist times, with gold being struck, land being settled, and the frontier pushed steadily west, it was often difficult to keep a physician in his job, as described in the *Deseret News* of September 18, 1852: "Two physicians have removed to one of our more distant settlements and gone to farming; three more have taken to traveling and exploring the country; three have gone to California to dig gold, or for some other purpose; and one has gone to distilling."

Male frontier physicians generally came from the rigors of the military—many were Civil War veterans, accustomed to performing surgical procedures under the most inhospitable (and unsanitary) conditions. They subscribed to the early-nineteenth-century maxim "Desperate diseases require desperate measures," and advocated liberal dosing with purgatives or cleansing the system with dangerous, extreme, and "heroic" bouts of bloodletting, cupping, blistering, poisoning, or puking. As if their harsh treatments weren't bad enough, many of this type of doctor were unreliable—often unavailable, late for a delivery, simply drunk—or worse. Ohio physician James Cross, suspected of "every crime in the calendar from drunkenness to rape," was finally forced from his teaching position in the early 1830s because of his reputation and left to wander from one post to another.

Gradually, people's attitudes toward health and medicine changed and they began to reject this kind of rough medical treatment. To middle-class Americans who once be-

lieved that sickness was more about spiritual retribution than it was about disease, good health became a priority, aided by temperance, nutrition, and a myriad of self-cures. The political tenor of the country—a strong, Jacksonian antielitism—provided further impetus to the medical breakaway. The common man became the common patient, who had grown weary of medical violence and welcomed grassroots reform.

Dr. Hilda Erickson.

Utah State Historical Society

Into the heart of such expectations sallied forth women physicians with gentle admonishments of fresh air, good circulation, adequate food, and fewer children. Female doctors had to function in a society that was deeply patriarchal and structured around men who held the upper hand both in public and in private, and who resented female deviance from traditional roles. In particular, male doctors feared that with women doctors to turn to, a significant number of their female patients would vanish. This fiscal fear often inspired a barrage of name-calling and innuendo, with epithets such as "unnatural female physicians" or "the third sex" hurled even by such prestigious organizations as the Boston Gynecological Society.

Men were accustomed to women of a delicate and ladylike nature, who might well swoon at the content of pulp novels, the condition of the world, or the thought of life's baser aspects, including disease. In fact, so delicate was the female constitution thought to be that a typical advertisement for tranquilizing medicines, printed in a Utah newspaper, the *Nauvoo Neighbor,* in 1845, refused to mention the word *childbirth:*

> *P. Meeks respectfully informs the citizens . . . that he intends keeping an assortment of the best Indian remedies now known, entirely vegetable; which he digs from the earth himself . . . also a certain root which entirely cures the enlargement of the spleen; also a certain root which is a sovereign remedy for the cramps likewise the same kind of roots*

which the squaws use to facilitate ———; those women that have not used it, will not be without it at such a time if possible to obtain it; which they should commence using two or three weeks before their expected ———.

Such assumed "delicacy," cited as one of the reasons women were not suited to the male-dominated public sphere, was bound up with the sexual repressiveness of the era, which in the most extreme cases even led to the performing of clitoridectomies on women. Ironically enough, such repression so discomforted women, they were unable to discuss their bodies and physical symptoms with a male doctor—much less be examined by one. This created a clientele of women who would welcome female physicians, thus encouraging these "unnatural women" who were determined to pursue the study of medicine.

Men accustomed to such wilting reticence were consequently shocked by the idea of women sharing scalpels, cadavers information, and dissection discussions. "No woman of true delicacy would be willing in the presence of men" to listen to medical discussions, protested a group of medical students at Harvard University in 1850, thwarting Harriot K. Hunt in her attempts to win a diploma. Her application had been submitted to the dean of the school, Oliver Wendell Holmes, who agreed to her entry but was daunted by the vociferous outcry of the male students. Furthermore, they objected to "having the company of any female forced" upon them, particularly one "disposed to unsex herself and sacrifice her modesty by appearing with men in the medical lecture room." Hunt eventually became a homeopathic physician with an M.D. degree from Syracuse.

Many other early female doctors gravitated toward such alternative or eclectic training programs, where they encountered less hostility. Despite the numbers of Mormon women who studied medicine—urged by Brigham Young because of the shortage of male doctors—the fact remained: Fewer women worked harder to survive as rural medics. In the dusty streets of Deadwood and along the heat-cracked gullies of west Texas, the U.S. Census of 1870 showed only 525 women physicians (0.8 percent of the national total of 62,383).

Despite the fact that some women eagerly sought out female physicians, often out of fear of male M.D.'s or a sense of shame, one obstacle to women's successes came from an unexpected quarter—from women themselves, many of whom rejected the ministrations of a female doctor in the belief that they would be better served by a male, regardless of qualifications. In the popular mind, a male doctor was "serious" while a woman, one step removed from a "healer" or "granny," was accepted only with reluctance. "As I stepped into the room [of a young farmer's wife], the expression in her face changed into one of disappointment," wrote Dr. Bessie Efner, whose first task as a practicing physician was to convince this woman that, gender aside, she had the same degree of professionalism as any of the local men. Oddly, it was the most comforting aspects of a woman's care—her ability to nurture and comfort—that spurred suspicion. Women patients associated the taciturnity of many male doctors with authority; in reality, many male medics lacked the knowledge to make a proper diagnosis and so said nothing at all, or else they deliberately did not discuss a patient's condition with her in the mistaken belief that women patients were unable to fathom a scientific diagnosis. "I have been to the doctor time and again," wrote a rural Virginia woman in 1917. "He gives me a pink tablet which I think contains calomel but I can never find out from him what causes this mucus to form."

Part of the reluctance to understand the role of female physicians came from the stereotypical association of women with nursing. "At one time or another every woman is a nurse," said Florence Nightingale, whether professionally or domestically in their roles as wives and mothers.

Yet sentiment aside, nursing was a low-paying profession, often lacking prestige, sometimes associated with promiscuity. Dorothea Dix, head of the army nursing corp during the Civil War, was concerned with the morals of nurses. She wrote to a friend: "No woman under thirty need apply to serve in government hospitals. All nurses are required to be plain-looking women. Their dresses must be brown or black, with no bows, no curls, no jewelry and no hoop skirts."

No such prohibitions deterred Calamity Jane, who, although medically unqualified to call herself a professional nurse, was frequently mentioned in newspaper accounts of her medical acumen and nursing skill. As cited in *Physicians of the Old West,* Calamity was praised in South Dakota's *Deadwood Pioneer* of July 13, 1876, for her care of a man named "Warren, who was stabbed on lower Main Street" and was doing "quite well under [her] care."

Another well-known caretaker was Julia Bulette, the notorious prostitute of Nevada City whose charitable nursing skills and general concern for miners during a raging epidemic impressed citizens who might otherwise have been outraged at her activities, no matter how discreet.

Eventually, the white-clad young women whose starched pinafores became symbolic of their profession managed to live down their earthy origins, but, like many early, rural "medicine" women, rural nurses were seldom licensed. Taking an exact count of nurses before the 1900s was difficult, since they were counted as domestics in the census, and, lacking a college education, were not listed on college rolls. Some were graduates of nurses' training schools; others worked as practical nurses under leading doctors, gaining skill and experience as apprentice handmaidens to noted experts in their fields.

Typical of the nursing profession was a black woman simply called "Carter," Bunyanesque in strength and stature and near mythic in reputation. An assistant to rural physician Charlotte Hawk, she kept the tiny hospital in the basement of the Hawks' Green River, Wyoming, home running efficiently as she tended to sick train passengers, or those wounded in the frequent accidents that occurred on the twisting, Union Pacific railroad fifteen miles away.

Despite the lack of official statistics, countless diaries, journals, and oral histories mention the presence of nurses. In particular, they assisted at numerous rural births, for out in the remotest areas, as Colorado homesteader Inez Whalin said, often "the children arrived before the doctor did." In attending birthing women, these nurses were close to the tradition of midwifery that had flourished in colonial times, producing such figures as Ann Eliot, a Roxbury, Massachusetts, midwife whose skills were acknowledged on her tombstone with the inscription "For the great service she hath done this town." Other midwives delivered thousands of babies, rarely losing a patient, and one, Janet Alexander of Boston, was so beloved by women there that she was paid $1,200—an enormous sum at the time—not to accept an offer to practice in New York.

If nurses were close to the female-centered world of tradition, providing comforting care and midwifery services, female physicians in the late nineteenth and early twentieth centuries served, as Judith Leavitt noted in *Brought to Bed,* as a bridge between that world and the more male-dominated world of scientific medicine.

Class, cadaver lab, 1892.

Minnesota Historical Society

❧

CHAPTER TWO

Medicine by Degree

❧

Women in Medical School

You can take my word for it; women will never be
acceptable to the medical profession.

—JOHN LUBCHENCO,

brother of Dr. Portia Lubchenco McKnight

IN THE FIRST FIFTY YEARS OF THE NINETEENTH CENTURY, MEDICAL education drew together the previously disparate disciplines of medicine, surgery, and midwifery, fashioning them into a rough approximation of a medical education. Private medical schools, essentially "diploma mills," asked only a high-school education and the fee for enrollment, with the standard course of study lasting only one to two weeks. By 1845, medicine was almost considered a layman's pursuit. Licensing imperatives had been lifted from most schools, and the ill-trained, unwashed medical offspring of such institutions were often more terrifying than the diseases they hoped to cure. Medical credentials were, in fact, often held suspect unless the practitioner had a proven record of local success.

As interest in medicine mounted, schools kept pace. By 1860, the country had nearly forty training institutes for doctors; many of the fledgling institutions were in dire financial condition, had only the scantiest admission requirements, and charged tuition by the course. Fees ranged from fifteen dollars for each lecture subject to ten dollars for the use of the dissecting room. Early medical schools were so rowdy that neighbors of the Geneva Medical College in New York tried to have the college declared a public nuisance.

The situation was somewhat less grim in the best national medical schools. Until the end of the 1800s, the standard medical education in these schools consisted of two five-month-long courses, followed by two or three years of apprenticeship, or preceptorial training, with an established local doctor.

Historically, the apprentice paid a fee of one hundred dollars annually to the physician for the privilege of learning by his side. The apprentice did much of the repetitive, laborious, day-to-day work, which was the major reason an apprentice was also called a "sweep and stable boy"—a phrase that reflects the very small number of women who took up medicine at the time. Rare examples of women doctors practicing with a preceptor-earned license were Dr. Mary Lavinder and Dr. Sarah E. Adams of Georgia; Dr. Lavinder's degree was a certificate titled "Testimonials of her qualifications to practice the obstetric art." Many women were apprentices for several years at privately owned, proprietary schools that could not issue degrees but did offer a respectable education.

Premedical education could fluctuate widely—typical studies usually included gross anatomy, gross pathology, drug use and dosage, and prognosis, with the greatest emphasis on immediate, gut-reaction diagno-

sis. Advanced medical studies included pediatrics, gynecology, physiology, and *materia medica,* with later forays into anesthesia, metabolism, serology, cardiography, roentgenology, endocrinology, aseptic surgery, and preventive medicine. Surgery, an elite specialty, was usually pursued by men and perfected by dissecting cadavers preserved in whiskey barrels; surgical procedures ranged from leg amputations to the removal of cystic or fatty tumors. Even mastectomies were explored as early as 1840. Anatomy was emphasized and recognized as the new cornerstone of medical knowledge. Lectures delved into diseases of the heart, ossification, veins, and piles. Disease diagnosis ran the gamut of complexity, including the simple sleuthing out of the presence of protein in the urine by heating a sample in a spoon held over a candle. A most exciting medical development students learned about was anesthesia—an American achievement of the mid-1800s, followed by the invention of chloroform in 1847 by Scottish physician James Simpson. Classes in histology and microscopic anatomy drew students into the microworld of embryology, pathology, and bacteriology, a world hidden far from the range of the human eye.

To impress the material to mind, students studied drawings, heard diseases described, repeated back the descriptions orally, then filled notebooks with the information. Unannounced reviews were sudden—any hour could be the unlucky time to recite the memorized terms: *clavicle,* collarbone; *scapula,* shoulder blade; *sternocleidomastoid,* a muscle that runs from the breastbone to back of the ear; *acute gastroenteritis,* the common stomachache. "I was utterly confounded by the strange, meaningless words that fell from the lips of our professors," wrote Helen MacKnight Doyle as she "groped slowly" through the "maze of Osteology, and Physiology and Medical Chemistry in which the freshman class seemed hopelessly lost."

Tested or not, student interns often found the pace of work excruciating. Bertha Van Hoosen, working as a trainee nurse in the Woman's Hospital in Detroit, felt the stress:

My physical, mental and emotional systems were kept at such a high pitch of activity that it became impossible for me to relax or rest. Night after night, as soon as I fell asleep, I jumped out of my bed and started to remake it. At this point I wakened, but again and again, when I lost consciousness, I repeated the performance. I outmaneuvered this emotional manifestation by sleeping on the bare mattress devoid of all bed clothing.

Even more disturbing was the night that her roommate had a nervous breakdown; Van Hoosen awakened to find the girl frantically wringing and "trying to empty her breasts." When Van Hoosen's family heard the story, they were "so alarmed" at the roommate's behavior that Van Hoosen was forbidden to return to nursing.

Stress could spring from the constant grind of poverty as well as demands upon time. Although most women medical students came from well-to-do families, there were those who could study only at great sacrifice, and to whom bill paying was as mysterious and difficult as any class in anatomy. Bertha Van Hoosen, who later was a surgeon in Indiana, became so inured to poverty that, when first out of medical school and working as a resident doctor, she often "blistered her feet" by walking across town to save carfare. In her limited fiscal condition, "days of study passed quickly, but it did not vanish so rapidly" as her money. Rosalie Slaughter, attending the Woman's Medical College in Philadelphia, wore a jacket of newspapers with a hole torn for her head. Although she had been raised in a wealthy family, her father automatically wrote her out of his will, assuming she would marry early. When she decided to study medicine, she had to deal with the necessity (and novelty) of being self-supporting.

꧁꧂

Although the first medical school was established in 1767, the first woman was not admitted until 1847. Elizabeth Blackwell was told that she might attend if disguised in male clothing, a ploy that had been successful for an Englishwoman, Dr. Miranda Barry, who spent her life disguised as a man and whose true sex was revealed only after her death in 1865. So successful was Barry's disguise that she had risen to the position of inspector-general of hospitals for the British army, a "gentleman" recognized for "his" medical acumen and skill.

Hahnemann Medical School, Chicago.

National Library of Medicine

Blackwell refused such subterfuge, determined to continue "in the light of day and with public sanction" to pursue her career. "The idea of winning a doctor's degree gradually assumed the aspect of a great moral struggle," wrote Blackwell, who was surprised to find she had an "immense attraction" for just such a fight in spite of an almost constant lack of respect.

Upon hearing that Elizabeth Blackwell planned to apply to the Geneva Medical College, the male students there thought it was a "great joke," and in that spirit held a mock vote in which they agreed unanimously to admit her; they were shocked when she was actually accepted in the school. Yet her graduation in 1849 provided a tiny opening through which edged an ever-increasing trickle of women. The graduation ceremony was a scene of wry amusement, during which the women of Geneva turned out en masse to see a "lady receive a medical diploma." Although the other graduates marched behind the band, Blackwell thought it unladylike and waited modestly in the church gallery. Conservatively clad in a high-necked black silk brocade gown, she opted for discretion throughout the ceremony, hiding her usual sharp sense of humor in order to present a demure figure to the wondering crowd. She bowed low upon receiving the diploma and humbly thanked the "most High" for the honor—to the resounding applause of the crowd.

Blackwell's medical degree from Geneva Medical College in 1849 heralded the acceptance of three women students at the Medical School of Syracuse University. Almost simultaneously, Dr. Joseph Longshore founded the Women's Medical College of Pennsylvania, leading to the establishment of fifteen more women's colleges. Seventeen women's medical schools and nine women's hospitals were founded between 1848 and 1895. The first women's medical colleges were staffed by men, since there were few women doctors available, and they were usually held in contempt by their male colleagues for their role in the unpopular process of educating women. So stigmatized was women's education that even as late as 1920, institutions such as Harvard only grudgingly allowed a woman to attend classes, but not receive a degree. Medical student Helen Taussig was permitted to attend histology lectures as long as she sat in an adjunct, open room by herself, forbidden to speak to the male students. One professor, according to Dr. Agnes Harrison, among the first female graduates of the University of Michigan in the late 1870s, "considered himself quite daring for talking to [women students] openly"; after all, in Toronto "he had lectured to the women students who were concealed behind a screen.

The New England Female Medical College began by moving from one private home to another for lectures and had a beginning enrollment of fewer than forty women. Eventually, a full regimen of lectures and clinics was added, covering chemistry, toxicology, physiology, hygiene, *materia medica* and therapeutics, anatomy, and surgery, as well as obstetrics and diseases of women and children.

Women practiced on leather obstetrical manikins, studied replicas of the eye and ear, and attended lectures by noted specialists of the day. Students were required to attend two full seventeen-week sessions in two successive academic years.

An important contributor to women's medical history was Dr. Harriot Hunt, who had already practiced as a physician for twelve years when she applied to Harvard Medical School for admission, but was still rejected twice, once in 1847 and again in 1849. Despite her rejection, Harvard apparently felt that even accepting her application was fair enough treatment. When a philanthropic female donor, Miss Hovey of Boston, promised the college a gift of ten thousand dollars on "condition of the admission of women students," Hunt was grudgingly enrolled against the wishes of a student body that felt threatened by the presence of a woman who, though matronly, stout, and not a bit provocative, was still a female and, as such, might possibly undermine their inherent masculine respect for the "modesty and delicacy of her sex."

By the last decade of the nineteenth century thirty-five medical schools had reluctantly tabled their objections to admitting women medical students, although national, state, and county medical societies continued in pitched opposition. Adrift in a sea of disapproval, women in medical school rigidly maintained the highest standards of excellence. Women students often received a top academic ranking, as did Anne Austin, whose extremely high grades earned at the Women's Medical College of Pennsylvania exempted her from taking the medical board examinations. Women students also knew that they would be carefully watched for any sign of weakness or vulnerability and that any break in their composure—for example, squeamishness about lab research, such as handling cadavers—would shrink their medical prospects. Surprisingly, such exams ultimately proved less startling to them than convention might have supposed. "My delicacy was certainly shocked," wrote Elizabeth Blackwell about a dissection, "yet the exhibition was in some sense ludicrous. I had to pinch my hand till the blood nearly came, and call on Christ to help me from smiling." Surely laughter at such a serious moment would have further endangered her position.

European colleges were more receptive to

> *Taken as a whole [women physicians] will probably never amount to much.*
>
> — DR. MCLEAN, MEDICAL DEPARTMENT OF THE UNIVERSITY OF CALIFORNIA, TO HELEN MACKNIGHT DOYLE

Instruction in obstetrics.

National Library of Medicine

women, and many American women physicians did postgraduate surgical study in Berlin, studied in Vienna for internal diseases, and went to Paris to study nervous ailments. Yet even European latitude had its limits, and propriety was occasionally invoked. Rosalie Slaughter recalled the reluctance of a dermatology professor to allow her in a class where the instruction involved a naked syphilitic man. The event proved too much even for the properly reared Slaughter; when she admitted her dismay to the professor, he offered to take her on his rounds and give her special instruction.

Academe seemed vastly confused over the appearance of women, demanding superior abilities in order to admit them, then, in a spate of chivalric confusion, often declining to actually test the women, since they were, after all, women. Bertha Van Hoosen, studying in 1885 at the University of Michigan Medical School, often questioned her own abilities and felt "tortured by a medical-practice inferiority complex." Hard as she had worked for it and as much as she valued it, her medical degree "brought . . . no sense of competency." Not only had she the usual sense, common to all doctors, of being "frightened" by the "responsibility for the life of the patient," but her fears were rooted in the school's own practice of not testing its female students. How could she judge her skills herself if she was never tested?

Breaching a male medical bastion was no simple task. On November 6, 1869, a slender, simply dressed Quaker, Anna Broomall, purchased "study tickets" for several surgery clinics at two dollars each—the usual procedure for attending a course, since individual professors "sold" their expertise, session by session. When male students discovered the "outrage" of her participation, they mobbed Broomall and her companions, terrifying them with a barrage of "hoots, jeers, caterwauling and paper wads" and chasing the women into a room, which was quickly locked for their safety. The women finally managed to escape by slipping out, a few at a time. Broomall's opinion of the event, told years later to interviewer Dr. Mary Harper, was: "Bless you boys! Nothing helps a good cause so much as well-advertised opposition."

When the College of Pennsylvania opened for women in 1850, it had no hospital facilities for bedside instructions. Eighteen years later, thirty-six females students finally managed to attend general clinics at the Philadelphia Hospital, where they filed into the amphitheater to a long rush of whistles, groans, jeers, and foot-stamping by the male students. According to medical historian Dr. Straight, a local newspaper cited the incident:

Ranging themselves in line, these gallant gentlemen assailed the young ladies as they passed out, with insolent and offensive language, and then followed them into the street, where the whole gang with the fluency of long practice, joined in insulting them. . . . During the last hour missiles of paper, tin foil, tobacco quids, etc. were thrown upon the ladies, while some of the men defiled the dresses of the ladies near them with tobacco juice. . . . It is but just to the ladies to say that . . . from their general appearance . . . none of them had ever been accustomed to the association of such unmannerly men before.

The experience was not much different for Lucy Wanzer, who entered medical school in California in 1872, expecting to take a course in medicine but finding the study of human nature superimposed. To taunt or to teach became the question, since not just her classmates but also her professors mercilessly harassed her in the dissecting room, once leaving a cadaver's genital organ obscenely propped up, by catheter, for her "discomfiture and embarrassment." As she had to go over the head of the dean and petition the Board of Regents for admission, the aggrieved dean, forced to accept her as a student, decided to make her miserable with hazing.

The Dean . . . announced to his students that . . . "We have to accept this woman student, as she has the best of us. The law has been decided in her favor, but you can make it so uncomfortable that she cannot stay. We will get rid of her in short order. Of course she will complain, but we will say we are very sorry but we cannot lecture to two classes. With just one woman we will make short work of it."

The men, according to Helen Macknight Doyle, M.D., a later graduate of Toland Hall,

had not "reckoned with the spirit of the woman who was struggling to gain for women the right to study medicine and surgery in California," nor with the sassy courage it took to maintain her independence. Characteristically, when a professor at an eye clinic snidely offered that "a woman had no business" studying medicine, and those who did "ought to have [their] ovaries removed," Wanzer retorted: "If that is true, the men students ought also to have their testicles removed!"

Helen MacKnight Doyle, attending the same classes seventeen years later, found male students just as antagonistic. She took her father with her to the lectures and dissecting room for the first few days, where he "glowered" the young male students into submission. Oregon rural doctor Corrinne Chamberlin had to wait for the male students to finish with the research materials before she was allowed access. Amelia Dann, at the Medical School of Syracuse University, found the same prankish behavior in the dissecting laboratory in 1875. At the first cut of the scalpel a gust of "ill-smelling vapor" was loosed from the cadaver —her male counterparts had spent the previous evening inflating the corpse's bladder with pipe smoke and "carefully suturing" all the other orifices until they were smoke-tight.

⸙

Pranks aside, determined women continued to storm the medical citadel, shoving aside the resistance of male students and faculty, and struggling to establish a record of scholarship. With time, grudging patronization gave way,

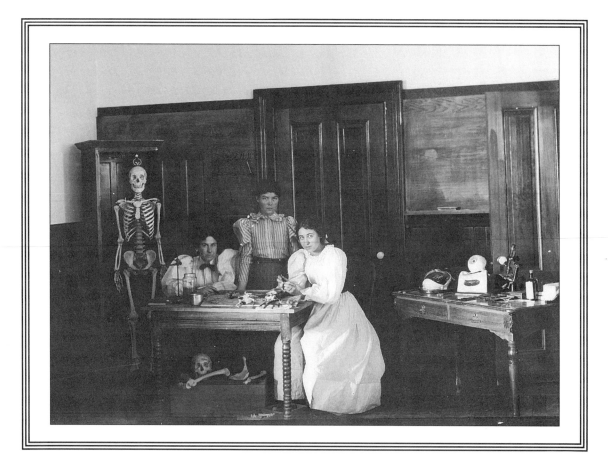

Medical school.

Courtesy Arizona Historical Society, Tucson;
Buehman Memorial Collection

finally, to a dawning appreciation, as noted by Dr. Kate Mead, who attended an all-female medical academy: "We smile when we recall that in the eighties the Board of Directors decreed that in all laparotomies in the amphitheater a man surgeon should be present. After a few such seances, however, these men refused to come in the capacity of critics for they acknowledged that [Dr. Anna E. Broomall, the presiding surgeon] was as skillful as any surgeon in the world."

By 1900 women physicians constituted nearly 6 percent of the profession, up from 0.8 percent in 1870. Institutional breakthroughs continued, and by the late 1880s some all-male medical schools began to admit women, including the University of Iowa and the University of California, although even at the coeducational Johns Hopkins, "women students were allowed to examine men only above the neck."

Nursing duties were often assigned to young female physicians, since in the eyes of male physicians, the two were closely aligned. Dr. Elizabeth Cushier, an 1872 graduate of the College of the New York Infirmary, found her first intern position at the infirmary itself. "Owing to the necessity . . . for the closest economy there was but one nurse employed in a ward of eight obstetric patients," Cushier noted. "This meant that the interns did a great deal of the work which would have ordinarily been the duty of a nurse, but we were none the worse for it."

No woman who suffered through such excruciating prejudice would be surprised at what happened to Dr. Josephine Baker, who in 1915 was granted the first doctoral degree given to a woman by New York University School of Medicine and then became a lecturer in child hygiene, when she attempted to teach a class.

They never allowed me to forget that I was the first woman ever to impose herself on the college. I stood down in a well with tiers of seats rising all around me . . . filled with unruly, impatient, hard-boiled young men. I opened my mouth to begin the lecture. Instantly . . . they began to clap . . . grinning and pounding. . . . Then the only possible way of saving my face occurred to me. I threw back my head and roared with laughter, laughing at them and with them at the same time, and they stopped, as if somebody had turned a switch. . . . But the moment I stopped at the end of the hour, that horrible clapping began again. Frightened and tired as I was from talking a solid hour against a gloweringly hostile audience, I fled at top speed. Every lecture I gave at Bellevue, from 1915 to 1930, was clapped in and clapped out that way.

Canadian medical student Elizabeth Smith was sure that her pain, "horrible beyond words to tell" with which she "writhe[d] inwardly," came from proximity to male students—those "blackest hearted roughs"—who constantly smirked and gossiped about the female students instead of pursuing serious study: "Injustice, injustice, injustice, rings in my ears & rouses me to bitter thought that sometimes I should dearly like to repay them [men] fourfold for what they make me suffer now & Try to crush out every resentful bitter, avenging thought. . . . I long for sympathy . . . yet I must study & I must go on & at times be merry, & social, & lonely."

Mary Canaga Rowland attributed the prejudice she suffered at John A. Creighton Medicine College in Omaha, Nebraska, to religion. At this Catholic school she found a "great difference in the attitude of the men." In the medical college in Topeka, Kansas, the men had treated her as a companion, often going over lectures with her. But at Creighton, she felt, the negativity was due to the "church's attitude": "Some of the students got me off to one side and told me they didn't think the other woman student should be there because she wasn't married, then they got her off and told her that I shouldn't be there because I was married."

Families often threw obstacles in the path of aspiring female medical students, hoping that a "storm of opposition" would deflect the young girls from an experience that was socially embarrassing, if not dangerous. "My family felt they were disgraced," wrote Bethenia Owens-Adair, whose own child was continually "influenced and encouraged" by unhappy family members to think that his mother was doing him an irreparable injury

> *If I am diligent I can accomplish — something.*
>
> — DR. ELLIS SHIPP

by continuing to practice medicine. Friends and neighbors "sneered and laughed derisively," sure that their "Christian duty" lay in advising her against taking the fatal step. Equally opposed were the family members of Southern belle Portia Lubchenco McKnight: "I sent an application to the South Carolina Medical College in Charleston. I was promptly rejected. . . . My family and friends were gratified that I would not be able to study medicine. South Carolina's rejection only gave credence to their lifted eyebrows. They had not really taken my idea too seriously; they had not wanted me to know disappointment."

Undaunted, she immediately applied to a school in North Carolina, traveling to Charlotte to apply in person. "I spent my hard-saved teacher salary money to get a black handbag, as though to bolster my courage with that facsimile of what I aspired to." To her utter surprise, she was accepted on the spot and told to begin classes the following day. Her presence was announced to the all-male class of seventy men by the presiding instructor, Dr. Mathison. "Gentlemen," he said, "we are delighted to have in our class a sister. We expect you to treat her as such." Her classmates adopted a brotherly, proprietary air; McKnight found her instructors "most encouraging," yet they did not let her off easy. "I did work extra hard at medicine," she wrote, "it was necessary for me to do so. I worked hard because I loved all of my courses, especially the laboratory work." She shared microscopes with other busy interns until, to her surprise, the head of the department gave her "the greatest impetus possible in a gift"—his microscope. After her four years of medical training and being "second in scholarship in the class of 1912," she was lauded as being the first woman graduate of the doctoral program as well as showing extreme fortitude in the dissecting room. As fainting male students were "stacked up together on a pile outside the door," McKnight simply requested that, should she faint, they "make an extra pile for her." Humor and assertiveness were hers, along with a deep love of medicine: "If I had ever any doubts about my interest in doctoring, they were completely dispelled," she wrote. "Medicine was in my blood, never, I knew, to be drained from it."

Others had positive experiences as well. Hilla Sheriff of South Carolina was supported in her gross anatomy class, when the cadaver issued to her was so enmeshed in its long, flowing beard that her shaving attempts proved futile. Students gathered around to watch her struggles with the razor, until finally a fellow student courteously produced a pair of scissors and snipped away the long beard.

Just as not all male students harassed the women, not all women instructors were patient, kind, and tolerant. By 1890, two thirds of the professors teaching at the Women's Medical College of Pennsylvania were women, many of them outstanding in their fields. According to Dr. Kate Mead, however, "rank and file" stu-

dents of Dr. Anna Broomall found her "rather alarming at times," particularly if the student was confused. Such impatience "possibly turned many a young woman from making a specialty of either obstetrics or surgery."

⁕

Women in medicine themselves had different opinions and philosophies about female physicians. Elizabeth Blackwell, for example, was convinced that medicine suited a woman perfectly because of her innate "nurturing qualities," and that women should naturally gravitate toward the areas of gynecology, maternity, laboratory work, and vaccination, harking back to centuries' worth of work as nurses, counselors, pharmacists, midwives, abortionists, "wise women," and witches, practitioners of a health care that was sited in the home and the village. Women had been "doctors without degrees" whose learning was often mystical or forbidden. Blackwell's antithesis was Mary Putnam Jacobi, an equally influential pioneer, who argued for equality of the sexes and who hoped that femininity had nothing to do with women's abilities to doctor; she believed that medicine was a science. As women claimed medical degrees and struck out for the West, adherents of both schools of thought found themselves belittled because they were women and, in the Jacksonian era of the "common man," eyed with suspicion simply because they were trained college graduates.

Despite all, women persevered, yoked to their own ambition, bound to their sense of

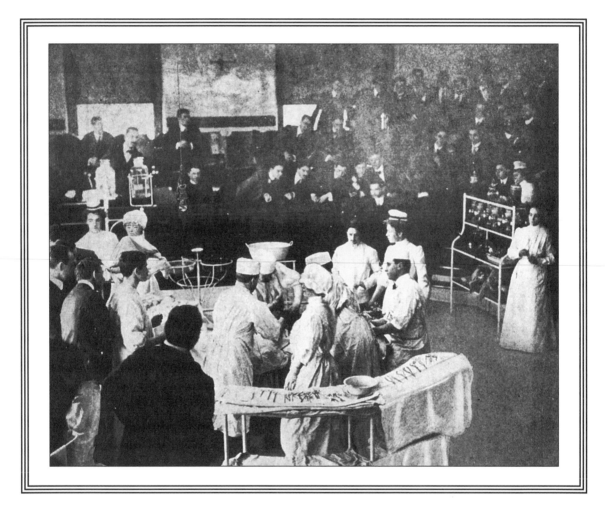

Cesarean section.

National Library of Medicine

mission, but also, in a countervailing sense, freed by the spirit of scientific inquiry, as described by Helen MacKnight Doyle: "I really liked the study of medicine. I wanted to go on with it more than I wanted anything else in the world. I wanted to win out. I wanted to keep the respect that I felt had prompted those young men to do what they had done that morning. I wanted to demonstrate that a woman could be just as good a sport as a man."

Dr. Bethenia Owens-Adair.

Oregon Historical Society

CHAPTER THREE

Women Scorned

Prejudice and Practice

By damn, there is something to be said for female doctors, after all!

—PAUL, A DOCTOR WITH MOLLY RADFORD, M.D.

ROM THE FIRST, RURAL WOMEN DOCTORS QUICKLY DISCOVERED THAT a crisp new medical credential, whether from a legally certified medical school or one termed "irregular," often seemed more like an authorization for discrimination than a passport for practice. The bias against women in professions in the nineteenth century was unique in its long-term effects—but also in its seldom-challenged jurisdiction. Even in remote mountain or desert enclaves, where the ethic of neighborly outreach was so strong that strangers could assume a ready welcome merely by swinging down from a horse, medical women found they had to "prove up," just like homesteaders. Practicing medicine, for women in a rural setting, could be a very lonely business.

The limits of medical knowledge and the rigors of the rugged frontier placed a heavy burden upon all practitioners, male or female, and within the profession antagonism reigned. "I can picture to myself . . . the deep malice [the doctors] feel for one another," wrote Illinois rural doctor

Hiram Rutherford. "And all this for a *living*." Such malice spilled over toward women physicians, so recently arrived in the field that they had yet to develop professional camaraderie with their male peers. Traditionally, men's and women's work was distinct, competition between the genders anathema, and sex segregation the rule. But by the end of the century, the role of women, as well as that of medicine, had subtly shifted. What had once been a female milieu of nurturance and friendly cooperation among neighbors became healing-for-hire, a flourishing and often lucrative business dominated by men. Emphasis on rational, scientific, "male" thought relegated women to the professional wings, where they gradually repositioned themselves to reclaim a place in the healing arts. No matter how efficient, a female doctor was relegated to the role of a folk practitioner, or leech.

Increasing numbers of women turned to medicine; the *Illinois Republican* of April 10, 1850, declared that "female doctors are becoming all the rage." Increased professional requirements, which included licensing and education, did not stem the tide of women, who, undaunted by prejudice and steep competition, were bound for a future in medicine. By 1900 the number of female physicians in the United States had risen to 7,382.

The arrival of women on the medical scene stirred up a long-held male fear: that women were rejecting the unspoken bargain struck between the sexes, namely, that men would give women the "sphere" of the home if women would agree to stay there. Professional women had a formidable task: to cure attitudes first, illness next, and their own self-esteem last of all. Such work proved daunting, since most women, despite the rigors of medical school, were little prepared for the rebuffs they met.

Male physicians acting as mentors were equally threatened. So fearful was one doctor in Rawlins, Wyoming, that the town would discover the presence of his female understudy that he forced her to lurk outside the office until the patient was anesthetized. "I wasn't to be present until after the first anesthetic was administered," wrote Dr. Lillian Heath. "I would wait in [the] drug store [until] Dr. put on a light in the window of the big front room. Then I would cross the street." So aware was Heath of her "irregular" position as a woman practitioner that when the state of Wyoming finally created its own medical society, Heath, who had belonged to the organization in Colorado since 1893, avoided membership. "I . . . would have been the only woman member," she wrote, "a fact that would have made all concerned uncomfortable." Dr. Amelia Dann sought the advice of an old family physician and mentor, Dr. Van Dun, about applying to the Onondaga County Medical Society; he cautioned her against optimism. When the governing board discovered that her specialty was treating the diseases of women, she was soundly rejected: bad enough that she *was* a woman, but to *specialize* in the ailments that were part of women's general inferiority? Never!

Nor was she alone in her ostracism. When it came to acceptance in state or county medical societies, the path was often impassable, invoking a near-visceral response in the medical fraternity. The attitude prevailed also among many male surgeons, who often refused operating privileges to women. Dr. Amelia Dann had to refer her patients to nearby male physicians, limiting her role to preliminary diagnosis and postoperative care. Those most opposed to the female medical presence were often fellow physicians who refused to bestow either respect or credit on their "petticoat" counterparts.

Some women resorted to disguise or name changes to counter the animosity, putting a lifetime of tailored tweeds or male attire between themselves and their sex. Although in 1870 the Montgomery County, Pennsylvania, medical society had voted to elect "Doctress" Anna Lukens as a member—the first female physician in the country so honored—six years later, the first American female physician to seek admittance to the American Medical Association did so by signing the roll as "S. Stevenson," rather than "Sarah Hackett." When her true identity was discovered, the entire issue of women as members was tabled for another forty years, while she was allowed to continue her practice.

Even on the East Coast, where feminism flourished and women's causes were routinely upheld in the popular press, women's inferiority was still practically an article of faith.

> *That a woman should not practice medicine because she is a woman, is absurd and intolerant.*
>
> — DR. W. H. WILLIAMS

Their appearance in the medical field had created a small number of mentors and some colleagues, but little sense of brotherhood-by-profession. In fact, shock and distrust often accompanied a woman on her rounds, and few women could avoid the waves of jealousy stirred by their presence. Sarah Grimké, a crusader for women's rights in the mid-1800s, believed that, to the world of men, women were simply a "lapse of nature and not an independent entity." A medical woman would seem to represent an even greater lapse.

Discrimination pitched back and forth between outright harassment and low-grade antagonism. Before federal antidiscrimination legislation, equal-opportunity advances in the medical community, and the feminist movement, to seek a nontraditional education and career and to realize one's intellectual potential were the mark of the exceptional woman. Yet many male physicians feared the "feminization" of medicine and believed that if medicine were taken up by secondary citizens—no matter how exceptional—it would become a second-class profession. "I thought I had mastered the technique of overcoming [antagonism in my four years of medical school and internship]," wrote Texas pioneer Claudia Potter, who learned not to fight back but to "use all a woman's wiles to win them over." Potter's first opposition was Dr. White, who bitterly opposed her employment at Temple Sanitarium, even though his partner, Dr. Scott, argued in her favor. "Dr. Scott hired me while Dr. White was away," despite his partner's admonitions, Potter recalled.

Even after being hired, in 1906, Potter's hard-won position was far from ideal. Not only did she work as an anesthesiologist, but "thrown in for good measure" were the duties of "pathologist, house doctor, stretcher boy and general flunky"—all for the paltry amount of $25 a month plus room and board. Hardly an adequate living.

Women often suffered in the profession, finding that each year added a layer of isolation and contributed to ever-sharpened sensibilities. "Not a day . . . passes . . . but something makes me shrink, something hurts me, hurts me cruelly, & why?" queried Elizabeth Smith of her journal. "[Nothing] in the whole range of medicine should make me blush or feel hurt in the tenderest part of a woman's nature." In agony about the invective of "ruffianly men," she wrote in 1884: "Oh it is enough to rouse such violent emotions as to make life's load too heavy. . . . I am grateful that I have the trait of forgetfulness."

Some rejection was rooted in the superstitious notion that women were conduits into the dangerous world of chance, misadventure, and general decline. Dr. Lillian Heath of Rawlins, Wyoming, was informed by a man felled by a heart attack while digging postholes for the rodeo and who regained consciousness in her office that he'd "rather die" than have a female doctor. Heath managed to calm his fears and allay the local skittishness about women in medicine; soon she found a growing clientele in the dozens of stomped, ruptured, and concussed cowboys who worked the local rodeos. Something about her gruff yet soothing manner appealed to them; while other doctors were often idle, Heath had the bronco-busted carnage of the rodeo to contend with.

In a rural setting that was isolated and far removed from patrician ideals, this sense of taboo and dread quickly turned into gossip and innuendo, forcing the female practitioner into either shamed isolation or belligerence as she struggled to justify membership in a male profession. If a woman wore skirts and hats, her feminine array caused the "lady doc" to automatically forfeit some of the respect due a man. Conversely, if she dressed as a man, her effrontery would provoke an opposite outcry, since women were already suspected of masquerading as doctors. Sordid imaginings forced young "hen medics" to tailor their personalities by either striking out boldly, with male dress, six-shooters, and rank language, or turning meek and circumspect. "I joined the local Methodist church," wrote Dr. Bessie Efner of Iowa. "[I] was forced to restrict myself to only such activities which no one could possibly associate with evil." Dr. Eleanor Lawney, Colorado's first female medical graduate from the Denver Medical College, noted the discriminatory dangers of practicing independently as a woman. Often she "dared not" accept a difficult case because, if the patient failed to mend, the result would be blamed on her gender. In

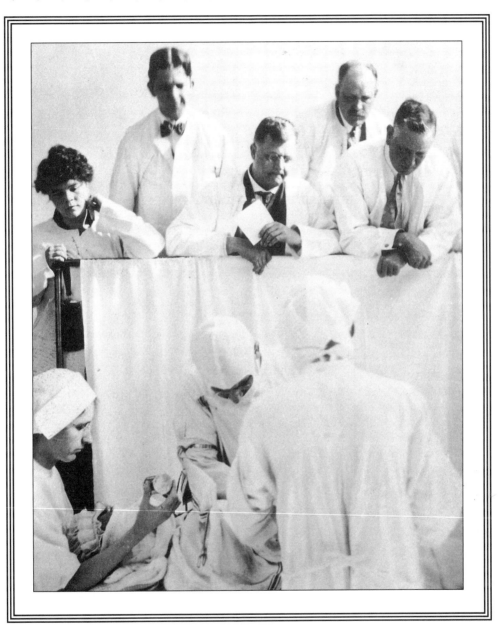

Operating room, St. Mary's Hospital, 1915.

Minnesota Historical Society

self-defense, she might transfer difficult cases to a male physician, fearful because she lacked the "prestige of custom." Indeed, she concluded, "a good deal of 'hedging' is still the 'better part of valor.'"

Women physicians had to be more circumspect than any man, as Dr. Georgia Arbuckle Fix unhappily determined. Despite seventeen years of service in the homestead community of Gering and dozens of loyal friends, when the doctor stepped outside the conventions of the day and divorced her husband, tongues wagged and rumors were rampant. In her notebook was found a comment, penned during this unhappy time: "You cannot sew buttons on your neighbor's mouth."

Women working as doctors often could not get their male colleagues to acknowledge their position. It was not uncommon to hear men say of a female M.D., "She's a good nurse." Predictably, many women turned in resignation to nursing work, where they were medically overeducated, socially ostracized, and viewed as even more aberrant a hybrid than if they had remained physicians. Dr. Susan Anderson quickly stirred up resentment in the nursing ranks with her ill-concealed knowledge, while the male physicians suffered the edge of her superior education, no matter how obliging she tried to be. In one case, she found a severely afflicted typhoid patient with an absent attending physician. She recalled that the male physician had once disparagingly called her a "good nurse." She mused: "He . . . said I was a good nurse . . . [so] I forgot ethics and took charge of the case." "Nurse" was the favored term in army hospitals during the Civil War, where women could not work as surgeons, and even degreed M.D.'s were listed as nurses. Many women adopted the term "ladies' physician" in an effort to avoid the term "doctor," reserved most often for men. In addition, animosity was often triggered by the very word "doctor"—partially from gender resentment, and partially in response to generations of unscrupulous, unlicensed men who called themselves "doc" in order to perpetuate fraud and malfeasance.

Indeed, any unlicensed man, regardless of education or medical acumen, could freely call himself a "doc" and even practice accordingly, while female graduates of medical schools were disparaged as "women physicians," "hen medics," and "lady docs" or were even hailed in familiar terms as "Granny," "Mrs.," or "Mrs. Doctor." Most women doctors found themselves inevitably diminished by the use of coy familiar names, perhaps subtle attempts to

Women doctors must be as quiet and inconspicuous as possible, so that when they are dead, no one will know that they have lived.

— ATTRIBUTED
TO PLINY BY
JANE E. ROBBINS, M.D.

undermine the authority of a gilt shingle ending in "M.D." But such names could also be a sign of affection; Helen MacKnight Doyle became "Dr. Nellie," despite the warnings of a medical school instructor to always insist on use of her proper title; Susan Anderson, practicing in the Colorado Rockies, was "Doc Susie." A serious professional such as Dr. Sophie McClelland, who practiced with her husband in the tiny agricultural outpost of Los Banos, California, became known as "Grandma," while her husband remained staunchly aloof as "the doctor." When Caroline Van Horne of Bergen County, New Jersey, went into practice with her brother Byron, the shingle that swung over the porch of their frame house in Englewood announced their dual practice as that of "Dr. Van Horne" and "Dr. Carrie." Jane Bruce Guignard, of Columbia, South Carolina, remained true to the formal tradition of Southern gentility by insisting that she be called "Dr." but, to her amused resignation, always ended up as "Bruce," while Mary Hays of Otterbourne, Kansas, was resigned to "Auntie May."

When Hannah E. Longshore, the first woman graduate of medicine to practice in Philadelphia, put out her sign, she was shocked at the "ribald derision" of passersby. So scorned was she that male doctors refused to consult with her and pharmacists refused to fill her prescriptions—she had to prepare her own medicines by hand. One pharmacist in 1852 who refused to fill her prescription advised her instead to "Go home and darn your husband's socks." Her ten-year-old daughter, Lucretia, was humiliated by a teacher who warned the girls against playing with a child who was "not quite respectable because her mother [was] a woman doctor."

How did women cope with such rough inequality? Dr. Charlotte Hawk, who moved with her husband, Dr. Jacob Hawk, to the barren cluster of shanties and railroad tracks in Green River, Wyoming, had weathered enough hazing, anger, and relentless criticism during medical school to prepare for the most grueling practice. Yet she found herself underutilized—fluttering about in her husband's wake and handing him instruments when needed, but barred from treating, diagnosing, or bandaging wary male patients by both her husband and the collective contempt of the town. A professional upturn finally occurred when a pregnant immigrant woman demanded to "see Dr. Hawk." Jacob Hawk automatically stepped forward, but the woman shrugged him away, insisting upon "a woman right now—Dr. Charlotte!" With the support of this first patient, Charlotte would no longer function simply as a nurse and assistant for her husband's patients; her first delivery in Green River produced a fine, healthy boy.

Nor was the path any easier for female medical instructors, who found intellectual sexism at the academic level nearly insurmountable; those who did breach the barrier of a quota system were felled by a network of professional male patronage. In 1917 Dr. Florence Sabin was the first female full professor at Johns Hopkins, and she would later

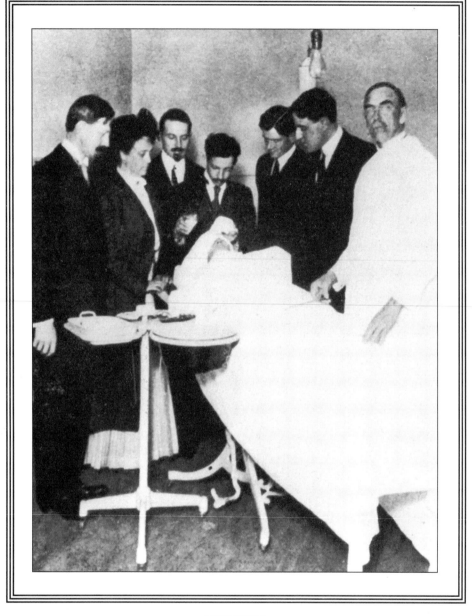

Women in medicine.

National Library of Medicine

be called "the greatest living woman scientist and one of the foremost scientists of all time." Yet Sabin was passed over for the position as head of the department of histology—a logical one for her to fill—in favor of a young man who had been her student. She had always staunchly maintained that talent and skill would take a woman to her goal, but she now faced a rebuff that would involve her in numerous women's causes as well as the promotion of her own efforts. Eventually she became head of the histology department.

Few examples of male exclusion are as poignant as that suffered by Bertha Van Hoosen, whose "dream fulfilled" was the creation of an obstetrical department at Loyola University Medical School. After her efforts secured a grade-A rating for the school, she was shocked when the American Medical Association overlooked her candidacy and placed a man at the head of the Department of Obstetrics. At Northwestern University she found herself in the same antagonistic milieu, caused by her popularity with the students. Van Hoosen had applied for an instructorship in anatomy at the Woman's Medical School, apparently a position so unpopular there was no salary attached. Yet anatomy was her love and she enthusiastically taught every afternoon, managing to see patients before and after her teaching hours. Van Hoosen "especially prized teaching women medical students," and in class she was inevitably drawn to the young women who gazed hopefully at her, seeing her as a model of medical success as well as feminism. So popular was her course

that at the end of the year a group of students asked permission to pay her for a private course, to which she happily acceded.

Van Hoosen apparently forgot that even a women's college was governed by male precepts and that the male hierarchy was where true power lay. She was reminded of her essential vulnerability when the students requesting credit for her course were informed that, if they wished credit, they could study under the director's nephew instead—"an excellent demonstrator of anatomy and a very good teacher"—who would welcome their financial offerings. The students refused, and shortly thereafter Van Hoosen was dismissed.

Sometimes prejudice faltered in the face of overwhelming skill, causing a talented female physician to be viewed positively, or at least without malice. Oddly, the Women's Medical College of Pennsylvania had a rule that each laparotomy held in the amphitheater needed a male physician in attendance—a policy probably instituted to placate financial backers and critics. Before long, male-dominated teaching clinics began to echo the words of Dr. Alfred Stillé of Philadelphia Hospital's Blockley Almshouse, who said: "I not only have no objection to seeing ladies among a medical audience, but . . . I welcome them."

Such courtesy was not extended to Claudia Potter, given a probationary period at the Scott and White Hospital in Texas that lasted for forty-one years. When she finally questioned the arrangement, she was surprised to learn that her chief critic had "no quarrel" with her medical abilities but simply figured that, being a woman, she would have too strong a personality. After all, the "conceit of a normal woman with the conceit of the average doctor" together would be more than he could handle.

Some prejudice was simply based on a woman's perceived lack of strength. Was she strong enough to wrestle down a hysterical male patient or turn a toothkey enough times, pulling all the while, to extract teeth? Bertha Van Hoosen had to face the question of strength and endurance in her hospital practice:

> With one exception I had been able to conduct all of the deliveries without calling upon the visiting staff. My last case, however, proved to be a Jonah.... The labor showed no progress.... I began to worry about the advisability of calling for assistance.... But when? If too early, I ran the chance of being ridiculed and mortified by facetious remarks about over-solicitous women physicians. Too late, and I become responsible for a death, perhaps two deaths. Preferring to suffer ridicule rather than the torments of a guilty conscience, I called Dr. Longyear ... a handsome gentleman, very courteous and kind, [who] made me feel inferior because I was a woman — an irremediable condition.

One spry physician, "Old Doc Anna" Darrow, had settled in Okeechobee, Florida, in the early 1900s—one of four local M.D.'s in the area. One of the male doctors resented her presence, complaining that "Doc Anner" was continually quoted to him as an authority, and vowed to "run the 'petticoat doctor' out of town." In a plot twist worthy of an ancient Greek playwrights, the envious and sulky male physician accidentally drank a toxic chemical, "High Life," which reeked with the stench of rotten eggs and was used around trash cans to discourage dogs and stray cattle. Thinking it was water, he chased a tumbler of whiskey with the potent chemical. "I can't remember putting up a bigger fight to save a life," Doc Anna recalled. She pumped his stomach and flushed his system with bismuth subnitrate to coat the burned mucous coating of his stomach. None could recall such a case before, and Doc Anna could only wait for each succeeding, unfamiliar symptom, unsure of all results save one: that the unfortunate man would ultimately be forced to acknowledge his female competitor was a fine doctor, even an equal— if he lived. Fortunately for him, the symptoms finally abated, and he was in Doc Anna's life-long debt.

A revealing and acerbic account of gender competition came from Dr. Worthington, an army physician stationed at Prescott, Arizona, in 1877, who wrote of his bitter animosity toward a local woman physician practicing in the area. He scorned the few women "so unfortunate" as to be "so nearly men" as to have masculine minds and be only fit for "masculine occupations." Indeed, he opined, he "hoped to be delivered from such 'monstrosities' who were not "in the strictest sense of the word *women* and they are not *men*."

His troubles with Mrs. Murray, M.D., began casually enough at a military reception hosted by the people of Prescott on May 7, 1877:

> It was quite a grand affair, especially for me, the fortunate one of the seven bachelors from the Post . . . who were eligible for the one young lady. . . . After supper we slipped off up to the ballroom until the rest came up. Mrs. Murray M.D. . . . was the first and so I had to give up my easy chair to her and then had a long medicine talk with her. She can talk medicine "like a little man" and is very well [educated.] It's lots of fun to [kid] her. She of course took a sisterly interest in my affairs.

By September, Worthington had totted up his earnings from his practice and marveled at the amount, $1,181—all from "side speculation." But, he wrote a friend about his medical practice, "there is millions in it. Millions." Apparently, however, even the "millions" were not enough to share with the "woman doctor in Prescott," and he refused to treat families who had consulted with Dr. Murray without his knowledge. A patient's consulting her was "a break of professional etiquette" that he could not stand. "And," he blustered, "I do not regret that I took the stand" against the shameless woman, this "free thinker" and "free lover."

> [Going to Dr. Murray] showed a want of confidence in me that I resented and told Mr & Mrs Thomas that I would not attend any of their family again unless they should be at some place with me where no civilian physician could be gotten.
>
> Shortly after this "Mrs. Murray" (She was Murray's mistress and not "Mrs Murray") left her two patients still requiring treatment and went to San Francisco promising to come back in six weeks and complete the cure. In two months we heard she had gone to Oregon after Senator Mitchell whom she had got stuck after! Dr. McKee had told me I was right in refusing to treat Mrs. T when she had treated me so and that he would support me; yet when "Mrs" Murray left he treated the Martins and Thomases himself and whether from his own laziness or from the influence of these two families he went back on his promise and sent me away. He told my friend Dr. Goodfellow—"It is all the fault of that damned bitch Mrs. Murray."

Worthington was aggrieved and offended, for he had offered her medical counsel and informative medical discussions, and in return, in his view, she thanked him by stealing his patients! He now regretted having invited her on a tour of his hospital and, once, at her request, having consulted on a case with her. Had she been a man, he concluded, "I might have *shot* the M.D.!" Being a gentleman, he could only actively hope for her death, perhaps from the stone in her gallbladder: "I hope it will kill her soon." Much of his anger came from a deep-seated fear that a woman doctor would win away his female patients—a fear not without basis, judging from precedent. One of the best-known early women physicians, Elizabeth Blackwell, had treated Boston's "most cultivated, influential and high born women," to the exclusion of male doctors. What happened in Boston could also happen in the West.

Women physicians trying to open a practice in a new community had limited choices; they could specialize in "women's problems," namely, obstetrics and gynecology, and hope for referrals from nearby physicians, or they could seek the protection of an older male physician. Such mentors were viewed as kind big brothers, particularly if they chose to pass along business to the new, young general practitioner. Dr. Amelia Dann, for example, was approached by Dr. Van Dun at a formal tea at his home; he asked if she could "arrange valuable time" to help him by performing minor surgery in the home and changing dressings. Anxious to work, she delighted in her new status of "associate." Jane Bruce Guignard, returning to her native South Carolina as a new, young practitioner, found a few of the old-time doctors helpful—

> *Trust a woman as*
> *a doctor!*
> *Never! Never!*
>
> —FANNY KEMBLE,
> BRITISH
> ACTRESS TOURING
> AMERICA

perhaps from a true spirit of support, perhaps from condescension. Her first patient was sent by a venerable local practitioner with a note in hand: "Dear Bruce—I am sending you Mrs. Sims and her little boy, I think he has worms."

Another physician, Dr. LeGrand Guerry, "graciously invited" her to observe one of his operations, and she became such a regular that he finally allowed her to assist him. After a while she was able to perform minor surgery in her office, simply laying the patient on the table, giving a "whiff of chloroform," and using instruments sterilized in a pan over a gas burner. Also, some women teamed up effectively with male medical partners to forge a strong medical unit. One such was the partnership struck between Mary "Auntie May" Hays, a fifty-three-year-old homesteader who had worked for years as an unlicensed "horseback" doctor, and William M. "Dr. Win" Beaver, a sixty-year-old physician. They worked together as equals, but if Auntie May delivered a baby without Beaver present, he, as a licensed physician, would have to sign the birth certificate.

Other physicians, such as the president of the Colorado Medical Society in the late 1870s, were equally supportive. He believed that if women failed, they should do so because of their own shortcomings, not because of male detractors. "That a woman should not practice medicine because she is a woman is absurd and intolerant," he concluded.

Many women showed a lively, entrepreneurial spirit in setting up their practices. When Evelyn Frisbie finished her internship in the Chicago Maternity Hospital, she practiced first in Iowa, establishing a solid clientele, then decided to move to Wagon Mound, New Mexico, where, under the terms of the Homestead Act of 1862, she could claim 150 acres of land if she could build and till and "prove up" her holdings. Weekdays were spent delivering babies, stitching wounds, and removing tonsils; weekends were devoted to carpentry and agriculture. But a greater challenge by far was to wrest away, in a civilized manner, part of the practice of the town's beloved physician, a Canadian-born doctor who practiced there from 1908 through 1920. Undaunted, Frisbie began to "work the countryside," riding to Ocate, twenty-five miles distant, in her horse and buggy, charting her way through unfamiliar terrain by following the faint outline of trails. So rough was the countryside that she finally abandoned the buggy and rode horseback, her medical satchel securely strapped on behind. Sophie Herzog of Brazoria, Texas, was equally intrepid in 1905, when she applied for the position of chief surgeon of the St. Louis, Brownsville and Mexico railroad. With glowing praises from railroad workers she had already tended, Herzog easily won the job—yet local railroad officials were never informed of her gender. When that was discovered, their plea that she quit the job was soundly rebuffed. "I'll keep this job so long as I give satisfaction," she replied, and that was what she did for thirty years, riding the rails by boxcar, engine, and handcar to reach her patients.

PART TWO

Women Doctors
on the Emotional Frontier

Relief Society nursing school, ca. 1900.

LDS Historical Department Archives

❧

CHAPTER FOUR

Who Will Be a Doctor?

❧

Character, Style, and
Outlook of Medical Women

Life is woven of circumstances . . . will the shuttle
weav[e] ugly rags or fine and beautiful cloth[?]

—MARY CANAGA ROWLAND

HO WERE THE WOMEN DRAWN TO MEDICINE? USUALLY THEY WERE strongly driven, seeking meaning in life; scientifically inclined; and generally unorthodox, as reflected in their dress and behavior. Their dedication made it difficult to marry and raise families, although each coped in her own unique way.

Women doctors functioned in a Victorian society that was deeply patriarchal, structured around men who held the upper hand both in public and private, and who resented female deviance of any kind. Women were due vocations, perhaps, but not careers. To the popular mind, middle-class men could tackle the "wilds" of commerce and trade, taming and interpreting the world for women, while the women themselves stayed home to tat, sew, visit, give birth, and exchange sentimental musings, literary aphorisms, and prodigious numbers of letters. Theirs was a middle-class world of discreet gossip and stiff protocol in an oddball mixture of

Puritanism, Victorian stuffiness, frontier self-determination, and courtly love. American culture of the 1850s had laced women into a paradoxical situation. While still dictating morality to all mankind, the roles of legislator, politician, or preacher were forbidden them. This etiolated breed of women, no matter how culturally elevated, seemed nervous, unhealthy, dependent . . . often uninspired.

Medicine cut an interesting swath through the Victorian mire, inviting women with a scientific calling to abandon leisure pursuits and fashion madness to pursue independence. In fact, the route of female independence actually paralleled the growing breach between the American home and the complicated, impersonal demands of increasing industrialization, urbanization, and professionalization of the 1850s.

"I feel as a Woman, I speak as a Woman, and I hope, I *understand* as a Woman," wrote a columnist for *Ladies Magazine* in 1830. She might have added that the hallmark of a woman's success in medicine was the early security of a good home, a strong ego, driving ambition, and a deep sense of service to the unfortunate—perhaps maternal feelings that had been sublimated into patient care. Bravery and lack of squeamishness were also part of the medical persona; typically, Elizabeth Blackwell had not the "slightest hesitation" about the "the horrors and disgusts" that lay in store in the study of medicine. Since her mind was "fully made up" about medicine, she said, "I don't care one straw *personally*" about the opinion of people. By 1846 Blackwell had sev-

ered "the usual ties of life" and was preparing to "act against [her] strongest natural inclinations," no matter what.

Nursing figured significantly in the professional lives of female physicians, since, for many, the decision to become a doctor sprang directly from dissatisfaction with nursing. Young girls with a desire to enter medicine were often forced into nursing, which led to great dissatisfaction and eventual career changes. Eleanor Townsend, a fourteen-year-old student at Chicora College in Columbia, South Carolina, was trained as a nurse in 1913 and subsequently practiced until 1923. Yet a pervasive dissatisfaction with the profession eventually brought her to the study of medicine, an odyssey similar to that of Anne Austin Young, whose family's poverty initially precluded a medical career. She entered nurses' training in 1910 at the University of Maryland but despite every effort, could only conclude that completing a nursing curriculum was "a waste of time." In 1910 she informed her parents that she would work as a teacher to earn the money for medical school.

An innate desire to right wrongs and to champion the oppressed also led many into medicine. Mary Walker, one of the first women to graduate from medical school, was an ardent campaigner for individual rights, even studying law in order to help Civil War veterans secure their pensions. Another advocate was Dr. Rosalie Slaughter, born in Lynchburg, Virginia, in 1876 and named by the League of Women Voters in 1923 as one of the twelve greatest living women in America.

Martha Hughes Cannon, M.D.

Utah State Historical Society

Since childhood Slaughter had harbored a deep concern for the rights of minorities, which both propelled her into medicine and prepared her for a future of personal ostracism.

Others were driven by discontent with the status quo or by a thirst for information, accuracy, or truth. The need to ask questions, to doubt, to accept nothing on faith shaped the scientific pursuits of pioneer Florence Sabin, born in 1871 in a shaky frame house in Silver City, Colorado, and so driven by the incessant desire of the scientist to achieve excellence that as a lecturer at the Johns Hopkins Medical School, she would tear up her notes at the end of each series of lectures to force herself to re-create them afresh for the next year. Soberly dressed in a plain brown tweed skirt and scorning cosmetics of any kind, Slaughter was an oblate to her mission, utterly devoted to truth, facts, and evidence, a believer that every great educator must first be an investigator. Said Sabin: "[It] matters little whether men or women have the more brains. All we need to do to exert our proper influence is to use all the brains we have."

⌘

Because of their disregard for conventional rules, "lady" doctors were naturally suspected of being involved in feminist causes, dress reform, sex education, and other "irregularities," particularly if they were single and self-supporting. In reality, many of the medical women born before the Civil War were high-strung libertarians, reformers devoted to moral issues, suffrage, women's rights, and temperance. Those born after the war, according to historian Gloria Moldow, tended to be professionals first and feminists second, for whom medicine was less a statement of personal autonomy and gender worth than a profession that would lead to profit. Regardless of their generation, medical women were seen (usually wrongly) as a tough, stunted species incapable of striking up social or matrimonial links, who brimmed with male hormones, a desire to wear pants and to rewrite history, and who exalted in isolation—cut off from their sex by both profession and predilection. Moreover, they had often graduated from inferior institutions and were numbered among the less-respected botanic, hydropathic, or eclectic practitioners in the clinical world. Women physicians simply inspired no confidence.

No wonder they faced a dilemma. With a Western canon that hailed the results of opportunism but scorned its enactment, they were expected to be feminine, but in doing so were excoriated as weak. Bertha Van Hoosen honestly desired the "material necessities" that

> *It matters little whether men or women have the more brains; [W]e women need to . . . use all the brains we have.*
>
> —FLORENCE SABIN

accompanied the profession, which also included social status and personal servants. A decent income also motivated Baltimore physician Lillian Welsh, who was tired of scrimping at a teaching job and had a keen interest in science and human nature. But, as women, could they safely have voiced these financial motivations?

Respectability averted criticism; femininity drew praise; but what, they wondered, would bring in patients? Women doctors were already seen as eccentric. Should they grasp the moment, court vulgarity, flaunt male attire, and give in to odd personal vagaries, from cigars to six-shooters? Those who embraced pistols and self-expression exuded the rowdy atmosphere of the streets, their personalities already tilted into the realm of eccentricity—or so it seemed.

There was no better example than Wyoming's Lillian Heath, whose prankish humor proved shocking to the uninitiated, who might glimpse on her shelves a favorite keepsake—the grisly skull of an outlaw, Big Nose George, who died in the hands of her medical preceptor, Dr. Thomas Maghee. "We studied his skull," Heath recalled in an interview. "It was still bloody with a piece of hair on it when they gave it to me, [with] a bullet mark on the skull." Heath, like many of her day, was caught up by the study of phrenology—a fleeting, quasi-scientific fad that determined character by head shape and brain size, lending the gruesome memorabilia a kind of scientific credibility. She believed that Big Nose George had a "small mentality" because

of the thickness of the skull, since there could be no mental growth, or expansion, through such a thick barrier. But keeping a skull on the shelf was mild compared to what her medical mentor did—he removed the skin from the outlaw's chest to make a pair of shoes, after which the body was unceremoniously dumped in a pickle barrel.

Heath's taste for the bizarre surfaced again when she treated "a great big burly fellow, a blustery type" whose foot had been mangled by a hay press, with the little toe completely sheared away from the rest. She placed the toe up on the windowsill to dry out and kept it there alongside an ear that another doctor had removed, which turned "the prettiest amber color when dried."

Union Army surgeon Mary Walker regularly wore hip-slung pistols as well as an American flag tied with crepe. Even though she practiced in the rough arena of the army camps of the Civil War, the sight of an armed woman proved disturbing to nearly everyone in some basic way, whether she was a surgeon or not. Walker flaunted her disregard for female dress codes, even designing a rape-proof costume for women, and once, mischievously, wore the uniform of a Union soldier to a funeral, complete with pistols. Her highly shined cavalry boots and shoulder straps signifying her rank as major raised an immediate public outcry. No gentleman would pack pistols to desecrate a house of God—why should she? Dr. Walker denied the charges, but she could not deny the fact that she wore pants to her wedding ceremony, refused to take Albert

Miller's name, and insisted that any vow to obey her husband be omitted from the ceremony. The marriage was greatly ridiculed by society, and, indeed, was short-lived. The plague of publicity that swirled about her never eased. No matter how skillful or enterprising Walker was professionally, the stigma of her dress and deportment lingered, causing her surgical skills to be impugned. But eventually her repeated deeds of mercy and unwavering devotion to dress reform caught the public imagination, and she was seen as a reformer rather than a complete eccentric. The New York *Tribune* acclaimed her "jaunty air of dignity" as she made her way through the rows of wounded and sick, "dressed in male habiliments . . . [and] a girlish-looking straw hat, decked off with an ostrich feather." In typical fashion, her *"tout ensemble* [was] judged "quite engaging" but, in classic journalistic style, there was no mention of her medical skills. In fairness, male physicians were also judged sartorially, even labeled "dandies," yet unlike women, their professional success was not as strongly linked to dress and deportment.

Even as a war prisoner, Walker drew comment. Captured by rebel forces in Georgia and transported seven hundred miles to a prison camp in Virginia, Walker was touted as the "Yankee lady in bloomers" and viewed with great curiosity. Locked in fetid quarters with idle time on her hands, she was accused of flighty personal habits; she refused to read "medical works on sawing bones and the treatment of camp itch," but instead, according to the *Richmond Examiner* of May 13, 1864,

she devoured "all the novel nonsense and trash she [could] get hold of with a Negro character in them." Of further concern was the fact that she refused to shed her bloomer style and adopt the dress code of her sex.

But women wore men's clothing for reasons other than the commonly assumed one, that of usurping the male role. Lillian Heath's penchant for "special clothes" came from a need for personal safety as well as convenience. Before medical school, she had studied with a local surgeon whose classes were held after hours and in the late evening. "So that people wouldn't talk," the young girl was asked to disguise herself as a man, wearing clothing that her father provided by taking her measurements and altering a pair of boy's trousers. Not only was it unseemly for a woman to buy men's clothing, but it was also illegal in some states. Besides, said Heath, "the ready made wouldn't do . . . because my waist was so much smaller than my hips." The rest of her costume was a boy's jacket over a plain shirt and a flat-topped hat, an outfit that she came to enjoy.

Male garb served the needs of Jennie C. Murphy, of Yankton, South Dakota, whose legendary gruffness was in perfect keeping with her mannish clothes, custom-made for her by the firm of Lubitz and Taylor. She fastened her hat to the top of a piled-up bun with a long hat pin, once saying, "With my hat pin and buggy whip, I'm not afraid to go anywhere!" Equally brazen was rural practitioner Sophie Herzog of Brazoria, Texas, a petite woman whose soulful brown eyes and gentle expression belied her mischievous nature, and who delighted in charging up and down the streets on a galloping horse, her bouncy locks tucked beneath a man's fur hat, a glittering necklace of twenty-four polished bullets and gold beads clattering about her neck—a good-luck talisman that testified to a reputation for extreme dexterity in removing bullets. Herzog's mannish, divided riding skirt had been created by a local seamstress, and her hair was cropped in jaunty defiance of the accepted style of the day, usually long braided strands coiled about the head. A native of Austria, she harkened more to the call of the wild than the voice of decorum, and the record of her impressive medical skills was subsumed to the lore of her brassy bravado, numerous children,

Lalda Goggins and Cleo McLaughlin.

National Library of Medicine

Who Will Be a Doctor?

and the fact that the strand of bullets was buried with her—at her request. In contrast, early-twentieth-century Kansas physician Mary Glassen was noted for her "strong and capable" hands and distinctly feminine appearance. Although usually so busy and hurried that she appeared hatless on the street, she was still completely feminine in appearance. Her silvery hair was delicately upswept, and she often sported lipstick.

Surgeon Bertha Van Hoosen, typical of medical women, had been so caught up in her practice that fashion seldom occurred to her. Several years into her career she decided to apply for a residency at the New England Hospital for Women and Children, even though, "as a Western woman with limited clinical experience," she had little hope of "being the successful candidate." She set out for Boston, dressed in her usual style of home-made dresses. "Buy yourself some new clothes," advised a friend, who took her to a department store in New York and suited her up in leg-of-mutton sleeves and a ruffled silk skirt. She "bought . . . a hat covered with wings, suggesting a flight of birds—a remarkable fashion" to settle over her unruly red curls. "I feared my feather would mitigate [sic] against me," wrote Van Hoosen, but she won the appointment on a choice "narrowed down to two points: hair and training."

Dress was not the only element of women doctors' comportment that aroused interest. By her own description, Bethenia Owens-Adair of Roseburg, Oregon, was a "strange, anomalous being" who "shocked and scandalized" women and "disgusted but amused" men, particularly due to her reputation of having handled male genitalia during an autopsy. Unabashed, Owens-Adair boldly waged profeminist campaigns for more exercise, shorter skirts, and the outlawing of the torturous practice of riding sidesaddle—wouldn't women, she maintained, have better balance with a foot in each stirrup, just like men? Having survived the rigors of prejudice from fellow medical students, arduous study at the University of California, the Women's Medical College of Pennsylvania, and the Jefferson Medical College, her already tough temperament turned even more steely. Owens-Adair became a successful lobbyist for the Women's Christian Temperance Union, reminding young ladies that they could wield the persuasive powers of their sex to lead men to temperance.

Tough, obdurate, even theatrical at times in order to make a point, medical women knew how to take charge, make a point, and were relentless in pursuing their goals. "Getting mad" was Dr. Hilla Sheriff's response to incompetence, demonstrated one day when visiting a center for the care of premature infants funded by a demonstration grant she had received from the state of South Carolina. She found two sick babies—one with severe diarrhea and the other with pneumonia—placed in the room with the premature infants. She went to the kitchen, picked up a butcher knife, and confronted the hospital official responsible for admitting the ill babies to the nursery: "I want you to kill all those premature babies with this knife. At least she would suffer less than they would when they die lingering deaths from those diseases you've exposed them to."

⁓❦⁓

Femininity, however, seemed intertwined both with independence and compassion. As well as packing guns and changing legislation, many women doctors had nearly infinite compassion. Utah's Lena Schreier believed that a doctor should give each patient the amount of time he or she required, whether it was five minutes or an hour: "It is the cry of the sick that drives you and compels you to work hard, sometimes doing the work of 48 hours in 24 if necessary." And Bertha Van Hoosen wrote, "If I should leave the laboring woman . . . I would be unfit for any other professional work, for my mind would be filled with possible happenings to her whom I had deserted." Dr. Mary Glassen was unable to stop working over a dying premature infant, struggling for over three hours to save the child's life. When the breathing stopped, according to biographer Vera Chance Ward, the doctor "picked up the tiny body in her arms and held it a couple minutes with tears running down her cheeks." Glassen was a popular figure around Phillipsburg, Kansas; children would shout "Hello, Dr. Mary," knowing that she was "never too busy" to prescribe for their dolls, examine their puppy dogs, or treat them to sodas at Rankin's Drug Store. According to the pharmacist, her ice cream bill alone ran "between $300 and $500 a year."

Georgia Arbuckle Fix was never able to hold her tongue at the sight of some egregious action, particularly if it involved a young child or the demon rum. An ardent campaigner against alcohol, Fix once, after delivering a baby in a rural setting, happened upon twelve bottles of liquor on a shelf. Furious at the baby's father for daring to tipple, much less appear drunk, she destroyed every bottle. Mary Rowland's husband called her "the New Woman," in honor of her intrepid spirit; in 1916, years after he had died, a string of border disputes between the United States and Mexico flared briefly into a small war, prompting Rowland to try to enlist in the army. After all, hadn't her relatives fought in every American war since the Revolution? Rowland envisioned herself "riding a horse over the battlefield and giving first aid to the wounded"—a vision unfortunately not shared by the shocked army medical corps, who had "never heard of such a thing." The army did not take women, and she was further embarrassed when a local newspaper announced that she had tried to enlist. "I didn't know the first thing about the organization of an army," Rowland recalled. "I was unaware that women were not a part of the army."

Not all female physicians were so single-minded. Many considered themselves women first and doctors second, possessors of a feminine nature that constantly recoiled from society's affronts. Elizabeth Blackwell seemed curiously innocent, admitting that "it was not until 1869, when attending the Social Sciences Congress in Bristol, that my mind at last fully comprehended the hideousness of modern for-

Dr. Ellis Shipp.

Utah State Historical Society

nication." For Elizabeth Smith, "not a day . . . passes . . . but something makes me shrink, something hurts me, hurts me cruelly, & why?" To her journal, she confided that "[nothing] in the whole range of medicine should make me blush or feel hurt in the tenderest part of a woman's nature." She agonized about the duality of her role and the difficulty of incorporating femininity with professionalism.

Women often solved the dilemma by moving west, establishing themselves in tiny villages and scrambling new frontier towns; they often abandoned habits of the past, finding in their new lives the strength to fight sex discrimination, although their struggle often caused them to forgo marriage and childbearing. How, it was wondered, could a woman combine a home and office? Should she abandon her primary calling, that of motherhood and marriage, in order to tend to the needs of the sick?

Yet women were often well suited for both. Able to wear pants, crop their hair, and ride horseback with the men, women doctors could also sew, tat, and bear children, and often found that both motherhood and medicine utilized their inherent abilities, despite the difficulties faced by a young woman trying to attend medical school or practice with children at home. Wrote the recently widowed mother and physician Mary Rowland in the late 1880s:

I began to practice when my baby was a month old. If I had been wise, I never would have tried to practice while I nursed her. I was practically on the gallop all the time. I would hurry to take care of a patient and then hurry home to nurse the baby. I kept a girl to do the housework and Doctor's [her deceased husband] mother came and stayed with me for two years to help take care of the baby.

So determined to practice medicine was Rowland—and also lonely after her husband's tragic murder—that she married a German butcher, which she privately called "the greatest mistake of my life." They parted shortly thereafter, in 1908, after he learned that Mary wanted him to help her raise her daughter Nellie while she practiced medicine. So "pitiable" appeared this single woman trying to raise a child that a couple offered to adopt the girl. "[They said] I could not practice medicine and raise her, but I felt she was my responsibility and I could not turn her over to someone else for care." Texas physician Sophie Herzog raised fourteen children and hordes of grandchildren while maintaining a breakneck practice. Children were a dominant theme in the life of Mormon physician Ellis Shipp, who was always accompanied on her rounds by one child or another. She even gave birth to a child while in medical school. Shipp worked at an excruciating pace, causing a daughter to plead with her in a letter written in 1886: "Dear Mama, Olea and I are very lonely without you and I want you to come home right now. The boys left us all alone and let the fire go out and we put some coal in the fire stove and we made a nice fire and thought you were coming home. Good night from your kind and loving daughter, Ellis R. Shipp."

Parenthood plus medicine brought attendant fears. A mother-physician could vividly imagine the diseases or accidents that lurked in store for her own offspring. Like all of humanity, especially at that time, women doctors not infrequently faced the loss of children. Dr. Lucinda Hall, the first licensed physician to practice in New England, who was joined by her husband in the practice when he received his degree in 1856, had the tragedy of losing her son to an accidental death by gunfire and her grown daughter to childbirth complications several months later. Despite her domestic tragedy, she continued to practice in Lowell, trying to maintain an optimistic outlook, treating diseases of women and sinking gratefully and enthusiastically into her work. No amount of medical training could prepare a woman for the sorrow of maternal loss, no matter how many times a fetus had slipped lifeless through her hands, accompanied by the sobs of its mother.

Wrote Oregon physician Bethenia Owens-Adair:

> At the age of forty-seven I gave birth to a little daughter; and now my joy knew no limit, my cup of bliss was full to overflowing. A son I had, and a daughter was what I most desired. . . . For three days only, was she left with us, and then my treasure was taken from me, to join in the immortal hosts beyond all earthly pain and sorrow.
>
> I felt it was more than I could bear.

No amount of medical proficiency could shield a woman from the dread of losing her own child to accident or disease—she had to exert discipline not to brood over the incredible possibilities. "If I was in total ignorance of certain symptoms, I should not worry so," sighed Utah physician Dr. Martha Hughes Cannon, a Mormon wife who fled to England in 1886 to protect her husband from prosecution as a polygamist. She raised her young daughter while in exile, and her letters home swing from pleading admonitions to vague fears that were actually realized one day, when her daughter, Elizabeth, drank a tiny vial of ammonia Mattie had hidden away for safekeeping.

Jan 18—87

> She got into the little box, and poured the ammonia down her throat. The entire contents, excepting a few drops in [the] bottom of the bottle, went down the throat into the child's stomach. I think when she gasped, the teeth closed on [the] neck of the bottle so that none of its contents escaped outside the mouth. I caught her as she fell senseless, gasping for breath, and went through all the horror and agony of feeling she was stiffening and dying in my arms. Oh the terror of that dark hour; it makes me shudder to think of it now.
>
> I first dashed water in her face to make her catch her breath, next tore open the little medicine case for a bottle containing about a teaspoonful of con-

secrated oil [blessed olive oil used by Mormons for healing].... Elizabeth, after I had poured all the oil I had down her throat, began to vomit so violently that I really felt that if the burning from the ammonia did not kill her, the severe straining & retching would complete the work. The matter vomited produced a lather like soft soap while several good sized pieces of mucous membrane either from the throat or stomach were mixed with it. Then begged Mrs. H to go and get a bottle of oil [which] she did with all possible haste, and in our frenzy we asked the Lord to bless it as best we could. A half tumbler of this I then poured down her throat, when from the soothing effects of the oil and complete exhaustion she became more quiet — but during the above period she suffered the most extreme agony I ever witnessed in a mortal being....

I felt in my soul it was a case beyond all human aid, for she had taken enough of the poison to kill a number of grown persons. All that night she lay & moaned, being conscious only part of the time.... I forced a teaspoonful of the consecrated oil down her little throat twice & it was most pitiable to see her struggles.... Talk about human heartaches. I never knew what the words meant until that dark night.

Next I milked a teaspoonful of milk from my breast and dropped it drop by drop on the little parched lips, when she looked into my face with an expression of thankfulness that I can never forget.

Miraculously, the child recovered, but not before the doctor discovered the limits of her own emotion and professionalism. Said Hughes: "I believe positively I should have gone mad had [Elizabeth] been taken."

Martha Hughes Cannon, M.D.

LDS Historical Department Archives

Compassion was often a hallmark of women doctors. The motherly nature of Dr. Jane Bruce Guignard of Columbia, South Carolina, drew countless patients into her practice, men and women alike. No matter how busy her schedule, Guignard would sit all night, with "infinite patience," at a patient's bedside. Keeping a vigil was considered a mandatory part of the nursing and healing process, every bit as important as keen diagnosis or deft surgery. "Too many doctors actually abandon a family at a time when they are most needed," said one physician to his graduating class at the University of Syracuse. Physician Amelia Dann knew this to be true and she, as a woman and a family-care physician, determined to offer consolation and help along with medication. Many emulated the tradition begun by Dr. Mary Lavinder, whose midwifery and pediatric practice in Savannah, Georgia, in 1814 was the beginning of an ever-widening service to the poor of the community. Daily, in her old-fashioned carriage drawn by an aged white horse, she distributed coffee, sugar, tea, grits—even mattresses and blankets—to the impoverished and ill. Mary Walker once cut off all her hair to sell for a soldier's wife who was destitute and homeless in Washington. Dr. Hannah Longshore established a thriving practice in Philadelphia by her "personality and ability," yet also gave service freely to the indigent. Her sister, Dr. Jane Myers, also had a "sympathetic attitude" that won her enormous popularity with patients. Equally charitable was Dr. Ellen Smith, known as "Doc Ellen" in rural Salem County, New Jersey—a woman who cared for all patients, whether they could pay or not.

To treat patients with empathy and respect was the goal of many women doctors; they understood that the care of the patient began with caring *for* the patient. Where often the male doctor concentrated on technique, the female doctor often sought human meaning. This nurturing quality frequently translated well into their professional world. Isabel Davenport, assistant physician at the Kanakee Institute—one of the "largest and best hospitals for the insane in the world," according to the governor of Illinois—established a garden for female patients. She had seen that when male patients were put to work pushing lawn mowers, pruning trees, planting flowers, making walks, picking up trash, tending truck gardens, and herding cattle, "much less hypnotic and sedative medicine was being given." However, normally women were assigned to sedentary, indoor tasks: ward work, the kitchen, dressmaking, rug weaving. Davenport was troubled by the

> *Doctor, how very odd it is to hear a man called Doctor!*
>
> —SEVEN-YEAR-OLD ORPHAN IN 1854 TO HER NEW MOTHER, KATHERINE BARRIE (BASS)

image of her women patients "plodding along in . . . monotonous walking parties, scarcely speaking or being spoken to." She resolved that the women should have a garden. The gardener issued seeds and offered advice; each bed had a border of low-growing flowers and was bursting with radishes, lettuce, cucumbers, tomatoes, peas, and string beans. The first show of green sprouts piqued full interest; even weeding and raking had "immense interest" for the female patients. Harvesttime brought group dinners and the warm aroma of cooking vegetables from the kitchen. The hospital gave her three acres the following spring, and several hundred women were put to outdoor work. Some patients prepared the vegetables for cooking, while others made bouquets and carried them to the sick ward. "It was a cozy, busy sight," Davenport remarked, thrilled that horticulture could reach out to manic-depressive patients as well as the apathetic, the restless, the delusional, the epileptic, and the demented. Only the paranoic seemed "less inclined" to take part, but they enjoyed arranging flowers nonetheless. Davenport never again had to feel apologetic for her "feminine" solutions after her horticultural success. She, like Dr. Mary Glassen and so many others, could sum up her interests: "[W]hat more life can hold when you love what you're doing, where you're doing it, and the people you're doing it with?"

BETTER COOKS, BETTER FOOD, BETTER HEALTH.

Wilson County Sanitation Day Parade, Fredonia, Kansas.

National Library of Medicine

꒰⚬꒱

CHAPTER FIVE

Early Inspirations

꒰⚬꒱

Motivation and Mentors

I have no memory of a time when I did not
plan to be a physician.

— JESSIE LAIRD BRODIE

 EDICAL ASPIRANTS OFTEN SIDESTEPPED THE DRAWING ROOM, THE nursery, and for some, the bedroom and conjugal happiness to pursue their profession. No matter how supportive the home environment, medical women still braved prejudice, jeers, antipathy, and often the loss of lovers, husbands, and friends to become physicians, raising the often-asked question: What kind of women were they?

According to pioneer physician Elizabeth Blackwell, girls who aspired to medicine craved more than the usual academic regimen for young women of "music, German, and metaphysics." They desired philosophy, arithmetic, and science as well, and were so determined to pursue their studies that any opposition touched off the makings of a "great moral struggle," which possessed immense attraction for spirited and idealistic young women.

The love of learning drove Mary Harris Thompson, born in 1829, to the New England Female Medical College in Boston, where, at the age of twenty-nine, she prepared to study physiology and other subjects in order to teach. But her keen intellect drew her to the medical curriculum, which caught her interest and imagination. Elizabeth Cushier, a young girl growing up in the New Jersey countryside, vacillated between her love of English poetry and music until, in the summer of 1868, she read an article titled "Influence of the Ganglionic System in Producing Sleep." What was the ganglionic system? she wondered. She had to know: "This meant, I knew, a knowledge of physiology, and physiology suggested medicine and its study. I knew that there were a few women physicians, but I had never met one, and the thought of taking up the study of medicine seemed chimerical; however, it became a fixed idea."

Often, intellectually active women were raised by nonconformist parents—perhaps suffragists, freethinkers, or members of a purity league, an antivivisection league, or a settlement house—who nurtured the popular "isms" of the day and encouraged all visions. While traditional belles learned the etiquette of the curtsy and the blush, other young women were throwing aside the imprimatur of "virtuous womanhood," naming plants and planets and trying to cure disease. Dr. Rosalie Slaughter came from a strong medical heritage; seventeen of her direct ancestors and fifty-two other relatives had been practicing physicians. At the age of sixteen she told her mother she wanted to be a nurse, and applied to several schools. After being rejected, she voiced her true dream: "I really intend to be a doctor, like the boys."

Girls from such literate, political households breathed in abolitionism, the temperance movement, and women's rights; they read authors such as George Sand and breezily applauded the freedoms of masculine dress. They believed that women had lost their practical function in society and sought to replace it with scientific intellectualism. Often, their families touted communitarianism, praising the notion of communal living and shared resources.

Such freethinking influence showed up in many ways, even in family appellations. For Mary Walker, her parents' individuality could be traced to a dusty photograph that showed two young sisters posed side by side, one girl christened Mary, the other, rather artfully, Aurora Borealis. At an early age Hannah Meyers of Pennsylvania decided to acquire the middle initial "E" without any name to go with it, simply because she wished to be known as Hannah E. Meyers—a way to distinguish herself.

Family influence aside, some women doctors recalled having an instinct to help and to heal since they were young girls. "All my life from early childhood I had said I was going to be a doctor," recalled Claudia Potter, whose "burning ambition to make good" in her work was supported by unflagging energy and a "love of humanity, in particular." As children, these future physicians had "treated" dolls, puppies, and friends, and they considered themselves healers, with a strong awareness of their calling. Lillian Heath spent her childhood "patching up" neighborhood children injured in tin-can fights, long before deciding to attend the old Hughes College of Physicians and Surgeons in Keokuk, Iowa, where she obtained her Doctor of Medicine degree in 1893. Jessie Laird's dolls "thrived on senna and camomile tea and were more likely to be dressed in bandages than in clothes." Mary Wood Allen, born in 1841 in Ohio, had doctored "sick" dolls since childhood, but it was only after the death of her first child in infancy that she and her husband began their medical studies. Hilla Sheriff, as a young girl in Pickins County, South Carolina, remembered naming one of her dolls "the doctor," since that was what she intended to be.

Some were persuaded to appease their "unnatural" medical desires through nursing, an approved career for women if not associated with the military. Anne Austin Young, a gifted student and valedictorian of her class at Presbyterian College in 1910, made such an attempt, but it left her deeply dissatisfied. She then turned to teaching in a one-room school near Cross Hill, South Carolina, hoping to save money for medical school. One term's worth of teaching gave her enough money to enter the Women's Medical College of Pennsylvania, where ensuing scholarships furthered her efforts.

In fact, the women who successfully pursued careers in medicine in the nineteenth century were exceptional—as a rule scholarly, autocratic, and outspoken, they were often also malcontents. Many were attracted by the hope of financial and professional independence as well. Such sentiments were captured perfectly by Bertha Van Hoosen, a native of Stony Creek, Michigan, who in the 1860s systematically weighed the advantages and drawbacks of medicine and finally concluded: "I wanted to be my own boss." Young Elizabeth Cushier, one of eleven children, attributed her choice of a career in medicine to a "determination to lead an independent life." Although she knew of women physicians, she had never met one; she had no model.

Boredom with middle-class life drew Florence Nightingale to medicine. Because of the influence of two nuns she had met in her travels, who encouraged her civic spirit and convinced her of the idea of service, she began to find the social life of her upper-class family abhorrent and withdrew to the field of medicine for fulfillment, likening medicine to a kind of religious awakening.

Whether influenced by nuns or priests, parents, or family physicians, nearly every young girl bound for medical studies could cite a mentor, some person who either inspired her or actually guided her into the profession, furthering the tradition of apprenticeship that had existed long before the establishment of medical schools. Close friends, husbands, male relatives, and physician-fathers lent support and inspiration, as did male physicians outside the family who believed that medicine would be enhanced by the female presence. Men who encouraged their wives, cousins, and sisters in the study of medicine were remarkably broad-minded for the time, usually intellectuals and staunch supporters of the movement against slavery.

The oppression of race or sex repulsed them, and in assisting women into professions, they spurred on the country in its own journey toward equality and opportunity—concepts that were only beginning to be voiced.

Such was the country physician who inspired Lucinda Hall's career. As a married woman with two children, Hall seemed an unlikely candidate. Her husband worked as a lay assistant to Dr. Paige, a medical doctor who manufactured herbal prescriptions to sell through druggists as well as from the back of a wagon. While her husband and Paige traveled, Lucinda huddled in the doctor's library, avidly reading his medical texts. Her interest in medicine grew daily, tempered only slightly by the fact that no college existed where she could actually study *materia medica*. She finally found a group of three male physicians willing to lecture to her and eleven other women. After the informal course of lectures, she finally received a degree. Her example inspired her husband, Robert Hall, to also study medicine; he joined her in her practice after his graduation in 1854. Another husband-wife physician team was Dr. Anna Darrow, of southern Florida, and Dr. Charles Roy Darrow. Their division of labor allowed him to mind the pharmacy and tend to office calls while she traveled throughout four counties on a lame horse (or driving a buggy if the back roads were wide enough), fording swamps and dodging snakes and other vermin.

Lillian Heath was inspired by both her father and the town physician, Dr. Thomas Maghee, who recognized the importance of a female doctor in handling issues of Victorian modesty and called on her to assist in his obstetrical cases. He encouraged the girl to think of medicine as a career, since as a "lady doctor," Heath "could do things for the women folk that they would prefer to have a woman do."

As with Heath, fathers were an important influence on many. The father of Elizabeth Comstock, born in 1875, was a "staunch believer in opportunities for women" and encouraged his daughter to study medicine. Texas physician Dr. Sophie Herzog was inspired by her father, an internationally known Austrian surgeon, as well as by her husband, a talented surgeon. Gulielma Fell Alsop daydreamed of becoming a missionary in China as she whiled away her summers at her grandmother's summer home in Pennsylvania. After listening to her ideas, her father remarked that she had better study medicine, and by 1908 she had graduated from the Women's Medical College of Pennsylvania. Civil War army doctor Mary Walker, who was born November 26, 1832, and graduated from Syracuse University Medical School at twenty-two, in 1855, always

> *Only in working toward my medical goal could I be true to myself.*
>
> —DR. PORTIA LUBCHENCO MCKNIGHT

cited her father, physician Alvah Walker, as her path to medicine. He taught her everything he knew about medicine, including the treatment of farm animals. As a young girl, Mrs. L. C. Smith of Carbon, Wyoming, had her interest in medicine sparked by her physician-father; such early inspiration led to a career with the Union Pacific Coal Company, where she dosed and sympathized coal mine accident victims into recovery.

Mary Putnam's father, a publisher, was proud of her abilities, and approved of her so heartily that any choice she made was supported, even the "repulsive pursuit of medical education." Overcoming his prejudice, he encouraged her to study for a pharmacy degree as a stepping-stone toward medicine. The self-made, tough-minded Scots father of Sarah Campbell Allan was irritated when she was refused admission at the Medical College of the State of South Carolina in 1890. He believed that his intelligent daughter deserved more than the suffocating, near-indolent life of most privileged Victorian women, counting stitches and days between one social event or another.

Jessie Laird, who had "no memory of a time when [she] did not plan to be a physician," found paternal inspiration from "many an evening" in rural Washington, when she assisted her father in his rural practice by holding a kerosene lamp aloft while her father performed emergency surgery on loggers. Supportive as he was, he still protested when she announced her intention to enter medical school, for male students often sneaked body

parts from cadavers into the beds of female students, which caused him concern. Was this what his daughter wanted?

The dreams of youth became an adult reality for Bessie Efren, whose medical lineage included a father, grandfather, great-grandfather, uncle, and brother who were physicians, and whose "daily diet" at home was a compendium of "sickness, medicine, bandages, pills, poultices and splints." From her earliest years, she practiced "folding little papers for powders, filling bottles with medicine . . . or holding the kerosene lamp" to assist her father at midnight emergencies. Her one desire was that she, too, might someday become a doctor. After graduating from the Sioux City School of Medicine, she wrote: "A dream of my childhood days and the burning ambition of my youth had become a reality. I was now a doctor like my father. I was now a member of one of the most respected professions in society, and people would from now on address me with the title of 'Doctor,' an honor that in my previous experience had been the sole prerogative of men."

One woman was actually driven into medicine by her father's pitched opposition. Helen MacKnight Doyle's determination proved intractable: "I . . . had no wish to change. I really liked the study of medicine. I wanted to go on with it more than I wanted anything else in the world." She wanted to "win out . . . and . . . demonstrate that a woman could be just as good a sport as a man." The constant objections of her family honed her resistance into a firm career plan. Struck by her stalwart spirit, her father eventually changed his mind. After all, he reasoned, wouldn't her success prove a financial advantage—even insurance—in his old age? From strict prohibition his tactic switched to lavish encouragement, and upon graduation she was summoned home to treat her sick stepmother and persuaded to stay in a tiny, hardscrabble Nevada mining camp, where she fitted up the front room of the house as an office and hung her shingle from the porch.

I dreaded to go home. There is no one to whom my heart goes out in such quick sympathy as to a child who dreads to go home. I know what a tragic thing it is.

But I soon forgot everything else in my first hand-to-hand, unaided conflict with death. There were two physicians in the town. One was an old army doctor, who refused to consult with me. The other was a man who treated my degree as a rare joke. He said I might be a good nurse.

My stepmother needed nursing and tenderness more than she did prescriptions. She had been over-drugged. There were hours of terrible uncertainty, when it seemed she would slip away from me, but gradually she gained strength. She recovered.

My father was immensely gratified, not by the fact that his wife had been spared to him, but by my ability to cure her. He went about the town, telling everyone whom he saw: "My wife is get-

ting well. The doctors gave her up, but Nellie came home and cured her!"

I knew it was useless to ask him to send me back to San Francisco. My place in the hospital was filled. I fitted up an office in the front room of the house and put out my shingle — Helen M. MacKnight, M.D., Physician and Surgeon. My father was proud of the M.D., but resented the Helen. I had been christened Nellie. That was my name. But I remembered the words of the Dean [that a doctor must have a serious-sounding name], and the sign was not changed. I put in a small stock of drugs (it would be necessary to fill my own prescriptions), bought a medicine case, and started in.

My conveyance was a two-wheeled cart with a jump seat. I harnessed and unharnessed the horse myself. I would stand at the back of the cart with the reins in my hand, raise the seat, clamber in and start off. I used to smile sometimes, wondering what those professors with their carriages and coachmen would think if they could see me. . . .

Doctors are supposed to be able to bury their mistakes, but if they do not wish to have post-mortem discussions of why and how it happened they had best keep to the cities. A young doctor, fresh from medical college, can pass many embarrassing moments in the presence of the neighborhood midwife. Country people have been through the stress of illness, without trained medical assistance so often that they have an astonishing knowledge of human ills gained in the school of experience.

Doyle's early enthusiasm quickly turned bitter. Her father, a cold and harsh man, informed her that "he was ready to retire and draw the interest on the investment he had made," and promptly quit his job as a surveyor. Wrote Doyle: "He stayed at home and watched every move I made with a consuming jealousy." Male patients were watched, hawklike, and allotted only so much time with the young doctor, who found herself struggling to survive "his utter possession." She was his investment, and an investment surely could not marry. He began reading her mail, once greeting her at the train station "white and trembling with rage" after reading an innocent greeting written by a young male friend who addressed her as "my dear girl." Raging hysterically, he forced her to write a letter to sever the relationship. For a moment she wondered if he would kill her; then she shook free of her terror, jumped up, and left his home forever. "I saw my father for what he was—a cruel, selfish man, who . . . sent for me to come to him only when I was old enough to give him a possessive pleasure." Yet in later years she willingly paid the notes and debts he had hoped to pay with the proceeds of her practice.

Although the father of Indiana surgeon Bertha Van Hoosen never hindered her progress, he worried continually about her finances, failing to understand her passion: "I

was so much in love with the practice of medicine that even blistering my feet [walking to save carfare] gave me a sense of devotion to a great profession, rather than a feeling of abuse." Her father's death from unexplained neurological complications left her distraught and plagued by feelings of guilt because she had failed to identify his illness. "The loss of my father left me with a sense of loneliness. Hunger for his approval nagged me year after year."

The first woman in North Dakota to earn a medical degree was Fannie Quain, who was inspired by her father, a druggist; his brother, a doctor; and her aunt and cousins, who were nurses and doctors. "This background may have had its influence on my desire to study medicine," she wrote, yet these same relatives seemed strangely uninvolved in her actual progress. Born in Bismarck, Dakota Territory, in 1874, her career had been hampered by poverty—she had to support herself as a typist as well as teaching in a rural school, even running for the office of county school superintendent, although she lost. When money was offered to her by a sympathetic relative, her mother refused to let her accept it. When an aunt who had once studied medicine offered to take Fannie to New York, the mother refused this offer also. Quain managed to save the money for her medical education but only received her degree at the University of Michigan at Ann Arbor years later, in 1898. Afterward she became a pioneer practitioner in Bismarck in public health, specializing in diseases of the eye and ear.

Young girls also drew inspiration from

A homesteader
Patient.

"Cowboys from the
Range"

"Brother B"

Georgia Arbuckle
about 1875

"he drove a fast Team"

The Doctor was
Sympathetic to Romance.

"a Stubborn Typhoid
case requiring 18
bonate trips"

Eli Beebe owed his life
to the Woman Doctor who
inserted a Silver Plate when
his Skull was Crushed by a
whirling
windlass.

Dan Davis

Dr. Arbuckle saved his hand.
when it was Crushed by a
windmill fan.

"A Dinner was given in
honor of Dr Fix before she
sailed for Europe in 1908,
A ship was the Center Piece."

"A hired girl"

The Fix Sanitarium building
in later years.
John McComsey, the Doctor's Companion

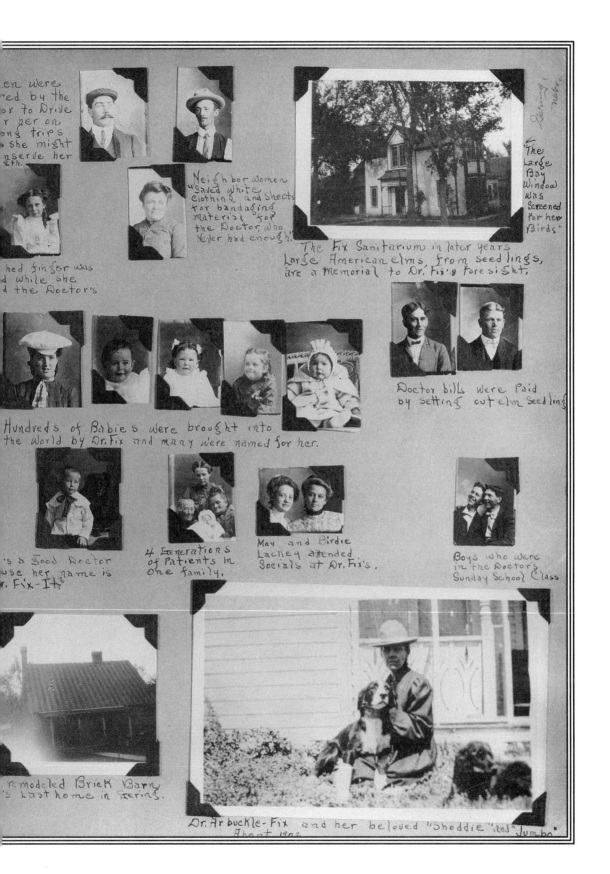

...en were
...red by the
...or to Drive
...r her on
...ong trips
...she might
...nserve her
...th.

Neighbor Women
"Saved White
Clothing and Sheets
for bandaging
material for
the Doctor who
Never had enough."

...hed finger was
...d while she
...d the Doctor's

The Large
Bay
Window
Was
Screened
for her
"Birds"

The Fix Sanitarium in later years
Large American elms, from seedlings,
are a Memorial to Dr. Fix's foresight.

Doctor bills were paid
by setting out elm seedling

Hundreds of Babies were brought into
the World by Dr. Fix and many were named for her.

...'s a Good Doctor
...use her name is
...r. Fix-It.

4 Generations
of Patients in
One family.

May and Birdie
Lackey attended
Socials at Dr. Fix's.

Boys who were
in the Doctor's
Sunday School Class

...remodeled Brick Barn
...'s last home in Gering.

Dr. Arbuckle-Fix and her beloved "Shoddie" and "Jumbo"
About 1902.

༄ཎ་ ༄ཎ་ ༄ཎ་

The picture book of
Dr. Georgia Arbuckle Fix.

Nebraska State Historical Society

female role models, often a mother who had either practiced medicine professionally or set an example as a healer. Mary Glassen's mother had wanted to practice medicine, a desire that translated into a heartfelt wish for the same for her daughter. "I decided she would be a doctor before she was born," wrote the intrepid mother. Mary's childhood had been a welter of home remedies brewed by her mother, including a cocklebur syrup for the whooping cough that was later proven to have healing properties when tested by the hospital where Mary practiced. Florence De Hart grew up in a household where her mother, Dr. Lucy Madana Fuller, was a full-fledged physician who practiced medicine in Jersey City until 1912. Dr. Elizabeth B. Ball, who graduated from the University of Illinois Medical School in 1907, credited her decision to study medicine to her mother's influence.

Economic necessity drove Emily Dunning's mother to suggest college to a daughter who was fatherless, without a dowry, and faced a future of poverty, not to mention possible spinsterhood and a lifetime of menial labor. The weight of community disapproval turned Dunning's mother "gray and drawn" as she informed her daughter: "Emily, you are going to go to college." Likewise, a financial

reversal in the family fortunes turned Harriot Hunt into the sole support of her family. She considered teaching, but the idea of such "daily heart-break," "underrated services," and "thankless toil" seemed grim. Her interest in medicine sprang from the mysterious illness of her sister Sarah, who was saved from death by a married pair of physicians, Dr. and Mrs. Richard D. Mott. Traditional allopaths had failed to cure Sarah's heart condition, but the Motts' gentle regimen of "Systematic Vegetable Medicines" and "Patent Champoos and Medicated Baths" was successful. "Here was my first thought of woman as a physician," wrote Harriot, who accepted the Motts' offer of a medical apprenticeship. She would learn the Thompsonian regimen of "herbes, roots, flowers, vegetables, gums and simples" before establishing her own practice in Boston as an unlicensed eclectic practitioner.

Just as some fathers discouraged their daughters from pursuing a medical career, not all mothers were supportive. The Quaker mother of Eliza M. Mosher remarked: "I would just as soon think of paying to have thee shut up in a lunatic asylum as to have thee study medicine." Dr. Mary Gaston wrote,

And then in 1885, from I know not whence, came the desire to enter the medical profession. Would I have the courage to practice? Mother thought not. I quote from a letter I received from her at this time: "You are a bundle of nerves," she wrote, "sensitive to every sight and sound, and so not fitted for the profession. You would soon come back broken in health and spirits. I would rather have you go to Europe for a year."

Georgia Arbuckle Fix of Princeton, Missouri, was born to an unwed mother and led an impoverished life. When her mother married a contractor and moved west, the nine-year-old girl decided to stay behind with the family of a Dr. Dinsmore, her mentor in medicine. Dinsmore encouraged the girl to study homeopathy, a method that influenced her later habit of diluting medicines with large amounts of water. Despite her poverty, she managed to attend the State University of Omaha's College of Medicine in 1883, and graduated as the lone woman in the nine-member class.

Poverty also drove Jane Bruce Guignard toward medicine. A southerner who grew up on a ramshackle, inherited plantation in Aiken County, South Carolina, the ninth of ten children, she spent her childhood in the bleak years of Reconstruction as her family fought to live after most of the livestock had been killed and the fields laid waste. Those bleak years had a lasting influence on her early life, as she saw her mother, from necessity, dispensing medicine, curing fevers, and improvising her way through various medical emergencies. Called "Brucie" by her family, Jane knew early that she would be a doctor, despite the family's desperate finances. As the family fortunes gradually improved, her dream was realized; financial support was offered by her brothers, who decided to let

"Brucie" "have her chance" at the Women's Medical College of Pennsylvania.

Jessie Laird, raised as the daughter of a pioneer doctor in Washington, was led to medicine by the memory of having to handwash her brothers' long black ribbed stockings and scrub the kitchen floor on her hands and knees. "By the time the suds were cold . . . I seethed with resentment. I . . . exclaimed to my brothers that I would never wash another floor in my life."

The few early female physicians were also a strong inspiration. Sarah Armstrong, born in 1857 in Newton, Ohio, received her M.D. degree in 1886, following a tradition established by her grandmother, the first woman to practice medicine west of the Allegheny Mountains. Sarah's great-great-grandmother had also been a doctor, although her only degree was the preceptor's license commonly awarded at the time. Likewise, Dr. Corrinne Trullinger Chamberlin, who practiced in Gresham, Oregon, owed her medical career to the inspiration of her grandmother, a doctor who had come to Oregon in 1848.

Hanging out the window of her parents' Golden Rule Hotel in the state of Washington, watching the traffic pass by, Esther Clayson was particularly struck by the colorful Chinese funerals and the sight of a sprightly, attractive female student going to and from classes in the street below.

At an early age I was first attracted to the medical profession, not because I felt the traditional urge to relieve suffering, but because of a beautiful young lady who used to pass every morning on her way to the Stark Street Ferry. She was a medical student at the old Willamette School, and if that's what women doctors looked like after they grew up I wanted to be one. Her name was Belle Schmeer, later Dr. Belle MacDonald of New York City.

Later she was impressed when another female physician, Dr. Callie B. Charlton, a graduate of the Willamette Medical School, delivered Clayson's sister's first baby. The birth was a "great occasion" at the Golden Rule Hotel, celebrated by all the transient boarders. The doctor was paid what seemed like a "grand sum" of $15 for her services, without even having to wash the baby. When the family hotel business failed, the Claysons moved to a farm, where Clayson observed the farm wife's ethic of "work and weep" and vowed never to be the "helpmate" of an Oregon farmer. Instead, she continued to dream of medicine, delighting in the presence of Dr. Charlton, who would gently appear to lend inspiration and professional help whenever there was sickness in the family:

[We] asked her to bring her medical case. She had gone homeopathic and was always glad to come, for our dinners belonged to the old school. We had confidence in her judgment and before deciding definitely on a medical career I asked for her advice. It was the best

vocation possible for a woman, she answered, and added that she loved her work and that her income was sometimes as much as $2,000 a year.

"The question was settled for me," Clayson wrote. She had a job selling dry goods but was unhappy in the position and was bullied by her supervisor, a "hateful" $300-a-year floorwalker. Wouldn't he be impressed, she thought, if she quit her job and came back one day with new, elevated status as a physician? Once she had her degree, she dreamed, the man would bow politely to her, just as he did to other favored customers.

꧁꧂

Many women assisted their husbands, thus developing an interest in medicine. Esther Hill Hawks, recently married to Milton Hawks and languidly collecting seashells along the Gulf of Mexico in 1854, also devoted considerable time to studying her husband's medical books—in fact, so thoroughly had she absorbed their contents that on their return trip home in the spring of 1855, sailing up the Mississippi River from New Orleans, she delivered public lectures on physiology in Vicksburg and St. Louis. Once settled into their married quarters in Manchester, Esther continued reading his medical books, clerking in his drugstore, and even visiting his patients, finally deciding to abandon her sporadic studies for formal enrollment in the New England Female Medical College. Many married older physicians, as did Marilla Downs Hemenway

The Schaefer sisters, proprietors of the first female-owned pharmacy,
in San Antonio, Texas.

University of Texas, Institute of Texan Cultures, San Antonio

Wilson, the first female physician in Oakland, California. From the age of eighteen on she learned to assist him, finally returning to school herself to study for certification.

Louise Abigail Mayo also learned as an apprentice to her husband, reading his books and journals, learning to apply splints and prescribe remedies. Rhoda Waters Summers's path to medicine was carved out by her spouse, Dr. James Kilgore, whom she married at the early age of fourteen. Although her medical specialty is lost in archival obscurity, records exist that show she did practice in South Carolina in the 1820s and 1830s, an activity she gradually curtailed as her ten children arrived.

Husband-wife collaboration sprang naturally from an amicable partnership, like that of Martha Spalding Thurston, a graduate of Boston Female Medical College who opened an office with her physician-husband in 1855. In 1847 Charlotte Wray traveled from New York to Iowa with her young husband, Thomas Scott, whom she assisted in setting up and maintaining his medical practice. Both of their lives were swept up in a tide of farm management, church life, and raising children; Charlotte helped him sort and prepare his drugs. "She makes the old iron mortar rattle," he wrote. "Every vial must be corked just so tightly, and every paper in just such style." They worked together happily, she taking delight in assisting him, he in "having her by me" when "at [his] books." Apparently his young wife grew so inspired that she, too, decided to study medicine. Charlotte wrote on November 4, 1847: "I have been studying med-

icine books, principles of midwifery. I am getting a good knowledge of that I think. Perhaps I shall go with Thomas to all such places. I have been twice. What think you of that?"

The following year, discussing the health of her in-laws, Charlotte found that one had a condition which caused him to lose the use of a hand and become lame; one had the ague; and one, Betsy, was "out of health." "I brought her home with me," Charlotte noted. "I think I can cure her." A year later she was still studying, "reading the work of Dr. Fitch, *Of Consumption Cured.*" It was a "grand work," she mused, which recommended "bathing in cold water every day," along with shoulder braces for anyone inclined to stoop. In the spirit of her research, she admitted: "I wear the braces."

Ellis Shipp, the "grand old lady" of medicine in Utah, found her natural ambition and keen intelligence directed toward education, then to medicine, by her polygamist husband, who "awakened in [her] soul its inmost determination to achieve." Ardently in love with Milford Shipp—a "perfect, noble, honorable soul, in his judgment unerring, in his integrity and faithfulness to duty, unfailing"—she joyfully accepted his every dictate, which included three new "plural" wives, her banishment to separate living quarters to make room for the "new" women, the temporary removal of her son for disciplinary reasons, and her designated role as financial caretaker of the family. Her husband emphasized that she must improve her mind by studying. Routinely, she began her studies at four o'clock in the morning and "put in three solid hours before the household began to stir."

Devotion and divinity, husband and church, word and deed intertwined in this thoughtful woman as she daily inscribed her longings in her journal. Each entry was carefully reviewed by her husband, who urged her to lessen her emotions, strive for tolerance, and simply cheer up. "I must curb my feelings. Oh I must never utter a word of discontent," she would lament. "Oh I have tried with all my power and energy to follow . . . his instructions. But of late I have become discouraged. He does not seem to appreciate my efforts." On January 18, 1872, she wrote in anguish: "O what an error I have committed! Despite all my resolutions to be cheerful and uncomplaining I this night spoke to Milford of the ills and hardships of life."

Older than most medical students, separated from her children, who remained in Utah while she studied medicine, Shipp was desperate to see her husband, yet was so penniless that she could scarcely buy food, much less travel home. She was twenty-nine years old, thousands of miles removed from her young children, and looked to as the potential financial savior of her husband's family, including the new wives, through her future earnings as a doctor. Money was scarce, although occasionally one of the new wives would send her "an order for fifty dollars." "I must not fail," Shipp resolved, "if only for their sakes."

December 15, 1872

I have been very sick, have suffered much in the past two weeks, and as is generally the case have been low spirited. I have felt at times that I had no friends, that no one cared for me.

December 31st 1872

What a day this has been! I have been so gloomy and despondent, I have felt discouraged—as if it were useless to try any more to do right, that I received no credit for my good acts.

1876

Oh, I must succeed for their sakes—and my dear husband. How anxious he is for me to persevere to improve and advance that I may gain a knowledge of my profession. How much I have to urge onward, how much to comfort me.

Jan. 13, 1876

I am very busy with my studies, feel more interested every day and more determined to succeed. How much force and energy is required, how much real hard work to gain a little knowledge. If I could only retain what I hear.

January 14th 1876

I am so anxious to study and improve every moment that I cannot sleep after four o'clock and I think it preferable to have a private room as I can concentrate my thoughts better when not disturbed.

January 20 1876

[My] one noble aim and desire . . . was to seek to do right to the best of my ability, hoping that my dear boys would be all that I once hoped I would be . . . I possessed not the time, education or means to bestow their advantages.

Dr. Mary Walker's path to medicine did not follow her husband, but led her to him. After receiving a medical degree from Syracuse University Medical School in 1855, where she was the only woman in her class, she married a fellow student, a man as "dashing and handsome" as she was militant and "odd," and who seemed to have no objection to her usual garb of bloomers, tunics, and sashes. Her affection quickly turned to disgust, however, when she found him philandering. She was even more horrified when he encouraged her to have the same privileges.

❦

Pioneer physician Elizabeth Blackwell's moment of decision came when a friend who died of a painful disease of a "delicate nature"

confided: "If I could have been treated by a lady doctor, my worst sufferings would have been spared me." The pleas of others also played a role in the career of Bethenia Owens-Adair, a diminutive, pretty young woman who had married at fifteen only to find that her husband was shiftless and unable to maintain a profession, no matter how many opportunities were given him. Finding herself a divorced parent while still in her teens, she embarked on a number of professions, often excelling in them, yet always returning to a "fondness for nursing," developed by years of tending to sick friends and neighbors. "I was more and more besieged by the entreaties of my friends and doctors, which were hard to refuse, to come to their aid in sickness, often times to the detriment of business, and . . . a desire began to grow in me for a medical education." Her decision to become a doctor was made one night in Roseburg, Oregon, in 1870, when another aspect of nineteenth-century life became clear to her: that often, the home-grown skills of a nurse-midwife far outstripped those of the old-fashioned, simply trained male doctor.

One evening I was sent for by a friend with a very sick child. The old physician in my presence attempted to use an instrument for the relief of the little sufferer, and, in his long, bungling, and unsuccessful attempt he severely lacerated the tender flesh of the poor little girl. At last, he laid down the instrument, to wipe his glasses. I picked it up, saying, "Let me try, Doctor," and passed it instantly, with perfect ease, bringing immediate relief to the tortured child. The mother, who was standing by in agony at the sight of her child's mutilation, threw her arms around my neck, and sobbed out her thanks. Not so the doctor! He did not appreciate or approve of my interference, and he showed his displeasure at the time most emphatically. This apparently unimportant event really decided my future course.

In some cases, the death of a loved one prompted the study of medicine, creating a desire to avert similar tragedies. Amelia Lamb and Edward Howard Dann were married in New York on March 24, 1868, with the mutual pledge of a shared life of "sympathy of mirth . . . sympathy of grief, [and] the delicious mystery of affection binding heart to heart . . . [in] perfect reverence for each other." The newlyweds were advised about "rough roads, dark nights and stormy days [to] be expected," an unfortunate prediction, since in the next year she lost her husband. He fell ill with typhoid when Millie was in her last weeks of pregnancy, grew feverish and crazed, and finally died. In a tragic two-week period, she found herself both a widow and a mother, skilled only in the decorative arts of china painting, oil painting, and dried flower arrangement. After a stint as a reporter and her own bout with typhoid, which left her "thin, drained of strength and almost bald," in 1875 she applied to the medical school of Syracuse University. At the age of twenty-nine, she began her studies, declaring a specialized interest in infectious diseases, particularly typhoid.

Dr. M. Charlotte Schaefer (1874–1927),
professor of embryology and histology, identified the hookworm.

*University of Texas,
Institute of Texan Culture, San Antonio*

CHAPTER SIX

꒰⸝⸝๑꒱

First Love

꒰๑⸝⸝꒱

Marriage or Medicine?

He did not speak of love and I was glad; I had seen too
many friendships broken on [its] threshold.

— HELEN MACKNIGHT DOYLE

ALLED "HEN MEDICS" BY THEIR CRITICS, FEMALE COUNTRY DOCTORS were seen as stern and dowdy, often of ample girth, whose pitched battles for position in a world of male-dominated medicine had turned them dour and resentful—unlikely candidates for romance. Yet love and medicine often flourished side by side, with surprising intimacies coming to bloom in dusty mining camps or boomtowns.

Medical women who trembled on the brink of romance had to ponder an important question: embrace science, domesticity, or both? And what about children? Marriage and medicine often seemed antithetical; to how many "callings" could a woman aspire? To obtain a medical degree might occupy seven or eight years, making it difficult for a marriage-minded fiancé to wait; such a lengthy obligation seemed to negate the idea of home, hearth, and childbearing. Many women were unable to resolve the conflict, although almost one third of the female physicians who began practicing before 1900 were married and living with their husbands.

Like the women themselves, society also perceived a deep incompatibility between medical practice and wifely duties. An article in the *Denver Medical Times* in the late 1800s stated that "medical women" should not marry, and that if a woman physician *did* wed, she should have the grace to "consent to a childless union," or else pursue some "narrow specialty" that made only limited demands on her time. Likewise, husbands often objected to a wife's practice, regardless of her skill or income level, and automatically expected that once involved in child rearing, she would leave the practice of her own accord. Mary McKibben Harper gave up medicine shortly after her marriage, although she was considered one of the most capable women physicians in the country. Nancy Talbot Clark, one of the first women medical graduates west of the Alleghenies, set up a practice in Boston, but after her marriage in 1856 she ceased her medical practice until 1874. Lucy R. Weaver married Nicholas Emery Soule, a physician who was seventeen years her senior. After two miscarriages and the birth of their only child, she ended her medical career.

In fact, because the marriage of two doctors had little precedent, no time-tested formula helped to decide priorities. Who would keep house, and who would keep practicing? So wondered Mabel Ulrich, whose attempt to make marriage and medicine coexist was only at great professional expense.

April 4, 1904: S. and I have decided to get married next year when we get through medicine.... We are going to divide up the care of the children exactly as we divide the housework.

September 23, 1905: It is no go. We have given up on the 50-50 housekeeping.... I have to laugh when I think how scared I was before we married lest I might be the more successful at the start! Would he mind?

June 5, 1907: Twenty-five today — a quarter of a century old. A doctor, a wife and a mother — yet I don't seem to have learned anything.

January 16, 1910: S. could stand and watch me cut off a leg or make the most brilliant of diagnoses and remain unmoved — but let him catch me in the kitchen with an apron on . . . and he is dissolved in loving admiration. This I have endured with a "twisted smile" for two years.

May 4, 1911: Have decided to try my hand as S.'s technician since Miss Johnson is leaving to get married.... I should by this time be getting used to my role of giving the anesthetics while he has the exciting operations.

Without the concerns of family, a woman's thoughts flew unhindered to her work. Living alone taught women doctors to improvise, to act with independence, to exist in solitary comfort, to live with loneliness and to substitute the needs of patients for those of family. The choice to remain single often reflected the rugged tyranny of nature and the frontier, in which women were pioneers first, medics second, and women—upholders of Victorian America's notion of true womanhood—last of all. Although such women could steer by the stars and face danger with determination, they often had trouble charting a romantic course. As noted before, Mary Walker forged her own version of equality by refusing to take her husband's name, wearing pants to her wedding, and insisting that any vow to "obey" him be removed from the marriage ceremony. The groom, Albert Miller, could only wonder what the future would bring. In fact, the marriage was short-lived.

Pioneer physician Elizabeth Blackwell spoke for many women physicians who would follow a nonwedded path in their future: "I felt more determined than ever to become a physician, and this placed a strong barrier between me and ordinary marriage. I must have something to engross my thoughts, some object in life which will fill this vacuum and prevent this sad wearing away of the heart."

Like Blackwell, homesteader and medic Georgia Arbuckle was a stranger to the idea of romance, a woman agonizingly ill-prepared when love suddenly blossomed and drew her close to Gwynn Fix, a dashing, younger man

> *I was the only one who did not dance except a deaf lady.*
>
> —DR. ELIZABETH BLACKWELL

she had treated for typhoid. The son of a prominent local family, Fix was a legend in the area for his racy, profligate ways and was seen as an unlikely match for the stolid doctor, a tall, mannish, powerfully built woman with her Native American ancestry revealed in her high cheekbones and tumbling dark hair that constantly had to be recoiled about her head. What was the attraction? Perhaps the doctor's maternal instincts were stirred, or, harboring memories of her lonely childhood, she felt the need for companionship. She had come west with her stepfather and half-brother in 1886 to settle a site on the north bank of the North Platte, a small claim marked by three tiny willow trees. Reason aside, the pair married in 1888 and were almost immediately plunged into conflict—his needs or her ambition? Should she stay home and tend to only *one* man—and one who had proved increasingly thoughtless and selfish, at that—when the entire valley of the North Platte clamored for her services? Her patients deserved prompt house calls, day or night, yet her young husband was childishly demanding, anxious for her to move to a claim closer to town and enraged by her refusal. Why should she continue to make the exhausting ride back and forth daily to visit her original patients? Rumors of their discontent abounded as well as rumors of his infidelity, but the most serious rift seemed to be financial. He continually spent her money, sold her cattle without consulting her, and pocketed the money for his own use. She continued to earn and he to spend until she could take no more; she filed for a divorce in 1909.

Of the nineteenth-century women doctors who did marry, many could be said to be happy. "More than twenty-one years have passed since I plighted my marriage vows," wrote physician Bethenia Owens-Adair. "Many sorrows have been interspersed with the pleasures of my married life, and during all these years, I have been as active and determined as in former days. I have never flinched from any undertaking." Quite a few chose to wed within the profession. Mary Putnam, who became a member of the New York Academy of Medicine in 1880, was instantly taken with Dr. Abraham Jacobi, the "father of American pediatrics," a winning, thoughtful man who had been twice widowed and had lost five children. Their medical interests and liberal politics were similar and they married on July 22, 1883, eventually earning the title of "first family of American medicine." He specialized in infant care, she in medical education for women, concentrating on the effects of menstruation on a woman's productivity. She was particularly interested in removing the unspoken stigma of shame and debility associated with the monthly cycle. Lena Fimpel Schreier fell in love with a fellow student while in medical school in Nebraska, while Esther Clayson graduated from the University of Oregon Medical School in 1894 in her wedding dress

—purchased for her upcoming marriage to her anatomy instructor.

Another to find connubial pleasure was Helen MacKnight Doyle, whose encounter with her future husband was an epiphany, both medical and emotional—surprising for both, occurring against all odds, and lasting, happily, for a lifetime. As a young physician, Doyle's days were a weary routine of horse-and-buggy house calls and impromptu patient visits by train, which scarcely allowed her time for recreation or reflection. On a house call to a tiny, one-store mining town to assist a child bride dying of puerperal fever, she found a medical satchel in the corner of her room in the local hotel. Nagged by curiosity, she wondered about its owner—who was he, and why had he left his bag behind?

"I looked through the Doctor's medicine case with interest," Doyle wrote, finding that the drugs he carried were similar to her own. The desk attendant told her that he worked as a miner at the nearby Wild Rose Mine, which proved even more intriguing. What kind of man would give up medicine for mining? Whatever his story, the presence of his bag invoked the standard response of physician etiquette; he had been there first, so Doyle judged him to be the physician-in-residence—the young woman she had come to treat must be his patient. She left the mystery doc a note about his patient and departed for home.

Weeks later, the "handsomest man [Doyle] had ever seen," nattily dressed in city clothes and a derby hat, graced by a "fine head, sensitive mouth, laughing eyes and curling hair," appeared on her doorstep one evening. It was the mystery doctor from the Wild Rose Mine. A moment's stunned silence passed, then they plunged into eager conversation. Both were the same age, both had graduated from medical school before the age of twenty-one, and each viewed the other as witty, humorous, well-informed, and attractive. "Ours was a horse and buggy courtship," Doyle recalled in her memoirs, describing long drives into the country, guitar serenades of haunting sweetness, and rapid-fire, fervent discussions that careened madly from subject to subject, save one: that of their tender feelings for each other. Doyle was hesitant—how could she love a man who had given up medicine and staked his fortune on mining? When his claim failed after yielding only a hundred dollars in profits, she delightedly urged him to return to medicine so that they could work together and build a joint practice as well as a conjugal future.

Medical women commonly waited until midlife to marry, when expectations had shifted from childbearing and rearing to the autumnal glow of achievement and community service. Eleanor Galt married at the age of thirty-seven, seven years after opening her medical practice. Another to stumble late upon love was the tough, wiry Lillian Heath, who began her practice in the sage flats of Carbon County, Wyoming, wearing tailored clothes and carrying "one or two" revolvers in her skirt for protection. Despite a mannish demeanor and a penchant for gunslinging, Heath's feminine side peeked through—she loved parties, enjoyed society, and always had time for a "fling," which meant traveling to a city to enjoy opera and to wear feminine clothing. By 1898 she was ready to wed, having savored the best of professional life. She married Louis J. Nelson on the day of his discharge from the army.

Another to claim romance late in life was Bessie Efner, who as a girl was engaged to an up-and-coming young banker—a "man in a hurry" for success and considered a "first choice" by the girls in town. His proposal flattered young Efner but also caused her to wonder if marriage was really her greatest ambition. She was determined to go to medical school—he would simply have to wait. She enrolled in medical school in Sioux City, Iowa, and was troubled for a while with "homesickness and the thoughts of [her] banker friend," yet found herself curiously unmoved when her fiancé met a woman who wished to be a traditional homemaker, unencumbered by ambition. Afterward Efner resolved to pursue only medicine, remain single, and build a practice, but soon found herself in charge of three foundling nieces she adopted in order to keep the girls together.

I . . . fully realized that with the three children depending upon me I could never expect to look forward to an acceptable marriage or a home and family of my own, something that every woman looks forward to as the final and full realization of her own womanhood. I considered all that and lost much sleep over it, but I always came back to the

*same conclusion: I have no choice. I
cannot do otherwise. May the consequences be for me what they will. God
will help me.*

Help came, indeed. Through persever-
ance, "Dr. Bessie" held on, becoming both
myth and institution on the Wyoming prairie
as she nurtured both the orphans and her
practice. The adopted girls grew healthy and
rambunctious, as did her practice. All that
remained was the hope, long withheld, that
she might someday find a partner for life.
Thus when Efner glimpsed a stranger in
town, a ruddy-faced young man who was the
new Lutheran preacher, she was delighted. He
was "in every respect normal, interesting . . .
versatile, interested in many things . . . in
short, he had everything required for the most
delightful kind of companionship one could
imagine." Their friendship deepened despite
the disparity in their age and her lack of facility in German, the mother tongue of the
Lutheran Church. At one point, she even considered the unthinkable: "A warm glow of
happiness had gradually filled my soul and my
life was beginning to take on new meaning,
new hopes . . . I had visions of a new happiness
such as I had not experienced before. For the
first time in my life I had met a man for whose
sake, if necessary, I was willing even to give up
my profession which I loved so dearly."

After careful consideration, Bessie and the
young preacher agreed to defy religious tradition and marry. She would study German as
well as the Lutheran religion and join him in

western Canada. "I . . . loved my practice and
never believed that anything could persuade
me to give it up," she wrote in later years. "But
I discovered that there are greater things in the
life of a woman than professional success,"
which included a family of her own. She married on September 28, 1912, finding in midlife
a new and fulfilling start.

In some ways, the marriage of Esther Hill
Hawks showed both sides of love—her husband's devotion *and* frustration. Hawks was a
beautiful young woman, with hazel eyes, profuse, curly black hair, and "quiet, serene . . .
good looks." She was a lovely and popular
young woman with many suitors when she
met Milton, her husband-to-be, in 1850.
Milton was so intent on finding a bride, he had
even frequented sewing circles. On their first
encounter he failed to see her as a candidate,
yet she was taken with the young doctor, and
a correspondence developed. When he moved
south, he met other women and had frequent
romantic notions. Yet, somehow, none mea-
sured up to the memory of Esther. They
finally married on October 4, 1854, and left
Boston for Florida. She eventually enrolled in
the New England Female Medical College,
causing some stress in the marriage. "I wish
Ette had never seen a medical book or heard a
lecture," her husband remarked. "It is not a
business man–like worker that a husband
needs. It is a loving woman." His resentfulness
occasionally surfaced; once, after she had
called his habit of distributing abolitionist
tracts "too blatant," he "silently hoped she
would fall off [a rock] and kill herself."

Men who stayed married to medical women were of a varied sort, with no commonality but the ability to weather exigencies such as last-minute house calls and random emergencies. Such was the spirit of the husband of Bethenia Owens-Adair, who was, by her description, an "optimist of a happy and cheerful disposition ... usually among the clouds" without "dark shadows," and so accepting of all vicissitudes that Owens-Adair constantly exclaimed, "My love for him knew no bounds."

The husband of Mary Glassen of Kansas was a successful publisher of a country weekly, yet he found the time to brood protectively over his wife, refusing to let her make house calls alone, announcing his devotion in the simple statement: "Her medical bag is heavy and I carry it." While he trucked about with her supplies, she dreamed up ways to tease him. He took pleasure in his wife's "prankish" nature, even when she once surprised him dressed up as an eerie figure perched on a broomstick who "pitched toward him" in a darkened room, or startled him with a "terrifying scream" that rent the air one dark night as he picked up her medical bag. Calm and unflappable, he simply laughed and went about his work, knowing these were simply little surprises from his wife, the doctor.

In her personal reminiscences, Mary Rowland of Kansas recounts the deep love she shared with her husband, the bliss of motherhood, and the sad and terrible tenuousness of her joy in the face of his loss. "How quickly one's whole life can change," she mourned, recalling one day, "sunshiny and calm" when she was "getting along just fine," feeling "at peace with the whole world," when her husband was brutally and inexplicably murdered by a businessman and fellow Mason in their community of Herndon, Kansas. The murderer, George Dull, was tried, sentenced, and later pardoned midway through his twenty-year prison term. Said Rowland: "When tragedy strikes it is like an avalanche, enormous, overwhelming. You think you cannot live but somehow you do. And life goes on." No explanation for his act was ever given, as the rumors that circulated of infidelity involving the doctor's husband and Dull's wife were never proven.

Not all romances were happy ones. The marital hardship of Utah physician Mattie Cannon stemmed from her polygamous union with an older husband, Angus, a high-ranking dignitary in the Mormon church. Cannon had met him when her career was in full swing, and for the first seven months of their marriage they lived in secrecy because of the growing persecution of polygamists in Utah. After the passing of the Edmunds-Tucker Act of 1887, polygamy was outlawed and plural wives were asked to testify against their hus-

> *You cannot get married and practice medicine, too.*
>
> — DR. BESSIE EFNER, 1880s

bands. In 1885 Angus was charged with "lascivious cohabitation"; in 1886 he was accused of "unlawful cohabitation," and to protect herself as well as avoid testifying against her husband, Dr. Cannon lived in disguise, unable to practice medicine openly.

Throughout Utah, a state of civil disobedience reigned, as "cohabs," or illegal families, fled from one hideout to another, pursued by zealous marshals. Marriages were disrupted, children boarded out with relatives, husbands were

incarcerated. As a physician who had delivered countless children to Mormon families, Mattie was arraigned and brought before a grand jury to identify these polygamous marriage partners. "If it can be proven that these children came into the world," she said, "their fathers will be sent to jail for five years." To Cannon, it was a "serious matter to be the cause of sending to jail a father upon whom a lot of little children are dependent, whether those children were begotten by the same or by different mothers." To avoid the conflicts she finally fled to England, sacrificing her career to keep her husband from prison. Even upon her return in 1888, the two were unable to cohabit because polygamy was illegal —even though she had begrudgingly subscribed to the practice. By her own description, she learned to tolerate polygamy because "we can't help ourselves," yet complained, in the language of Shakespeare, that "it [was] too much like having Greatness *thrust* upon us." The initial success of her medical career had been shunted off the track; her marriage turned out to be long-distance, as she and Angus never lived together again publicly as a married couple. Although she still loved him, she was irked by being uprooted and chased into foreign surroundings while his other wives continued to live in Utah. In exile for the actions of her husband, she was, as John Sillito and Constance Leiber explain, a woman divided between idealism and practicality. She commiserated with her husband over the "terrible life" he was leading, "hiding around." But she, too, had suffered: "I tell you, you would feel worse if you were here." For love, she had left her home and her hard-won career, finding in England "not the slightest opportunity of . . . practicing [her] profession," as "the people [were] too poor to buy their medicines, let alone pay a Physician." Upon her return she was able to revive some aspects of her private practice, leaning toward teaching classes in nursing and obstetrics, becoming best-known in the state of Utah, however, for her political activities.

Religion also intervened in the marriage of Dr. Nina Baierle, a Seventh-Day Adventist whose story of disappointment, abuse, and abandonment is a poignant one. As a faithful Seventh-Day Adventist, Baierle allowed the church elders to select her husband—an older man and ordained preacher who was indifferent to her personally, yet who was deeply attached to her earning potential as a physician. For years he siphoned off her money, deprived her of even the most basic comforts—including his love or approval—and would reappear in her life only for another infusion of money, increasing her anguish and sense of deprivation. On one return, the doctor refused him any further cash, and the enraged preacher physically attacked his slight wife, breaking a bone in her throat and paralyzing her vocal cords as he tried to choke her to death. She was saved by her son, who screamed and pulled the man's hair until he regained control. When Baierle filed for divorce, she heard her husband admit that he had married her because he thought she'd be "a great success as a doctor."

How to be a doctor and also be single? Women generally solved the problem of professional discretion by having offices that faced the street, so town gossips could see male patients entering *and* leaving. But they still had to reckon with the threat they posed to married women. Mary Rowland remembered the jealousy that could boil up—and did—one night at a dinner party when she was joined at the table by the superintendent of the paper mill. He sat next to her by way of a "friendly gesture," but his wife "sailed across the room, snapped her fingers," and told him to give her the keys to the house—she was going home.

He followed her "like a whipped dog," said Rowland, who "never saw him again." In fact, Rowland spent the years of her widowhood effectively dodging male attentions—particularly those of a man she met while in New York who wanted her to come back east and live with him. "My mind was not on being tied to anyone," she wrote. "But, he was a very fine man and I enjoyed all his courtesy to me."

There were those who never knew love's vicissitudes—rural doctors, often living in remote outposts, whose closest associations were with patients, often remained single throughout their long professional lives, either courting suspicion and jealousy from local wives or pitied for their loneliness. This was the life feared by pioneer medic Elizabeth Blackwell, when, as a young girl, she confided in her diary in 1836 a talk with a good friend: "Anna and I had a talk upon matrimony and she fully intends *courting some body.* . . . I really could not help crying upstairs when I thought of my situation. I know it is very wrong to be so ungrateful & I try very hard to be thankful but when I think of the long, dreary year's prospect, I cannot always help it." Later she confided to her diary that her mother had "seriously advised" her to "set her wig" at a certain gentleman. A later entry detailed her feelings of awkwardness at a party. "I was the only one who did not dance except a deaf lady," she noted—and this from a romantic girl who would have, as she noted in one entry, "knocked down my father, overturned my mother, and fled over my elder brother into my lover's arms"!

Medical pioneer Harriot Hunt had no qualms about choosing medicine over love; in the summer of 1860, she even staged a "silver wedding anniversary" with 1,500 guests to celebrate her twenty-five years in medicine. Flowers trailed from every nook and every surface, evidence of a ceremony as shocking in its day as it was sentimental. Seldom did single women have the temerity to celebrate great events in their "solitary" lives at a time when professional women were expected to pay the price of their professional success by great personal unhappiness. On that day, Hunt and her physician-sister wore double wreaths as Hunt "consecrated" her marriage to her profession with "a pure gold ring."

Other relationships faltered on the shoals of emotional defeat, regardless of how great the degree of mutual love and trust; the hardships proved too damaging, the damage was too extreme, and the love too frail to be nurtured back to life. To Susan Anderson, "life seem[ed] so useless and vain" after the death of her brother and being deserted by her fiancé. He had been summoned for a "talk" with Anderson's father, after which he immediately returned her photographs and left town. What had her father said? Anderson was distraught, believing that "no one now care[d] much whether I live or die." Her naturally ebullient spirits led her back to health and optimism, but she still maintained a genteel aloofness with the steady stream of lumbermen, rough riders and cowhands who came her way, brightening up "only when railroad brass or mill bosses . . . dropped by."

No matter how inspiring the challenge or how receptive their patients, to be a rural physician was a lonely lot, and no matter how accepted they were locally, such medicine women often missed the camaraderie of fellow professionals—or that of a mate. Helen Doyle, hidden from society by hundreds of miles of bleak, Nevada desert, recounted her joy at discovering that the celebrated author Mary Austin was teaching nearby. "She would come in the evening and sit with me and recount fragments of stories that afterwards took shape in 'The Basket Woman' and 'The Flock,'" Doyle recalled.

Even the humblest community might offer an eclectic variety of cultural events, including dinners, songfests, church gatherings, poetry hours, even long-winded debates about the Creator's view of the theory of Darwinian evolution. Yet such events were best enjoyed with a friend, a suitor, a mate. Dr. Elizabeth Blackwell, although not a rural practitioner, voiced the thought of many women as she went on a moonlight stroll with her friend Miss Buell. They "talk[ed] of hiring a beau" if they could "get one cheap." What good was a "beautiful moonlight night" and a "walk along the Battery" without a sweetheart? Indeed, they agreed, a beau "would be very pleasant."

Medicine inevitably demanded sacrifice, and only the most fortunate were able to give what was necessary and still have a reserve of strength left over. And part of what many med-

> *The first foreigner I had ever known became my husband.*
>
> —DR. PORTIA LUBCHENCO McKNIGHT

ical women lacked was support for child care. What to do with the children? Often, the consequences of years in medical school, extended fieldwork, and weeklong house calls was the puzzlement or even indifference of her children. One of the first women doctors, Romania Bunnell Pratt of Utah, recounted her family's alienation when she left them to obey the dictates of church leaders, who asked her to study medicine. She sold her house and piano to finance her studies in Philadelphia, and she had to leave five of her seven children with her mother. When she finally returned home, the house was "still, quiet, and empty." "On hearing voices in the orchard I wandered back and found my dear faithful mother and two youngest children gathering fruit. My heart was pierced with sorrow when my little ones opened wide their eyes in wonder and with no token of recognition of their mother. I wept bitterly that I had been forgotten by my babes."

However, she was convinced that "the happiness of a woman physician was no less desired, no harder won, than for any other woman of the nineteenth century. It was just as much a matter of luck, pluck and happenstance as heavenly blessing." And she might have added the nostalgic words of westerner Anne Ellis: "Romance is not dead; not in the heart of a woman, anyway."

PART THREE

Horseback Heroines
Head West

Dr. Susan La Flesche Picotte, second from left,
Native American church meeting.

Nebraska State Historical Society

CHAPTER SEVEN

Dangers Faced, Hardships Borne

The House Call

The snow came early and was four and a half or five feet
deep, no place . . . for a woman to practice medicine.

— MARY CANAGA ROWLAND

WHEN EMERGENCY CALLED, THE RURAL DOCTOR WAS BOUND TO respond—weather notwithstanding, payment aside, undeterred by danger or distance. To live with risk, steer by the stars, gauge weather by the wind, and heal on demand became the credo of the buckboard doctor, to whom raging streams were nightly torments, as were roads as tricky and narrow as "mere deer-paths," hardly allowing one vehicle to pass by another.

A narrow path set high on a cliff could be indescribably frightening. A buggy driver might be forced to dismount and guide the outside wheel by hand, pushing it away from the cliff's edge —a hair-raising and acrobatic maneuver difficult for anyone, gender notwithstanding. "I had to depend entirely on the good sense of my horse," Bessie Efren wrote, narrowly missing death one night as she veered in her buggy through the dark, unable to distinguish the cliff's edge. By daylight, she returned along the same route and trembled to see how close the wheel marks were to the edge. Death had stalked her that night, she believed, but grace had brought her to safety.

Nor were raging rivers a barrier, at least to Jennie C. Murphy of Yankton, South Dakota, who crossed the Missouri River by pontoon bridge and ferryboat to serve her rural patients. One night, responding to a frantic call, she was picked up by rowboat and set out across the icy, raging river, dodging huge ice floes. They had almost made it when the boat capsized. Fortunately, the water was shallow. Dr. Murphy pulled herself ashore and retrieved her medical kit; soaked through, she made it to the remote farm, where she delivered a healthy baby.

The pioneer doctor was helpless without horsepower, and each woman learned to coax cooperation from her animal with whatever method at hand—apples and oats, or the whip and the spur. Fear and vigilance prompted Nevada physician Helen MacKnight Doyle to warily assess a new horse for skittishness before mounting; she could predict her fate by the rigid position of an ear, the quiver of a nostril. Once Doyle noticed that her rented horses had been tied to separate hitching posts, where they strained to brush shoulders and nip at each other. Could this edgy pair really drive her safely a hundred and fifty miles to the bedside of a dying typhoid patient? Doyle was fully prepared when the horses bolted "like scared rabbits for the first ten miles, sometimes . . . in the road, sometimes just hitting the high spots

through the sagebrush," speeding toward the "gaunt ugliness" of the mining town that was her destination. Thrown helter-skelter, Doyle managed to keep her seat, her hat, and her medicine case until they reached the tiny settlement of Candelaria close to dawn.

Mary Canaga Rowland drove her team of horses late at night, alone, over rutted, snow-covered trails. During the summer she was so covered in dirt, with her "eyes filled with dust," that it was impossible to tell the color of her hair. She harnessed and cared for her own team, then had to go home and feed her child. Often, late at night, she silently cried at the burden of her profession. "Once caught out in a violent storm, my horses turned around in the road and wouldn't travel a step. The wind and rain together with the thunder and lightning made it terrifying. Suddenly lightning struck the fence not fifty feet from the place where I sat in the buggy. My horses were cowering and wanted to run, but I held them until the storm abated."

Jennie Murphy so trusted her horse that she often fell asleep behind the reins, wrapped in a lap blanket as the buggy rocked rhythmically through the night. By dawn she would awake, her house in sight, offering silent thanks to her reliable animal for carrying her safely home. Likewise, Mary Babcock learned to trust the intuitive sense of the horses and mules that bore her up and down the mountains, maneuvering through narrow passes to reach outlying patients. Before beginning her rural practice, Babcock knew little of animals, but over the years she developed a degree of trust—even expertise—as she rode daily to her job as physician for the Gold Leaf Mining Company in Montana.

As soon as my horse is fed . . . was the first thought of Oregon doctor Bethenia Owens-Adair, arriving saddle-weary and horse-wise after days and nights of traveling to patients throughout Oregon's wet, coastal forests. Her husband would admonish her not to ride out on the nearly impassable trails during the drenching Pacific storms—particularly one dark night when she was awakened by the sparkle of a lantern on her window at 4 A.M. and the high-pitched pleas of a man begging her to attend a sick patient. As the man shivered, his lantern flickered crazily; he had scarcely made it to Owens-Adair's compound as rain-sodden trees crashed across his path, and was forced to abandon his horse along the trail and wade the last mile on foot, determined to fetch the doctor. How could she refuse? The patient lay suffering, six hours distant; there was no medical help closer than Dr. Owens-Adair. "Saddle the horse," she insisted, over her husband's objections. "I must go."

I succeeded in reaching the barn without being blown off my feet. . . . After I was in the saddle, a blanket with a hole in its center was drawn over my head, and its corners, sides and ends made fast to the saddle and cinch. Thus, in true Indian fashion, my wraps were held in place, and I could not be blown off. The messenger and my husband armed themselves with axes and lanterns, and

we started for the woods. We found five trees in the road, and after two hours' hard work, we got around and past them. After we got out of the woods, the horses found great difficulty in facing the storm, and my good, sensible old horse wanted to go home. I was so bundled and tied up, I had little control of him. . . . After daylight the storm began to abate, and by ten A.M. it was over, and the sun was shining. We found many more trees across the road, but we finally reached our destination at eleven A.M., and found the folks anxiously hoping for our arrival. . . . I quickly relieved their anxiety, and was ready to return.

Rural life seemed an admixture of delight and despair, presenting the doctor with a host of medical puzzles to solve, from disease to drink, animal attack to industrial mishap—perhaps a powder mill explosion, machine injury, or locomotive derailing. Among the "Accidents, Catastrophes, Etc." that could occur were a "fall from a span of the old bridge . . . [a] foot [caught] in the machinery at the Ice-House; a drowning in a bleach vat at the paper mill; an explosion of the soda-water generator at Smith's Drug Store," cited in a diary kept by Charles Baldwin of Catskill, New York, in 1860. Where else could a young physician gather such varied—and vital—experience?

Occasionally, the doctors themselves were victims of the unruly frontier. Mary Jane

McGahan, a beautiful young doctor with shining hair and sprigged, ruffled dresses, was the first woman to practice in Idaho's rugged Shoshone and Benewah Counties, as well as the first woman physician known to die by violence. McGahan presided over a thriving medical practice and had recently purchased a drugstore in the bustling timber town of St. Joe. She would often carry narcotics in her satchel as she trekked back and forth from drugstore to patient. One day her horse-drawn buggy returned empty, her bag plundered; her body was never found. Her tragic death occurred in 1912, shortly after the passage of the Federal Narcotics Act.

How to minister to the ill but still maintain safety? On dark nights, the unsuspecting traveler might happen upon animals, Indians, or worse—who could know? For Mary Rowland, "worse" was a train ride from Topeka, Kansas, to the tiny hamlet of Herndon, her base location for a series of difficult, day-long house calls made by livery team over the prairie. As the train rolled west, a storm struck in the dead of night and stalled the train in a pounding deluge of wind, rain, hail, and thunder. The doctor huddled in her seat, feet in icy water, while men milled anxiously up and down the aisles, slapping themselves to keep from freezing. Heavy winds and ice had blasted out all the windows on the north side of the coach and blown off two boxcar tops, filling the compartments with ice. "I held my medicine case up to my shoulder to keep the hail off," wrote Rowland. As the only woman on board, she was praised for her equanimity; a number of men "had never seen such nerve." On the other hand, a few of the men thought she was the cause of the storm. "Some of the men on that train said I was a hoodoo . . . [that] bad luck followed me," wrote Rowland. Had she lived a hundred years earlier, she feared, she might have been "tried . . . for witchcraft."

For Bertha Van Hoosen, an Indiana surgeon practicing in the late 1800s, danger might lurk along the way to any house call, but she was never deterred, no matter the hour or the disreputable location.

Fear was never my companion. . . . I had crossed and recrossed viaducts considered dangerous after dark; I had passed saloons from which drunken men had been hurtled by burly bartenders. . . . I had waited on a lonely corner for a streetcar at two in the morning, and had seen a man with a bag held up by a thug, who was in hiding behind a pole. . . . I had seen the man move on, leaving me with the robber, who came across the street to my side, where it seemed as if he remained for an hour before . . . finally on padded feet, he ran in pursuit of another victim.

Women (and men) doctors occasionally encountered an even worse scenario: abduction by a desperado who wanted the physician to treat a wounded fellow outlaw. Such surprise skirmishes often ended with the unlucky doctor bound, blindfolded, and transported respectfully but with determination to the hideout of a wounded felon, to stitch and suture, bind and bandage during a long, nerve-racking night—usually for little thanks, no pay, and occasional rough handling. Dr. Charlotte Hawk of Green River, Wyoming, also had numerous encounters with outlaws, one when a man galloped into town towing a riderless horse, yelling that a gang member was "bad shot" by the bullet of a Union Pacific guard and needed medical care. He insisted that she should come along. Resigned, Hawk mounted the horse and was blindfolded, feeling insulted by the outlaw's lack of trust. After all, didn't he know that she would never betray information about patients, medication, or destination? Didn't he know her reputation? As the horses galloped toward the felled bandit, questions raced through her mind. Would the outlaw survive? What if there was infection?

And worse, could she trust his companions not to blame her if he happened to die? No physician wanted to be the harbinger of death, particularly in outlaw country.

Despite the long ride and dire conditions, Dr. Hawk worked steadily, disinfecting the wound, swabbing and binding, trying not to imagine her fate if the man should die. After the successful surgery, she was blindfolded, ridden back to the outskirts of town, set free, and given a ten-dollar gold piece and a polite appraisal by her outlaw escort: "Thank-you, Ma'am ... you know your business." Her "business" was also to forget every detail of the outlaw's camp and not inform the posse. Hawk was proud of her status as the first woman doctor in Wyoming, to which she could now add her status as the first to treat a wounded bandit. Anna "Doc Anner" Darrow of south Florida was also forced, blindfolded, to a hideout deep in the palmetto groves to tend a sick bandit, after which she was reblindfolded, bundled into a wagon, and escorted back to town.

Eleanor Galt, the first woman physician to practice medicine in Dade County, Florida, occasionally found herself pressed into another kind of "volunteer" service. She lived in Coconut Grove, a village so tiny that Main Street was merely "two pitted ruts worn by wagons ascending the gentle grade" and so drowsy that panthers were often found padding softly through the undergrowth. Along the shore of the bay rocked and swayed the battered dinghies of sponge fishermen.

The doctor was a "petite, blonde, well-groomed [woman,] conservative [in] dress and manner," who could whip up her green mango pie on demand and was known for her femininity. She liked to wear frilly dresses from "beneath which peeped high-buttoned shoes." Galt was also "friendly, easy to talk to, walked with a quick step ... [and] made her medical rounds in a single-horse road cart driven by the Doctor or her houseboy."

One day in 1894 she found herself summoned to treat a victim of outlaw Sam Lewis, who had killed two men in broad daylight and wounded a third, being hit by gunfire himself in the process. Surrounded by a posse, Lewis retreated into a shack, shooting and shouting threats.

Lewis's surviving victim had been felled by one bullet in the neck and two in his body. After making him comfortable, Galt demanded that Lewis let her in to treat him. According to the account in the *Miami Metropolis* of 1895, she "removed two bullets from his right thigh and one from his left leg, dressed his wounds and splinted the compound fracture of the leg" but refused his request for enough chloroform to commit suicide. Instead, she convinced him to surrender, and a few hours later the outlaw gave up, racked with pain, thirst, and hunger but chastened enough by his injury and his intimate conversation with Galt to face his fate.

Some physicians found themselves embroiled in legal testimony, calling into contest the vow of patient privilege and duty as a witness and citizen. Because of their position in the community, women doctors were often summoned as character witnesses—taking the stand to deliver information. "I had to tell the truth," Mary Rowland sighed, testifying both in a lawsuit and a criminal case in which her patient, the same defendant, was accused of shooting the town marshal. Nebraska homesteader and physician Georgia Arbuckle Fix observed a murder in 1888 in which she knew both the victim—a rancher—and his murderer, a disgruntled hired hand who shot his employer in an altercation about pay. As a key witness, she had to recount her role in trying to save the rancher.

Response to risk varied; some women fled to the safety of a city practice after a stint on the frontier, while other female doctors never left the urban centers. Yet other women physicians opted for self-defense—sure that they could defend themselves as well as any man.

Male medics armed themselves, toting either a buggy whip on their house calls or else a loaded "piece," ready to fire. Or they would bolster up courage with swigs of whiskey. Physician J. J. Best of the Ft. Berthold Indian Agency in the Dakotas completed his daily route of "twenty-five miles, twenty-two patients" armed with "large Colt revolvers and a Winchester repeating rifle and ammunition and a self-acting revolver" to ward off surprise attacks. A horseback doctor in Fisher County, Texas, whistled his way through outlaw country, hoping that the tune would identify him as a doctor and healer, a man not to be shot as he rounded the bend.

To go armed or not? Women doctors who yielded to wartime hysteria or the random danger of the frontier and decided to carry guns followed in the tradition of militant matrons such as the indomitable Mary Walker, who wore high boots, a waistcoat, and a "six-shooter tucked inside her jacket" during her stint as a surgeon for the Union Army. Although she was elaborately prepared for action, her actual encounters seemed mild enough. One night, fully armed and out for a stroll, she found herself stalked by a "dude," who sidled up to her. Before he could even speak, she flashed her firearm and was satisfied when he ran away. Walker's reputation was legend: she was a tough woman, able to pack a gun, shock a crowd, act with abandon, and spin tall tales, as well as be paid for her medical work by the U.S. government.

Another to go armed was Dr. Lillian Heath, of Rawlins, Wyoming, who packed a pistol as routinely as a medical kit for her rounds of house calls. "I pulled a trick," she confided to an interviewer. "I had two deep pockets set in front of some garments in which to carry, among other things, a revolver." As a woman alone on the streets late at night, she feared untold hazards, both real and imaginary. With her father's help she had a suit of men's clothes tailored to fit, confident that the anonymity of the stiff jacket and men's pants would provide a male demeanor that would allow her to pass unnoticed through strange neighborhoods. Swinging a lantern as she walked, she grasped that "most women wouldn't think of doing such a thing." To South Carolina physician Portia Lubchenco, "making the rounds" in her ancient Ford "tested the courage" almost to the breaking point. In one event, the police gave her a pistol to use in case she encountered escaped members of a chain gang. "I did not know how to use a weapon and would likely not learn," she decided. Without a gun, she sang "hymns of faith" and talked to her horse, Maude, to bolster her courage.

Masculine methods also appealed to fearless Texas physician Sophie Herzog, so convinced of her own powers of self-defense she refused to carry a gun. Once she brandished a poker to drive a troublesome patient from her office. "I want no odds because I'm a woman," she declared.

Nor would Mary Gaston of Somerset County, New Jersey, carry a gun. An energetic young physician, she made her night rounds on foot, no matter what hour, riding in a horse and carriage by day. When her father insisted that she carry a gun for protection, she countered that she was more fearful of the gun than of any harm that might befall her.

Women, often scorned by male medical society and marginal in their political and social positions, frequently felt they would lose further respect if they gave in to timidity. A woman needed enterprise and daring in a rural site; she had to analyze danger, act in a flash, redefine the meaning of "brazen," and, if worse came to worst, exploit her femininity to advantage, relying upon the civic spirit of male supporters. And why not? To practice freely, women sought any shortcut, embraced any means. Julia M. Carpenter, who became a practicing physician in Boston in the late

1800s, traveled west in 1882 after her children were grown, often stopping to deliver lectures. In Austin, Texas, she presented a letter of introduction to Ben Johnson, a man who "seemed mighty friendly" and promised to help her if necessary. His chance came soon enough. Cowboys at the local hotel discovered that a *woman* would be lecturing publicly and protested. It was one thing for men to deliver lectures, but the cowboys did not want public discourse by a woman. The hotel manager urged the doctor not to create a fuss, to just give back the money. Carpenter turned immediately to her champion, Ben Johnson, who handed her a silver whistle and told her to blow it loudly at the first sign of trouble. All went well until half past seven, when "eight or ten cowboys in a gang" led by a "tall powerful looking rascal" began to curse, swear, and terrorize the crowd. "I up and struck him in his face," she recounted. At the same instant, "I [pulled] out the little whistle and put all the breath I had into it." The shrill blast summoned a dozen young men who "was up them stairs like a flash," accompanied by Ben Johnson himself, who finished off the confrontation by raising a pistol and shooting off the ear of the offending ringleader.

As the twentieth century neared, women physicians faced changes in technology, from the latest surgical techniques to the advent of the automobile—the "four-wheeled buggies" that would broaden their rural access and add a measure of safety to their nightly appoint-

Dr. Hilda Erickson.

Utah State Historical Society

ments. Many older residents of La Jolla, California, still remember the attractive, outgoing Martha Dunn Corey, who bought one of the first automobiles in town—an air-cooled Franklin, which she paraded "up and down La Jolla Boulevard with flags flying, bells ringing, and chickens running," according to a local newspaper account. Assisted by her sons in the actual driving, her one-cylinder vehicle took her upon her round of calls up and down the coast, often along the main highway from Los Angeles to San Diego, through a snake-infested pass called the "Biological Grade," through scrubby terrain in which bobcats were often seen and where, the newspaper reported, "on a Sunday it was a safe bet there would be one or more accidents." Weekly a car would plunge off the hillside or collide squarely into an ongoing auto hugging the inside of the blind curve.

Even more primitive conditions existed for Anna Darrow of rural southern Florida, who drove her Model T Ford at night along rutted cowpaths through the dank sawgrass, her headlamps ebbing and glowing according to her speed. Windshield wipers were hand-operated, and drivers often had to halt to clear away the rain and snow. The car cranked up only if the spark handle and the manual accelerator handle were properly placed, and even then, the motor only continued if the driver could skillfully maneuver the gadgets and controls. If she drove fast, the lights faded, so by night she had to inch along in low gear in order to see ahead. Especially treacherous roads caused the wheels of the car to "skid and

finally stop and dig deep into the muck." Once her rickety Model T "shook and quivered all over and stopped," its fenders resting on the wheels, the front spring broken. Miles from a garage, she found a piece of two-by-four, "got out the jack and the ax and wire, raised up the body of the car, drove the timber in, wired it," and headed home. Other times she was forced back into a buggy pulled by a crippled horse, or worse, onto the back of the horse, which she "had to saddle . . . and ride out into the back country . . . through marshy sloughs."

Although Helen MacKnight Doyle and her physician husband finally gave up their swift team of horses for an automobile, they, like others, found the results uneven at best:

We struggled through the sand and over the hills, always wondering at the bottom if we would ever get to the top. We cut sage-brush to lay in the sandy roads to increase traction. We had a puncture every few miles, and bent our backs over a hand pump to inflate the new tire. I have had many a Panama hat ruined when I was thrown into the top of the car as we leaped the irrigating ditches. Many a time our engine flooded and died when we plunged into bridgeless streams.

The automobile further taxed the intuitive and scientific skills of women practitioners; in addition to doctoring, they often had to be mechanics. Dr. Claudia Potter, assisting two surgeons in Texas on their late-night rounds, recalled the "bright red Pennsylvania cars" they used that were worthless in rain-storms. When the headlights faltered, their way was lit by lightning flashes; finally, they borrowed a lantern from a nearby farmer and as Potter and Dr. White navigated, Dr. Scott would sit on the hood or fender of the car, shining the lantern on the road ahead.

In general, automobiles made it easier to make rural house calls. Potter recalled riding through frosty Texas mornings, her feet warmed by hot bricks and heavy lap robes tucked about her, the car wheels cutting through mud and ice, "half hub deep in places." Her account of one operation in Lott, Texas:

We began the preparation of the room.... I was still thawing myself for I think I was as nearly frozen as I have ever been. The table was prepared and we boiled lots of water on the stove to use as sterile water. I put the sterile linen on a side table together with the instruments, then prepared the table and helped Dr. White and the family doctor scrub up and get into their sterile gowns. I then took my mask and ether, [and] took the child to dreamland. The surgeon and his assistant then proceeded to remove an acutely distended appendix.

The house call was a great leveler; no matter what educational or societal background the physician came from, no matter how committed a feminist she was or how strident her views on temperance and coeducation were a long journey on a dark night, and the reassuring greeting of a small farmer or storekeeper at the journey's end, seemed to be the reward of frontier medicine.

Northwestern Hospital supply room, surgery, ca. 1913.

Minnesota Historical Society

❧

CHAPTER EIGHT

Rural Outbreaks

❧

Plagues, Scourges, and General Afflictions

It seems to be [men's] ambition to cure disease and very seldom do any of them think it worth their while to teach their patients how to prevent a return of their maladies.

—DR. AMANDA PRICE

HARDLY A DAY WOULD PASS IN THE LIFE OF THE WESTERN SETTLER without exposure to some illness or another. "Disease has laid us all low and robbed me of the strength of my young womanhood," wrote Idaho settler Agnes Reid in 1879. Communicable diseases leaped like wildfire through overcrowded coaches, hotels, and waystations where sanitation was nonexistent and slop jars fouled the bedside air. Guests at waystations and hotels overflowed into tiny rooms, often less than ten by ten feet, where one dingy, dirt-stained mattress might serve as a shared bed for two or three timbermen, cowboys, or sheepherders, who were unwitting recipients of one another's infections. Fortunate were the few who bunked on separate bedrolls, which afforded some separation from the miasmic broth of foul air and fetid body contact. Contagion also tainted trains, where aisles were sunk deep in dirt and spittle that dried and was swept up by broom, spiraling into the air to choke and contaminate. The popular cure-all for such airborne filth was to clutch a vinegar-soaked cloth to the nose to "purify" the miasma, or to fend off contagion with bags of camphor worn about the neck as a preventative.

Human and animal wastes were trodden underfoot, and germs were swirled through the air by hosts of flies or transmitted by unwashed hands. Tents, privies, and kitchens shared the same space and often the same water. Illness plagued filthy, congested towns that had yet to devise means of providing pure drinking water and disposing of waste. Even the earth seemed threatening at times, particularly when settlers camped on wet and swampy turf that bred mosquitoes and disappointment in equal amounts.

The idea of germs was still unfocused. Despite general recognition of Louis Pasteur's germ theory and its surgical applications by Lister, the notion of linking germs to infection seemed dubious and a "new bit of nonsense"; the use of carbolic acid as a disinfectant was seen as a sham. Vaccination was virtually unknown, and measles, whooping cough, diphtheria, and other diseases took their toll by way of epidemics.

By 1879, awareness of germs and contagion had increased, and even citizens of rural Idaho could understand the relationship between germs and diseases. Wrote settler Agnes Reid: "I regretted to take my tiny infant among people where might lurk the germs of every dread disease. We never go anywhere to expose the children." "It's a wonder we didn't die," remarked a Colorado homesteader after drinking sediment-laden river water that, in a feeble attempt to purify it, had been allowed to settle overnight. But this awareness didn't mean that everyone changed their ways. Warm weather brought an upsurge in illness—few understood that a shovelful of dirt thrown into the privy hole would discourage flies and thus reduce contagion.

Some diseases were so rampant they were considered scourges—including malaria, which affected countless settlers west of the Appalachians to one degree or another. Water that stood in puddles and clogged streams offered tranquil breeding grounds to legions of mosquitoes, and the risk of malaria to every passerby. In Wisconsin in 1841, malaria killed eighty of the six hundred residents of Lake Muskego, and before the last third of the century, death rates from malaria ran as high as 5.7 per 10,000. Imported from Europe by early settlers and known as fever and ague, pestilential fever, or intermittent fever, it cut a death swath through the entire Mississippi Valley into Canada, jumping from swamp and lowland to river town, halting only at the hot, clear reaches of the Southwest and the Rockies.

European visitors were fascinated by the vision of "pitiable looking" men and women whose teeth chattered as if freezing even while the sun was at its powerful, smoldering zenith. There was virtually no escape while in mosquito-infested lowlands, and any medical

The pharmacy.

Murphy Library, University of Wisconsin, La Crosse

Child in Pacific Grove, California.

Photograph by C. K. Tuttle; Eureka Bank Museums

practitioner, man or woman, knew well the language of sallow cheeks, sunken eyes, distended spleen, and depleted energy. "I find myself very weak," wrote Kansas settler Miriam Colt, one of thousands of emigrants who simply worked "the shakes" in with their routine, convinced that any family existing *without* a case of chills was a curiosity. "I had to sit down twice while mixing my bread. When I began to feel faint and dizzy, I would sit down on a stone, and when the dizziness passed off, go on with my mixing." So common were the tremors associated with malarial fever, that a typical observation offered the prospect of health if an individual was free of fits "since dinner."

Those already infected were bitten by local mosquitoes, who spread the malady to others. No setting was safe, and so common was the contagion it was dubbed the "American distemper," often passed from one to another in crowded settings, particularly at camp meetings, where men and women joined rousing revivals for days at a time, often sleeping helter-skelter in tents overnight, some in raised bunks, but others nestled side by side on straw on the floor. Dr. Hiram Rutherford's wife, Lucinda, died from disease contracted such at a camp meeting, where she "staid all night in a tent . . . [lying] on some straw on the ground," despite her medical husband's warnings that "sickness was raging like a devouring element all over the country."

Asiatic cholera raged during the gold rush, with its victims dying within two days of infection. Incipient tuberculosis brought its own kind of despair. The respiratory distress associated with the disease, also called "a decline" or consumption, was a foremost cause of death in early America. The disease was difficult to diagnose, and even upon identification, its victims were often unconvinced that they were ill. Consumptives who still felt well enough would simply ignore the physician who had given them an honest diagnosis and go to a physician who said they were merely "run down" instead. Since the treatment demanded a long, slow cure, patients would often lose heart and veer away from the program. With tuberculosis, a heart-to-heart talk was often needed to gain the patient's confidence and win cooperation.

Typhoid also terrorized the frontier population. Wrote Oregon physician Dr. Esther Lovejoy in the late 1800s:

Typhoid was . . . endemic and we were used to it. . . . Week after week we observed the cases, carefully watching the rise and fall of the temperature and other significant symptoms, until the patients recovered or died. We were all qualified to treat typhoid fever, but just as we were hanging out our shingles the Portland water system was changed. Infected water from the Willamette River was turned off, and pure water from the mountains turned on and typhoid fever, a seasonal blight on the community and a regular source of income to the medical profession, practically disappeared from the city.

❧

Little attention was given to preventive medicine beyond quarantine—the frontier was a raw, new country that seemed to lack all sophistication concerning cleanliness and the spread of germs, save the pesthouse. Dr. Eleanor Galt Simmons, hidden away from the mainstream of Florida life in the tiny hamlet of Coconut Grove, witnessed the devastation of several sweeping epidemics. One flared up in 1898, when seven thousand troops from the Spanish-American War were housed in squalor in a campsite near Miami. The soil was too dense to dig latrines, and the barrels used as toilets were seldom emptied. Soldiers excreted directly on the ground, tainting the water supply and sparking a surge of "typhoid, dysentery and measles, among other troubles." Even after the soldiers had decamped, yellow fever flourished, prompting hygienic efforts so exacting that "mail was disinfected by punching holes through the envelope, letter and all, and placing it in a fumigating box with burning sulfur. Newspapers were similarly fumigated but were not perforated."

Often patients wondered which was worse, the disease itself or fear of its morbidity, as witnessed by a panic that was triggered by the fear of skunk-transmitted hydrophobia, or rabies. A woman bitten on the hand by a coyote became so panicked at the thought of rabies

that she shot herself. Some victims who fell ill walked helplessly in place, frothing at the mouth, until death. Those fortunate enough to reach a physician could look forward to a cleansing with hot water and soap and treatment with tincture of citron seed applied to the wound, followed by carbolized Vaseline. Admitted one doctor: "[R]abies might still develop, but the wound would heal."

Illness was often rooted in poverty, attacking "mostly [those] who live on coarse food and in open houses," according to an Illinois country doctor who believed that "those who live comfortably are seldom sick." For the less fortunate, it can only be supposed that "death was doing its work" among them. Colorado physician Susan Anderson grew tragically acquainted with the dread symptoms of scurvy in infants, often induced by ignorant attempts to substitute for natural milk a canned substitute that contained nothing but fats, water, and sugar. Advanced scurvy in an infant was terrible to see—and irreversible. The swollen eyelids, emaciation, dehydration, thin bones, rapid respiration, spongy gums, and faint heartbeat of an afflicted infant were immediately identifiable and all too common among marginal backwoods families who scrimped on vegetables and fruits and replaced fresh milk with canned.

Other nutritional disorders were rampant as well. Children in the gloomy, fog-shrouded Pacific Northwest often had rickets, with bowlegs and misshapen heads and chests, resulting from a lack of vitamin D; diets were boosted

Deseret hospital.

Utah State Historical Society

with cod liver oil during childhood to starve off the disease.

As if disease and violence were not enough, people could be felled by accidents that sprang from the simplest routines of life. Choking was not an uncommon cause of death; Margaret Coffin quotes an entry from an eighteenth-century doctor's diary, in which "Widow Adcock died of a hot bread supper," while "Justice Billings [died] of eating Brown Bread for breakfast, a Thing he never used before." Even the ice wagon loomed dangerous for young children, who risked being crushed by the huge wheels if they darted into the street.

Death could also come from the quick hiss of a rattler, from spiders or insects, or from obscure herbal toxins. In the insect-ridden Everglades, Anna Darrow had to react quickly when "two men bitten by the black widow spider" rushed to her, sweating and nauseous. She dosed them with a preparation from her pharmaceutical store left over from her graduate days from medical school. Lloyd's Preparation was also used to manage reactions to tarantula and centipede bites. From these, she had "no fatalities." Helen MacKnight Doyle of Nevada was appalled at the number of Greek workmen drawn to Nevada by the Tonopah silver boom who were lured by the "succulent, poisonous wild parsley" growing everywhere, and upon eating it, died.

In addition, the rural physician had to diagnose pea-size bladder stones, swollen joints, "summer complaint," pneumonia, "scarlatina," headache, heartburn, cankers, chilblains, bruises, bronchitis, coughs, colds, croup, earache, eyestrain, blistered feet, jaundice, and even lockjaw. "No person need die of lockjaw," instructed an early pioneer journal. The remedy was simply to heat the afflicted area "as hot as the patient can bear. Don't hesitate to . . . put hot wood ashes into water as warm as can be borne."

⁓

Physicians, male and female, were called upon to treat a population inured to hardship and often able to self-medicate. They were strong as leather and tough enough to treat their own wounds, as did Os Chase, a North Dakota man standing six feet two inches tall in stocking feet, who traveled to the Badlands and had the misfortune of freezing both large toes. With no doctor within forty miles, Chase simply took out his hunting knife and amputated both toes himself. This same intrepid westerner, when bitten by a rattler one day, slit the fang mark, sucked out the poison, then applied a wad of Peerless tobacco over the wound, fastened it with strips torn from his shirt, and went on his way as if nothing had happened. Such were the "patients" who considered their own skills and needs long before committing themselves to professional medical aid.

Overlander Martha Heywood thought nothing of tending to a cholera victim. She "felt so keenly" that she "went at once to render . . . assistance." Acting as the wagon train's physician, Heywood wrote in 1850: "Though the symptoms were dangerous in that stage of the disease, I used the knowledge I gained on my trip from St. Louis to Kanesville and in due time brought [him] about."

In fact, settlers were willing to countenance the most terrible afflictions before voicing their medical needs. "Rebecca's abscess occasionally runs a little . . . but that does not allarm us," one father wrote. ("Allarm" wouldn't settle in until the deathbed arrived, it seems.) They were able to tell from her "gaining strength and flesh and . . . straightening up" that things were better with their daughter's health.

Noncommissioned officers' mess, Company D,
93rd New York Infantry, Civil War.

Keystone-Mast Collection

CHAPTER NINE

Medics in the Military

No Women Need Apply

*I never wish to go through the same scenes — Blessed be
the veil which hides the future!*

— DR. ESTHER HAWKS

HEN THE CIVIL WAR BURST UPON THE AMERICAN SCENE, WOMEN
as well as men were stirred to patriotism, and no less women physicians. Tent
hospitals overflowed, doctors worked from dawn to dusk, and nurses, often called "laundresses,"
washed soiled linens and worked for months without salary. Yet no matter how deep the need for
their services, women physicians, with one exception, were not invited to participate, except as volunteers. The usual hospital corps consisted of a male surgeon, a hospital steward who would fill
prescriptions, an assistant surgeon, a ward-master, four nurses, two cooks, and a general worker.
The sick were treated as kindly as possible, but as fatigue and sheer numbers of wounded
mounted, supplies and sympathy were stretched thin. There is no record of the number of women
physicians who volunteered, only select stories of those few who managed to participate.

Elizabeth Blackwell helped Dorothea Dix, Mary Walker, and Amy Barton organize nursing
for the Union Army during the Civil War, but they were unable to smooth the path for female

physicians. Women were hired only as nurses; at the beginning of the Civil War the federal government refused to take on female physicians, which denied them very real advantages. Union Army pay to contract surgeons was generous, and there a doctor would receive more surgical experience than he could get any other way. Where else could a physician learn to improvise in the absence of yet-to-be-discovered antisepsis, antibiotics, or intravenous fluids? Or apply daily the standard treatments of amputation and debridement (the surgical removal of tissue), or pour whiskey down the throats of typhoid patients? Although rounds were a terrible gauntlet of dying men, some as young as fourteen, some as old as sixty, women still wished for the experience.

When Dr. Esther Hill Hawks tried to join the army to support the war effort, she hoped to be employed as a physician, or, failing that, a nurse with the Fifty-fourth Massachusetts Infantry—a black unit. She was refused a position as a doctor but remained in Washington for several months as a volunteeer worker in the hospitals. On returning home to Manchester, she served as secretary to the Soldier's Aid Society, which provided the troops with clothing, linens, and other items. Her husband, Milton, became a U.S. Army acting assistant surgeon on the staff of General Saxton in 1862, assigned to administer physicals to men enlisted in the nation's first black regiment, the First South Carolina Infantry Regiment. Although Esther was never assigned to the hospital with him, her diary entries for 1862 through 1864 reveal her efforts to help black soldiers.

> *October, 1862: Our Chaplin marked out a new Cemetary for the soldiers, and about 20 poor fellows were laid in it, during the six months, we occupied the Camp. [The] Comissary tent was very dirty but by turning over the boards and a little cleaning it was rendered usable and here I opened school for the plantation children and such of the soldiers, left behind, who were able to come. . . . My most remarkable pupil was one of our soldiers, too old for active service, [who] has been detailed as nurse.*

In April 1863 the first general hospital for black soldiers was established in Beaufort. Although her husband was appointed its director, Esther Hawks "worked hard to get it in order."

> *Here in Hospital we could keep them as clean as we chose, so I circulated among them with the greatest freedom — prescribing for them, ministering to their wants, teaching them, and making myself as thoroughly conversant with their inner lives as I could.*

Occasionally she could practice surgery. She wrote in October 1862: "For three weeks I performed the duties of hospital and Regimental Surg[eon] doing the work so well that the neglect to supply a regular officer was

not discovered at Hd.Qrtrs." Realistically, she admitted that the opportunity would not have happened if her brother had not been the hospital steward—or if the patients had been white men." She worked steadily in fetid conditions, where "severe cases of gangreen poisn'd the air" and the "tainted atmosphere and overwork" caused her a "relaps." Working at Camp Saxton with a group of black soldiers who had been routed by larger Confederate forces, Hawks tended wounds that were in some cases "comparatively light," in others severe. A small hospital fund supplied her with "many little comforts" for the patients.

Sympathetic and interested in her soldiers "of color," Hawks prayed with them when asked and would playfully help them write "vigarous love-letters" to their sweethearts. She slept in a palmetto-covered cabin made of logs, with windows and doors covered by swinging army blankets hardly thick enough to keep out the freezing winter air. Part of her duty was to act as commissary sergeant, providing the soldiers' rations during the sergeant's absence. "I think now, the only thing remaining to fit me for some important military position is to have command of a Company or Regt. for a short time," she wrote. "I have no doubt in my *ability* to command them—providing they be *colored* troops."

Riding with her husband at the rear of the retreating Union soldiers, Esther Hawks was obliged to see that no one fell by the wayside. Retreating from the enemy under a full moon was close to being a "jolly march" to Hawks, until she discovered fifty wounded men quartered in a church. "Sending for rags and bandages," she wrote, "we commenced work." She carefully removed fragments of clothing embedded by a bullet in the fleshy part of the arm of a black soldier—luckily, the ball had been "nearly spent" when it hit him.

At times doubts would creep into her mind. At a camp near Jacksonville in 1864, she was separated from her husband. Nightly, loneliness would crop up, and she lay on her cot, wondering: "[Is] it my *duty*, really, to live this way—[am] I wasting time which should be devoted to my profession? Shall I ever resume its duties[?]—sometimes I say *no* to the

question." Further, she often wrote of a "feeling of *dread*" connected to her military experience, which she was unable to "shake off."

When Hawks left in September of 1863 the hospital had "passed into other hands" and she regretfully discovered that the succeeding surgeon was a "young, inefficient disipated negro-hating tyrant" who was "heartily hated" by the men. Before she left, she noted that the "tyrant" and his chief medical officer had prostitutes on hand, and also insulted the white nurse to the point of forcing her to leave. They also, she claimed, were eating the fruits, jellies, wine, and chicken that had been sent to the individual wounded.

In October she transferred to another camp at Hilton Head with her husband, where life was "monotonus but pleasant," and she spent time riding horseback. After Dr. Hawks left the camps, she established a successful practice in Boston, becoming a revered public figure and an honorary member of the New Hampshire Association of Military Surgeons. She was also active in charitable associations, the New England Hospital Medical Society, and the school board.

Another to assist in the war effort was Quaker physician Mary Thomas, who practiced medicine in Iowa for a short time, followed by a stint in Richmond, Indiana, near a large colony of Friends. Her husband, Dr. Owen Thomas, was a contract surgeon stationed at the army hospital in Nashville, Tennessee. Although she was a proficient surgeon, army regulations prohibited the hiring of women doctors except as nurses. The only exception to the rule forbidding women as doctors in the military was Dr. Mary Edwards Walker, who graduated from Syracuse Medical College at the age of twenty-two, in 1855, and was accepted by the Union Army for volunteer service in 1861. Women were not commissioned as army nurses or doctors until three years later, which made Dr. Walker an acting assistant surgeon and a first lieutenant, with pay of $100 per month.

Walker was captured by Confederate forces near Chattanooga and spent four months in prison before being traded with twenty-four other captive doctors for seventeen Southern surgeons. Although she was cruelly harassed while in prison, she pressured the prison overseers to improve the food, ultimately managing to obtain occasional wheat bread and vegetables amid the steady diet of cornbread.

She fulfilled her military contract until the war's end, after which she relentlessly campaigned for recognition. Presidential correspondence reveals Walker's intrepid letter-writing skills; she sent missive after missive, first asking and then demanding her past-due money and credit for her war efforts. In 1864 she was finally awarded the sum of $432.36.

After the Civil War, Dr. Mary Edwards Walker received the nation's most prestigious military award, the Medal of Honor, from President Andrew Johnson on November 11, 1865, for her war efforts as a surgeon. But she was not without her critics. In 1867 Roberts Bartholow, once an assistant surgeon in the Union Army, met Walker in Washington at Lincoln General Hospital. As a member of the medical board that examined her qualifications, Dr. Bartholow wrote that "she betrayed such utter ignorance of any subject in the whole range of medical science" that he found it difficult to conduct the examination. He was sure that an "ordinary housewife" would be more skilled, and he also believed that her "riding about outposts alone" had been a deliberate bid to be captured.

The Medal of Honor was rescinded in 1917 by a change in national guidelines that specified the award could only be won by an armed man in combat; thus she was disqualified. Undaunted, Walker refused to return the medal to the government even though she was forbidden to wear it. Only in 1977 was her case reinstated and the medal reawarded.

The military prejudice against women physicians is illustrated by the comments of the young surgeon John Lauderdale, who wrote of "three ladies on board" a hospital steamboat, whom he derided as "acting the part of Florence Nightingales" who "pretend" to minister to the patients but "take some liberties." His fellow medic, Dr. Hoff, did not appreciate their attentions since they "appeared to be the strong minded variety of femininity." Were they nurses? Disgruntled physicians working as nurses? Lauderdale did not say. Such prejudice continued even as late as the Spanish-American War.

Nurse visiting the Navajo.

National Library of Medicine

CHAPTER TEN

Ethnic Outreach

Women, Medicine, and Cross-Cultural America

Plenty of air and sunshine — that is Nature's medicine.

— SUSAN LA FLESCHE PICOTTE ("BRIGHT EYES")

F ROM THE TIME OF THE FIRST EUROPEANS' ARRIVAL IN THE NEW World, the lifeways of the American Indians were severely disrupted by this utterly different people. Currents of misunderstanding ran deep—and their influence over the the practice of medicine was no exception. Yet often there was surprisingly positive interaction. "Many of the early Botanic physicians of America appear to have obtained their first . . . medical knowledge from intercourse with the natives," wrote Alexander Wilder in his early text *History of Medicine.* In fact, native remedies were the "chief remedial agents" in the colonies. Indians of the upper Mississippi Valley used a number of practical herbal remedies to treat illness, including emetics, laxatives, and coagulants in the form of poultices and teas. But there were differences in the style of practice of Euro-American doctors and Native American shamans. The Euro-American physician often opted for invasive techniques, namely surgery. In Indian healing ceremonies, the shaman sang, used smoke, or sucked the afflicted area to draw out the illness. While Anglo physicians relied upon Western science to diganose, Indian healers relied upon second sight, the smell of sickness, or even an object brought from the sickroom to identify the ailment. For many Indians, well-being came from living in harmony with family and surroundings, or as the Navajo describe it, "walking in beauty." Much illness sprang from an imbalance in the harmony. Native Americans credited other serious illnesses to spirit activity or the malevolent actions of another person and were most concerned to discover *who* caused the illness, in order to heal it. Songs, dreams, and voices of departed ones were all part of the healing process, but medicines were used as well, often suggested to the shaman by spirits while he or she was in a trance.

Among Indians, death was perceived differently than in Anglo society. In many Native American cultures, the mortally sick should be segregated and left alone to die, since if death occurred in a camp, the entire village would have to be burned. Thus, when Helen MacKnight Doyle found her Indian patient gone, with "no other information forthcoming," it was only by chance that she "spied a rude sapling shelter by a tiny stream" where the man had been placed to die. The shelter was built across the stream so that the failing man could lie in his rabbit-skin blanket and dip water with a cup. Doyle responded with compassion and sorrow, as well as respect for the tribe's decision—thère was no record of intervention.

Sometimes, though, Euro-American physicians did intervene. When rural Florida physician Anna Darrow found an ailing Indian child tied up in water up to his neck as "punishment" for his illness, and was expected to "die [at] sun up," she could not stand on ceremony or tradition. She persuaded the family to release him instead and bring him in for treatment. A keen diagnostician, Darrow found that the boy had acute pericarditis—she invited the family to listen to his "friction rub" in the heart through a stethoscope. Her remedies eventually turned the child into a "normal happy Indian boy."

❧

Like pioneer families, ordinary Native American women used home remedies for simple ailments, calling in the shaman for only the most difficult or serious illnesses. Women used charred wood powder for dyspepsia, and pounded raw honeysuckle root was used to drain a boil. They used joint grass ash or powdered sand dock root to cure running sores, and powdered primrose root to reduce inflammation. Colds trailed away under the ministrations of horsemint tea, meadow rue tea, or tea made from mountain mahogany. Mountain mahogany also served to cure lung trouble or tuberculosis; the outer bark was for colds, but the inner bark was for more serious ailments. Women were healers of their own hearths.

An interesting cultural dichotomy existed between Native American women shamans and Euro-American women doctors. Native American shamans received their ability through dreams, an endowment that allowed them to treat specific diseases and gave them a

Prenatal class.

National Library of Medicine

position that was seldom questioned. Their powers were believed, their practice trusted, and their remedies unilaterally accepted. A traditional medicine woman, or healer, had to know not only methods of preserving, preparing, and applying herbal remedies, but also the medicinal use of prairie plants, their geographic range, and their time of harvest. She also had to have extensive spiritual knowledge. What she visualized as the cause of disease was taken as fact.

In Western culture, women's medical aspirations might also be called "dreams" of a sort, though sometimes not even medical training and a degree gave them the authority they sought in order to help patients. Their paths were arduous, strewn with societal obstacles that a Native American female healer did not have to face.

As tribes were herded into settlements and reservations, an inevitable mingling of lore and habit took place, all too often leaving the

Native Americans adrift culturally, each tribe learning to create its own spiritual and health care through a bastardized mixture of Anglo and Indian practices. From the cultural confusion, occasional leaders surfaced: Lillie Rosa Minoka, a Mohawk Indian raised by Quakers in Philadelphia, was also a graduate of the 1899 class of the Women's Medical College of Pennsylvania. She and her husband, Charles Hill of the Oneida tribe, lived on the Oneida reservation, where she was known as "Youda-tent," or "she who carries aid." She practiced for five years, but her husband objected, allowing her to care only for neighbors and relatives. Finally, in 1934, she applied for a medical license in Wisconsin.

Another was Susan La Flesche Picotte, an Omaha from Walthill, Nebraska, who crossed both gender and racial barriers to study Euro-American medicine at the Woman's Medical College of Philadelphia, graduating first in a class of one hundred. La Flesche was the daughter of the renowned chief of the fur-trading days along the Missouri River, Joseph La Flesche, whose prestige was such that when her office opened, the young Indian doctor immediately attracted "an immense practice . . . among whites as well as Indians," according to a newspaper tribute at her death in 1915. Her patients numbered 1,244. They lived in tipis and earth lodges on the Omaha reservation, and those unable to come to her office at the Indian school in Macy were visited by La Flesche, who rode to visit her patients daily, saddlebags packed with bottles and thermometers that often cracked from the jarring impact of the horse's hooves. As daughter of a chief, she fell easily into a role of authority, serving in a complex medley of roles: physician, mother, financial and legal adviser, and domestic intermediary. "The name of La Flesche means the arrow," she wrote in 1914, a metaphor for her surely aimed life. "I have lived right with them for over twenty years practicing medicine, attending the sick, helping them with all their financial and domestic business and anything that concerned their personal and family life."

In a typical day, La Flesche might diagnose mild tonsillitis and apply an alcohol sponge to a baby, call up the hospital to discover that Lizzie Blackbird was no better, try to "help the Johnson boys" get their money, then consult with "White Horse and wife . . . about [the] new home they wanted to build." Often patients boarded at her home to recover. She was often asked to interpret: once on behalf of a tribe member being dunned for $30 rent money, another time to clear up a land title, and yet another time for a man and wife about to make out wills—"40$ each for children after death." She would advise a couple to have their teeth attended to, or write a letter for an illiterate man.

She was equally connected to the community's spiritual needs. When one of her patients was ill, La Flesche called on her and "played some hymns for her," promising to come some Sunday and play and sing hymns for her again. "Henry Lyon came in and talked about his efforts to better himself spiritually as well as temporally," she wrote on November 3, 1910.

She consoled a little girl who complained that in the district school she got no attention because of the many white children in the school. She attended an "old mother" who was very feeble, and she listened to the recounting of one man's personal demons in his "struggle to better himself in every way." As a wise elder, she offered the finest of what medicine had to offer—emotional as well as physical comfort.

The doctor had much over which to despair; although the federal government had endowed each tribe member with salable land, it often ended tied up in trusts or being blindly sold for a quickly dispersed profit. Alcohol left a trail of destruction through the reservation, sickening and incapacitating many. When asked to testify in the investigation of the death of an Omaha man, the forty-seven-year-old La Flesche gave an impassioned plea for the decline of her tribe, a "very moral people" torn apart by the white man's poison, and whom she endeavored to heal with the white man's medicine. The challenge was extreme, the litany of deaths wrenching, as she recorded in her journal.

They did not know the taste of [liquor] until it was brought to them by the French voyagers in trading. They first used liquor sometime before 1865. It brought them disastrous results. There were murders, lawlessness, and vice. Joseph La Flesche or Iron Eyes, my father, was chief at the time. Realizing the ultimate disastrous effects liquor would have on them, he took drastic measures to put a stop to the drinking. . . . It was during the year '88 when Joseph La Flesche died . . . that politicians came among the Omahas and told them that now since they could vote they had the same rights as the white-man, and that they could drink just as much as they wanted to. . . .

Men and women gave themselves up to drunkenness. Liquor was given to children. There were about eight men who did not drink. The church stood empty. Women who would not have dreamed of doing so while sober, committed immoralities. . . . The people have been idle [now] for over eighteen years, we find a marked effect on them physically from this idleness. . . .

Then in 1910 . . . a great many patents in fee were released to the Indians. [Many] immediately sold their land and proceeded to spend the proceeds in dissipation. Since then, each year a few men have fallen away.

– In 1894, Harry Edwards fell from a buggy, was not missed by his drunken companions and in the morning was found frozen to death.

– In the same year Alvin Reese, a young man, had a runaway while drunk and was dragged to death.

– In 1895 George Parker, an Omaha Indian was shot by a drunk Winnebago and died instantly.

– In 1895 Washington Baxter, a young Indian man, died in one night

from convulsions from drinking alcohol.

–In 1894 Philip Watson, an elderly man, while drunk died from exposure and pneumonia.

– In 1896 James Walker, an Omaha Indian, while drunk, was run over by a train in the city of Omaha.

– In 1898 William Parker died in a few hours from drinking alcohol.

– In 1903 Charlie Reese, a young man died from drinking alcohol.

– In 1904 Henry Guitar, a mere boy, while drunk, killed his father Stephan Guitar, and he was sent to a penitentiary where he spent about seven years, being paroled in 1913. James Blackbird, while drunk, shot Gilbert Morris who recovered after a long and tedious illness.

– In 1905 Nathan Lyon was killed while drunk by John Walker who died in the penitentiary in 1913.

– In 1905 Sam Parker killed Andrew Honson, but escaped any punishment. Both were drunk.

– In 1906 Silas Wood while drunk, killed George Phillips, another Omaha Indian who was also drunk. He escaped punishment. Wolf Chief while drunk in the State of Iowa was hung by the Vigilantes. Spafford Woodhull while drunk killed a New York Indian about 1896. He escaped punishment.

– In 1906 Stephen Walker died in a few hours from drinking alcohol.

– In 1890 Philip Porter or White Swan, died from drinking alcohol.

Furnas Robinson while drunk lay in the fire and had his leg burnt so badly that it had to be amputated.

– In 1909 Richard White while drunk lay out in the cold and died from the exposure. Frank Grant died from drinking alcohol.

– In 1905 Brian Preston while drunk was drowned in the Missouri River. Arthur Hallowell, a young man, was killed in the runaway while drunk.

– Eli Sheridan in 1906 died from drinking alcohol. The following women died from the results of alcohol: Levi Levering's mother, May W. Walker, Henry Warner's wife, William Frost's wife, and William Callon's wife.

– In 1911 Louis Levering died from the effects of alcoholism and tuberculosis.

– In 1911 Sammie Freemont who had served five years in the navy, shortly after his return from the navy committed suicide. While drunk he had signed away his patent in fee to W. E. Estill; after finding out what he had done, he shot himself.

– In 1913, Shagaduba, an old man while intoxicated drove into a ditch and was killed. The following died from alcoholism: George Grant, Ozoogacha, Willie Harlan, and Sioux Solomon. Joseph Drum while drunk was injured in a runaway so badly that he died.

– In 1912, Jeremiah Parker while drunk was shot and killed by a white man.

– In March 1914, Joel W. Tyndall, an educated Indian, died of alcoholism and general dissipation. In April, Henry Warner, an old man, was killed while drunk. The young man who was accused of killing him committed suicide. He was also drunk. These two deaths resulted from Lemon extract sold to them by George Phillips, a white man.

Native Americans confined to reservations were often forced to turn to American doctors for medicine—some were accepted, others rejected. Ironically, white female doctors were often accepted more readily by the Indians than within their own society; Oregon physician Mary Rowland worked with Crow Indians at the Chemawa Indian School in Salem.

ꙮ

Because the house call was an integral part of the medicine of the day, women physicians on the frontier might be summoned to unfamiliar, cross-cultural settings. When Wyoming homesteader Bessie Efner opened her door one night, she found two "grim-looking, swarthy Mexicans" who handed her a note. They were from a distant small town in Colorado and had come to fetch her to attend a childbirth. Would she accompany them on a railroad handcar? Frightened by their appearance and the thought of speeding through the moonless night on a hand-pumped handcar, she hesitated—but only a moment. "I wonder how I did have the

courage to risk some of these calls," she mused in later years, but on that dark night the doctor's sense of duty prevailed—a human life was at stake. "I quickly finished dressing, grabbed my medicine and instrument bag, took another glance at my sleeping girls, and then stepped out into the darkness with these two Mexican strangers." After hours speeding along beneath the waning moon, they reached the remote town; she was courteously escorted to the expectant mother, delivered a healthy baby, then returned home the next morning by train.

Cultural crossovers also occurred in the back alleys of San Francisco's Chinatown, where young intern Helen MacKnight Doyle often rambled, "watching the children dancing in and out ... gay as butterflies" and studying shop windows packed with herbs, powders, roots, dried lizards and snakes, and assorted other pharmaceuticals. Ancient customs dictated medical choices, yet occasionally, in the Americanized Chinese culture, Anglo physicians were called in. According to Doyle, the Chinese preferred American women doctors to minister to their women during childbirth, even though "there were two Chinese women physicians practicing medicine in Chinatown" who had graduated from medical school in Shanghai and Beijing and kept spotless, Western-style offices.

I spent one of the strangest nights of my career in Chinatown. While I was an intern in the Children's Hospital, a woman physician, who was on the visit-

ing staff, invited me to go with her to attend a confinement case of Spofford Alley, one of the most notorious places of Old San Francisco.

The Chinese preferred American women doctors to attend their women in confinement. At that time no respectable Chinese woman or "family girl" was allowed on the streets and the alleys of Chinatown were no place for a white woman to be seen alone at night. But the black medicine case that the women physicians carried insured safety. They were never molested. Just the same, the strange odors, the shadowy figures that shuffled along the streets and alleys, the weird screeching of Chinese fiddles, and the wailing of oboes, all gave me a feeling of dangers.

We climbed stairways where slant eyes peered through peepholes and heavily hinged and barred doors were opened to us. We were ushered into a room where gorgeously embroidered panels hung on the walls, elaborately carved teakwood tables held priceless ornaments and our feet sank into soft rugs of exquisite design. There was an altar to Joss and incense was burning before the shrine where Chinese lilies bloomed.

The prospective father, a wealthy Chinese merchant, received us. He was wearing a mandarin coat stiff with embroidery and a round, black cap with a jade button set in the top. Chinese women attendants in wide trousers and wide-sleeved coats of somber hues padded about noiselessly. The mother-to-be lay on a bed of red and gold lacquer; on the floor beside it stood her tiny, high-heeled, embroidered slippers. She was one of the beautiful ladies whose feet had been bound since childhood. Her hair was securely glued to form an elaborate head-dress and was ornamented with jade. On her fingers and arms were beautiful jade bracelets and rings. A dainty brocaded coverlet was on the bed and she lay between paper sheets, soft and fine as silk.

She did not understand or speak English, nor did her attendants. The husband was our interpreter. As the labor progressed, the doctor realized that the woman was about to give birth to an acephalous child—a terrible monstrosity. We had no chance to talk over the situation. That imperturbable Chinaman was watching every move.

The doctor knew the danger to us. She knew that the Chinese considered a deformed child a curse upon the house, and that the doctor was held responsible for any deviation from the normal. But she was a match for that imperturbable Chinaman. With perfect calm she faced the difficult task of preparing the father for the tragedy that was about to occur in the room that had been prepared so ceremoniously for an auspicious event.

I shall never forget that night. The smoke of the incense stung and blinded *our eyes and choked our lungs. The only relief we could find was to put our heads out the window, which must be hurriedly closed again, and inhale a few breaths of fog. The cries of the mother, about to be disgraced by her offspring, the stoical, sinister calm of the father, and the soft padding feet of the attendants were the only accompaniment to what seemed an endless labor.*

The child was born. Fortunately it took only a few breaths. Then the father sent for his friends. When they came there was great gesticulating and high-pitched argument. We knew they were discussing how far we were responsible for the monstrosity and what should be done. It happened that the doctor had been away on a vacation during a certain period of the prospective mother's pregnancy and the consultation resulted in the decision that the woman who had attended the patient during the doctor's absence was responsible for the condition.

The doctor restrained them from throwing the child out into the alley, as they wished to do. She insisted that the birth must be recorded and the child buried. We were told that in China such children were thrown out to be collected by the street scavengers, but the father finally reluctantly consented to do as she directed.

I have never been more thankful to get away from any place than I was to leave that house where the prayer papers

fluttered from the windows as we left Spofford Alley in the early morning.

Primary accounts from the nineteenth century have countless references to gender discrimination, but fewer concerning race. Racial attitudes were often revealed in the dealings of white physicians with black patients. One insight comes from surgeon Bertha Van Hoosen, who became a staff member of Chicago's Provident Hospital, an institution for the training of black nurses. Remarkably free of prejudice for her time, Van Hoosen had once inadvertently demonstrated her "color blindness" by giving a quick kiss to a black patient. Shocked, the woman reacted as if Van Hoosen had struck her in the face. The doctor vowed never to repeat the blunder, yet maintained her standard of gracious manners.

In the case of black women physicians, the issue was dual, concerning both gender and race, and affected every aspect of the black female doctor's life. For one, in many cities in the South hospitals did not accept black patients, which meant that black women physicians would have to treat their patients at home or work in collaboration with a white physician. According to historian Gloria Moldow, black women formed a very small part of the corps of practicing women physicians—in the twenty-five years following the Civil War there were 115 black women physicians in the United States—and were often separated from the activities of their white female colleagues. Nearly all of these black women were reform-

Mamie Hale, midwife.

National Library of Medicine

Sra. Leonor Villegas de Magnon y Jovita Idar curando el primer herido constitucionalista que capó en ma' de los federales en la batalla de N. Laredo, de las fuerzas de Jesus Carranz Mayo 17-1913 Fot. E. Montoy.

Leonor Villegas de Magnon (left) and Jovita Idar, organizers of La Cruz Blanca, treat a person who was wounded during the Mexican Revolution, Laredo, Texas, ca. 1912–1914.

University of Texas, Institute of Texan Cultures, San Antonio; Courtesy of A. Ike Idar

minded women from an elite black society that developed after the Civil War.

Because influential black families had struggled hard to achieve a certain level of comfort, there was widespread prejudice in these families against young black women entering the medical profession. In part this was a result of attitudes acquired during slavery, a kind of mimicking of the aristocratic fears and dislikes of past masters. On the southern plantation, work was not associated with the privileged class.

On the other hand, as pointed out by historian Gloria Moldow, black women understood the strong possibility of slipping downward in class and status because of a lack of eligible men of their own status to marry. Thus, maintaining self-reliance through a career, particularly a lucrative one, was essential.

Those black women without family fortunes to launch them in a medical career often found support in the black women's social clubs so popular in the 1890s. The Lucy Brown Club of Charleston was one of the foremost. Brown, a doctor, was so accepted in her field that, according to historian Ruth J. Abram, she joined a group of eight black male physicians to establish a hospital and training school—part of an effort to focus on the care of "the colored sick." The separate facility was necessary, since black nurses were not allowed in the public institutions. Born in North Carolina in 1863 to a poor family, Lucy Hughes Brown was even further burdened by the death of her mother while Lucy was young, which left her with the responsibility of caring for her brothers and sisters. She began her education by studying at home, then graduated from the Women's Medical College of Pennsylvania in 1894 and started her own medical practice in Charleston in 1896.

Matilda Evans was one of the first black physicians native to South Carolina to practice in the state after receiving a degree from the Women's Medical College of Pennsylvania in 1897. Supported by scholarship and her own part-time work, Evans's huge capacity for hard work resulted in many professional laurels. "I have built up the most enviable reputation," she wrote in a letter on behalf of a black female applicant to the medical college in 1907. "I have done well and have a very large practice among all classes of people. I have not lost one day since I left college." She established the first black hospital in Columbia and founded several free clinics.

Dr. Rebecca Cole, the second black woman to receive a medical degree in the United States, was a graduate of the Women's Medical College of Pennsylvania in 1867; Rebecca Lee had received a degree from the New England College of Medicine in Boston in 1864. Mary E. Pritton graduated from Berea College in Kentucky in the 1870s, and worked as the first black female physician in Lexington.

If questioned about their commitment to health and healing, all the women, matters of race aside, would probably respond in the spirit of Native American physician Susan La Flesche Picotte: "I cannot see how any credit is due me. I am thankful I've been called and permitted to serve. I feel blessed for that privilege above all measure."

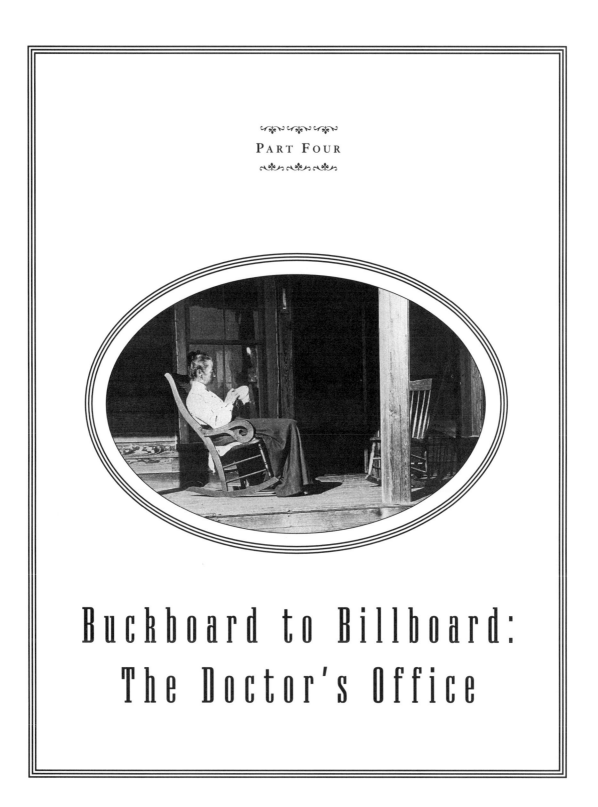

PART FOUR

Buckboard to Billboard:
The Doctor's Office

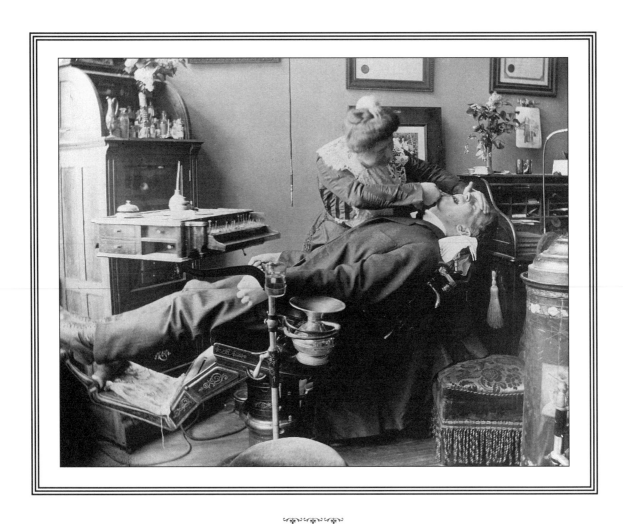

Dr. Olga Lentz, a St. Paul dentist, ca. 1920.

Photograph by Albert Nunson;
Minnesota Historical Society

CHAPTER ELEVEN

The Doc Is In

Setting Up a Rural Office

*When a woman goes into business she must look sharp
and not break her health.*

—MARY CANAGA ROWLAND, M.D.

O MATTER HOW REMOTE THE SETTING, HOW CRUDE THE DWELLING, OR how fledgling the practice, the female physician presided over a medical realm that began with a stationary site—her office. From the moment she first hung out the shingle, she was flooded with a sense of pride and inevitability—the result of years of college, complicated finances, pitched discrimination, poverty, bank loans, and grueling hours—that would be the burden of her early years. That so many female graduates of medical colleges were able to establish themselves in rural nineteenth-century America, despite male opposition and the general reluctance to view women as professionals, attests to an extraordinary degree of determination and will. Private practice was the ultimate medical dream, usually achieved by the bold, the well-financed, and the well-connected, since establishing a sizable middle-class patient base took time and resources as well as a promotional effort that might involve word-of-mouth recommendation, flyers, calling cards, window notices, picture cards, and paid advertisements in local papers and periodicals.

Setting up shop nearly always began with the hanging of a shingle. Lillian Heath's simple black-and-gold sign graced the front door, inviting patients into the parlor of her parents' home, which served as the young doctor's office. Hannah E. Longshore proudly established herself as Philadelphia's first female doctor with a jaunty new shingle that belied her despair over the ornery refusal of male druggists to fill her prescriptions. Optimism swung high with Mary Putnam Jacobi's first shingle, proudly nailed into place by her father, who was delighted by his daughter's success.

In fact, the question of the sign became one of the practitioner's first and most important decisions: When the shingle was hoisted, what should it say? Acknowledging her gender by spelling out her entire name—not just using initials—risked male antipathy, yet attracted women seeking private "female consultation." Or, to deflect criticism, the doctor could disguise her sex and hide behind her husband's name. Cautiously proper, this approach would ensure a minimum amount of resentment from adherents to the idea that women were unfit for "the professions." Mary Glassen opted for caution when ordering a shingle, hand-painted by a schoolboy in Phillipsburg, Kansas. She instructed him to paint the cautious designation "M. Townsend DeMotte, M.D.," which would downplay her gender. Dr. Marilla Hemenway Wilson, the first female practitioner in Oakland, California, was equally circumspect; she had practiced jointly with her husband for years, but after his death in 1877, decided to remain "Mrs. Dr. M.D. Wilson," a "Ladies' Physician."

Medical pioneer Elizabeth Garret took another stance. Her hard-won admission to the Society of Apothecaries in 1866 and arduous course of study were too precious to disguise—she was determined to advertise her entire name on her shingle. "I don't like 'Miss Garrett' on the door," she maintained. "It is only like a dressmaker."

Most women physicians practiced at home, where medical duties melded with domestic chores and the cost of a separate office was saved. Sophie Herzog held consultations in her daughter's house when she first arrived in Brazoria, Texas, in the 1890s, but her popularity and growing patient following quickly forced her into a three-room office with tiny living quarters in the back, where she lived alone.

South Carolina's Jane Bruce Guignard lived and practiced in a large, two-story house in Columbia—her office was never separate from her residence, and domestic arrangements had to flow around the line of patients that snaked from the waiting room to the consultation area, with space edged aside for a nurse-assistant. After graduating from Creighton Medical School in 1905, physician Mary Rowland built herself a twelve-room house in Topeka, Kansas. Value lay in character, not possessions, Rowland believed, but her initial reluctance to build such an ostentatious edifice gave way when she recognized that it gave her "a certain social standing" as well as providing convenience. The house was "planned like a hotel," with two stairways, two landings, and a liv-

ing room fireplace. One room near the kitchen was insulated with charcoal and served as an icebox, where a hundred pounds of ice were delivered twice a week. Indeed, to the pleased young doctor, "the whole house was a wonderful creation."

Most private offices were drawn on a smaller scale, often so simply furnished and so tiny only the doctor and patient could share the space. Georgia Arbuckle Fix began her practice in a lowly sod hut but eventually moved into the town of Gering, Nebraska, to set up her office in an old brick building, once a schoolhouse. A flourishing patient load soon forced her to buy an additional site, which she "fixed up" with two already-built houses, dragged by teams of horses across a frozen river, placed side by side, and remodeled into a combination home and office for herself. This soon became the site of a women's shelter and missionary society, literary club, church, boardinghouse, hospital—even a wedding facility—as well. "The Sanitarium" became a refuge for all the town citizens, and also offered a haven to animals: several birds, including an owl, and various mongrel dogs.

Those who questioned the propriety of a woman's treating male patients were appeased by the typical office arrangement—a room with access to a main street, which would thwart rumors of unseemly dalliances with male patients. Propriety was also served by the use of a parlor or the back sitting room of a large family dwelling, preferably while family members were at home. "In the house I had an office for my very own use, with an outside entrance," wrote South Carolina physician Portia Lubchenco. "It consisted of a room for examining patients and a waiting room. It tended to draw more of my practice to the office and lightened the duty of calls somewhat. The advent of the telephone tended to bring more folks in through appointment, also."

Those without permanent homes rented office space or lodgings, an ordeal that presented interesting challenges to women unaccustomed to living away from home, including the very young or the recently widowed. Dr. Mary Rowland, a young general practitioner, marked her exodus from a tiny borough in Kansas to the sprawling, unfamiliar city of Omaha by a comic mishap centered around her first apartment, rented in a rough part of town. After several weeks, her roommate noted the steady stream of male "company" always buzzing about the landlady. Was it the woman's cooking? Suddenly, the two women realized she was a prostitute. "The very next day," Rowland wrote in her journal, "I went in search of another apartment and secured an entire house."

Such innocence might also translate into financial loss—unscrupulous landlords were quick to recognize that medical education had nothing to do with economic sense. In one rented apartment, Rowland was persuaded to pay forty-five dollars to repair burst pipes that were the landlord's responsibility. "He said I should pay to fix them because I lived there," she mused, sensing some subterfuge but hesitant to protest. Later, in 1910, she moved to Lebanon, Oregon, a rustic town completely without sewers; the streets were muddy and water "stood everywhere in the town," so people walked on raised board sidewalks. She rented a battered old house on Main Street and hung out her shingle. "People went by and I heard them remark, 'Dr. Mary C. Rowland. A woman doctor. Well, well, well.'" If the "well, well, well" was tinged with jealousy, it came from the enigma of a professional female's supposed prosperity. How to view such success? Rowland humorously pointed out that even when she could afford to have her own house built, the young contractor whom she hired refused to allow her to enter while the house was under construction. He was "willing to take a woman's money but not willing to have her supervise its spending," she wrote. "I was amused."

Furnishings reflected individual personality and taste. Rural patients, hard-pressed to pay and fearful of medical attention in general, distrusted finery, thinking it meant the office was "too grand," thus too expensive; they preferred efficacy to antimacassars, price to polish, and were more interested in the medical trappings than the architectural one. In the early 1930s, Mary Glassen equipped her first reception room with "a settee, two matching arm chairs, magazine rack and floor lamp bought from Montgomery Ward for $29.50." She covered the floor with a rag carpet. Amelia Dann used an old dresser from her bedroom to hold instruments and medicine bottles and a kitchen table for her laboratory. Helen MacKnight Doyle found her fixtures at an emporium—an old counter with built-in shelves, where she could easily sort and stack her potions, pills, and dressings. Kept cozy by an "air-tight heating stove," the room also held a cot for sleeping and a rough-hewn, splintery table for patient examinations. Dr. Dann kept a few toys on hand for children—blocks, a wooden train, a few washable animals, and some books. According to Harriet Belcher, her office on State Street in Santa Barbara, California, was ideal: "The office is about 8 by 12 feet, is prettily carpeted and papered [with] a lounge, wardrobe, office chair, and large desk of stained wood. [There is also] . . . a pretty towel rack which I have filled in with English Embroidery, my diploma, books, etc."

Typically, a doctor's office would always include brass scales, a magnifying glass, test tubes and measuring cylinders, and a stove for sterilizing instruments. Amelia Dann hired a young woman to clean her house and sterilize the instruments, but Dr. Dann would allow no one else to pack her precious medical bag, which held a special rack for medicine bottles above and her stethoscope, thermometer, tourniquets, syringe and needles, catheters, bandages, adhesive, and other first-aid items below. The year was 1878—Dr. Dann was ready for patients.

Equipment was necessary—ideally, something more sophisticated than a kitchen table for surgery. Bessie Efren, the lone doctor in a small Canadian town, noted, "When fracture cases were brought into my office, I had at least the advantage of my office equipment and a professional table to work on." When she made house calls, often she "had to resort to the kitchen table as the most convenient place to do the work."

❧

Physicians unable or unwilling to either rent or own offices became part of a loosely organized, medical affiliation of traveling doctors who would hold consultations in hotels, and who attracted many patients because of lower prices. Such physicians, women included, would tout their specialties in billboards and newspaper ads, set up tables in hotel lobbies, and pass out patent medicines to cure all ills, including bed-wetting and weight loss. Citizens in the vicinity were "respectfully informed" of their medical presence, often by the offer of a free consultation or lecture series.

Individual practitioners had office hours of their own choice. "Hours 1–3 except Saturday," advertised Marcia B. Cleveland of San Francisco. "Hours 1–3," echoed Elizabeth Yates. "Hours 7–8 P.M., Tuesday and Friday" simply conducting a genteel ancillary practice is unknown. Mary Glassen of Phillipsburg, Kansas, who practiced in the mid–twentieth century, had an office open from 9:00 until 6:00 daily, and her house calls were made at night. In a fledgling practice, often a doctor saw an average of three or four patients daily, with the number increasing yearly. Records kept in medical daybooks list the many costs of doing business as a doctor, including the long-running pharmaceutical accounts. Increased income was generally matched by climbing expenses—a doctor could earn additional money through drugs, consultations, coroner's business, and special clinics.

Procedures for illnesses and prices for procedures throughout the country were standardized by the passage of the Medical Practice Act of 1876. Colorado instituted licensing standards in 1881, while in Utah, a local Salt Lake City ordinance relating to physicians was published in the local news on October 22, 1856. "Any person" practicing "physics, medicine or surgery" within the city limits had to obtain a license from the city council and have his or her qualifications examined by a committee of three appointed by the city council—failure to obtain legal permits would result in a fine of "not less than five nor more than one hundred dollars for each offense."

Although such physicians were licensed, the entire question of licensing was suspect. The success of a practice hinged upon a physician's credibility, which was defined by, among other things, medical school training, special-

were those offered by Adelaide Brown, also of San Francisco. Whether the women were on house calls during the remainder of the day or ization, and licensing. In Europe, the quality of American licensing procedures was held in contempt—one physician from Indiana practicing in Britain was fined for claiming a degree that, the British believed, "was one of those American titles which could be secured for about thirty dollars." Until licensing went into effect, state by state, it was impossible to identify medical school graduates. Frequent travel, no fixed address, and the lack of regulatory penalties made licensed and unlicensed difficult to oversee. With or without licenses, stationary doctors with local addresses and community standing were easier to oversee. The medical examining boards of each state stood between medical school graduates and the public, making it their business to protect the public from poor training.

The first woman to practice medicine in Dade County, Florida—Eleanor Galt Simmons—was issued an occupational license for $1.00 in 1894. But the way a license was granted to Nina Baierle when she applied for certification in West Virginia in 1914 was rather unusual. A medical emergency had flared up suddenly, and a special process was set up to quickly certify out-of-state doctors. Each was given a test tube of urine and asked to identify the disease. Baierle was an excellent diagnostician; after several minutes of intense concentration, she suddenly dipped her finger into the "urine" and sampled

> *In my hotheaded infatuation for Chicago, I had begun practicing in a city where I had not a single friend or acquaintance.*
>
> — DR. BERTHA VAN HOOSEN

it. "The specimen [was] water, sugar and a coloring agent, and no one yet has died of it," she said. Dr. Baierle was notified the next day of her certification to practice medicine in West Virginia, beginning immediately. Not all applications were successful. In 1909 Mary Canaga Rowland failed the Idaho state medical examination and went immediately to Oregon, where the state examination was being offered to 132 men and 2 women. "I think only thirty-six men passed," Rowland wrote, "they caught one man cheating, handed him his examination fee back, and dismissed him," adding, "but both women passed."

As in any profession, the doctor's first months depended, financially, upon her ability to charm, wheedle, cajole, or tempt patients to her practice—patients who had reserved judgment as to whether the "young lady doc" was "worth her stuff." In beginning a practice, women had to gently insinuate themselves into the rhythm of the community, often confronting intense prejudice from both men and women.

If the town had male practitioners, attitudes swung from indifference to generosity, and competition might flare up—or not. Friendships with other women doctors sometimes provided new patients; Dr. Margaret Ethel Fraser, during her internship, met two other young interns during her years at the

Medical Women's College of the University of Toronto—Elsie S. Pratt and Margaret Long, both of whom became lifelong friends. But more often it was elder male physicians who welcomed the women, hoping that they might be willing to relieve the men of more irksome patients, mainly other women and, in some cases, young children.

Mary Glassen's medical practice, based in a four-room frame house, was so desperately slow at first that boredom would drive her "over to . . . the restaurant" across the street to "sometimes . . . help with the dishes." Amelia Dann's first patient was a ten-year-old boy carrying a wounded puppy in his arms, "a fishhook hanging ominously from his left eyelid where the hook had snagged." The puppy howled as the doctor quickly snipped away the hook—her payment was a grateful thank-you and a wave of the hand. Mary C. Rowland began her practice with a ten-year-old boy who came to her late one night, waking her to take a look at a finger he had hurt while bowling. "He was crying and I asked him how he happened to come to me and he said, 'Cause I know'd you're a woman, and you'd be careful.'" Rowland counted among her many satisfied patients the boy, who grew up to become the county sheriff.

The "first genuine sick call" to which Bertha Van Hoosen responded provided both a moral dilemma and a professional turning point. A one-year-old German immigrant child was ill from cholera infantum—two siblings had just died from the disease. Van Hoosen examined the child, then irrigated the baby's bowel with a catheter and funnel. After teaching the mother the same technique, she advised that the child be given only boiled water for a time. A fellow boarder, a "young Eastern doctor with fine offices," grew upset at her action. To him, immigrants were incapable of carrying out complex medical procedures and were content only with prescribed medicine. "You must always give medicine to that type of patient," he exclaimed, "even if no more than sugar or bread pills. And never tell them not to feed a baby." Van Hoosen was horribly upset.

I went to my little hall bedroom office, sat down and had a good cry, then and there resolving to give up the practice of medicine and go back to teaching anatomy. If one practiced medicine just to bamboozle the public, I would have none of it. The teaching of anatomy was honest and honorable, and I felt I had been foolish to start into a high-class swindling game.

Yet Van Hoosen's technique had worked. The mother, ecstatic, went from door to door, telling her neighbors, "If your baby get sick, don't send for them mens doctors. You get the lady doctor. She gives you no medicine. She just tell you what to do." Van Hoosen's first case was happily concluded: "From that day the solution of the problem of clientele (so difficult for many young physicians) was assured, with little effort on my part."

᷒᷈᷒

Childbirth was an area in which distrust mingled with curiosity, and in which patients with limited incomes were loath to gamble on the unproven skills of a woman. Dr. Margaret Stewart, a practitioner in San Francisco, recounted reasons that a few of her patients had given: "One patient engaged me because when her last baby was born, the doctor put a bottle on her mahogany dining-room table, and she had never been able to remove the stain. Another woman said they had four boys and wanted a girl so much that they decided if they had a woman doctor, the next baby would be a girl."

After Helen Mac-Knight Doyle successfully delivered an unexpected set of twins from a frightened army wife, who had already borne three girls and been warned that future deliveries would cause her to "surely die," her practice was assured. The woman's desire for a boy exceeded her fear of death, and when Doyle was called in for the labor, she had the unique pleasure of delivering first a girl and then, to the father's amazement, a boy. Despite threats of "dire misfortune," the mother had borne twins with no difficulty whatever. "Everybody in the valley knew about it," Doyle exulted. "My practice flourished." Dr. Harriet Belcher waited a month for the arrival of her first patient, a "young girl who imagined she had cancer" and to whom the doctor responded, "The purest fancy!" The doctor was correct.

Lillian Heath began her practice in a tiny Wyoming community to the buzz of local gossip; who could imagine a woman who rode alone through the desert, lived by herself, and treated male patients? Scandalmongers buzzed when Heath was summoned to the bedside of an elderly man who lived far from town. Harnessing up "buckboard and bronc," Heath cut through wash and gully and traversed miles of sage to find the patient "bright and chipper as could be," and up and about his chores. Puzzled, Dr. Heath examined the elderly man, quizzed him about his health, and secured a specimen; then, as it was too late to ride back to Rawlins, she stayed the night. Inadvertently, she overheard a conversation that explained all: when asked how he felt, the sly fellow replied that he was fine. He simply "wanted to see what a lady doctor looked like."

Dr. Esther Hawks, beginning her practice in Manchester, Connecticut, found that her "splendid sense of humor" sustained her through the first years. Prejudice kept patients away, and before she finally established a patient base, she found herself every afternoon at her husband's drugstore, fitting women up with "shoulder braces, supporters, trusses and the like.

> *I have sat in that damned office for three months without a real call.*
>
> — MABEL ULRICH

Child care and hygiene, ca. 1915.

National Library of Medicine

CHAPTER TWELVE

Fees, Bills, and Payment in Kind

That horse was my first patient in Wyoming, and the 75 cents
the first professional fee I earned on the Western frontier.

— BESSIE EFNER

SHROUDED IN MYSTERY, BESET BY DOUBT, AND CONSIGNED TO THE CAT-
egory of "questionable" and "a poor risk" by banks and other lenders, women in
medicine faced financial prospects that seemed dim indeed in a profession that often earned more
payment in chickens and baked goods than in currency. Although both male and female doctors
envisioned a future with at least a steady income, the fledgling profession of medicine was beset
by a "significant disproportion between the amount of services doctors rendered and the fees they
were paid." Often, it took years to earn a decent living; according to one study in 1889, only 11 of
390 women doctors were able to support themselves. A female physician had to overcome pervasive prejudice against professionals in general, coupled with an unspoken expectation that medicine was really only nursing and charity combined, and should be offered without a price. The
other false expectation was that women had no need to support themselves, even though a national
survey taken in 1892 showed that at least 32 percent of the nation's practicing women physicians

were their own, sole support, or were financially responsible for other family members. Even Bethenia Owens-Adair, one of the better-known physicians of her time, author of many well-publicized health campaigns for women, and head of a thriving rural practice, suffered financially. Although this stalwart, authoritative woman had been independent since the age of fifteen, no number of patients or amount of community recognition seemed to free her from financial burdens. "I have often looked back over my past life not with a shudder," she wrote, "but to gain strength and courage to meet the financial difficulties... [that] threatened to engulf me." Elizabeth Blackwell, the country's first practicing woman physician, found her first seven years in medicine were "very difficult uphill work." Not only did patients come slowly, but her "pecuniary position [was] a source of constant anxiety." She had "no medical companionship," since the profession itself "stood aloof" in a society that was "distrustful of the innovation [of women doctors]." And worse, she received daily "insolent letters . . . [that] came by post," impugning her morals, her femininity, and her medical skills.

Despite such impediments, Blackwell's growing practice caught the attention of her old college professor, a man who had once tried to thwart her academic career because of her sex and who now, viewing her success, believed that his former student was the recipient of a financial windfall. Ironically, he now decided that she should join him in a "benevolent partnership," in which he would manage her practice "on condition of sharing profits over 5,000 dollars." Certainly, he believed, she could earn this amount easily in a year! Blackwell's actual income, like those of most women physicians, was far less. Women found they generally bore out Plato's opinion that "the true physician . . . is not a mere moneymaker."

By the beginning of the twentieth century women had been practicing medicine for over fifty years, yet their financial worth was still undetermined, their suitability questioned, and their skills and education seldom acknowledged as the basis for bank loans or credit. In 1927 Jessie Laird Brodie tried to use her medical education as security for a loan to start a medical practice in Portland with her husband, but she was rejected. No American bank of that time would view a medical education as security. Had they any other collateral?

Generally, male physicians could expect a brighter future, even if immediate earnings fell below expectations. "A doctor can always

> *I charged him twenty dollars and he started cursing me. He said, "Why did I ever call for a woman doctor in the first place?"*
>
> — MARY CANAGA ROWLAND, M.D.

collect a debt," wrote Charles Forbes of Buxton, North Dakota, in 1888. "He can seize anything and everything that a man has got until the debt is paid, by the laws of Dakota. Fees are high too." To James Rutherford, a self-satisfied Illinois practitioner in 1841, "the Doctor is the greatest man in the country," whose reputation drew patients from "nearly all the good families in the country," earning "about $150 per month" during the summer, "with a peak of $250 in August." Such prominence prompted a certain grandiloquence, as he boasted: "Here I walk a lord of the soil." Despite a fiscal downturn in fall and winter, his income seemed quite satisfactory, with fees ranging from "$5.00 to deliver a baby, $2.00 to set a bone, $.50 for a dozen quinine pills, .25 to staunch bleeding." From this generous total was deducted the cost of quinine, drugs, smelling salts, and some instruments. Never a humble man, Rutherford seemed well pleased with his position: "Wasn't it pleasant to do good & see a community [so] grateful for [its] benefits," he marveled.

A particularly brash Irish immigrant, Richard Somerset Den, who practiced in California under Mexican sovereignty, had so many devoted patients that he never made a house call for less than twenty dollars. Once, according to a fellow physician, Dr. Lindsey, Den took in "more than one thousand dollars . . . for his fee," a most lucrative house call. Such income allowed the doctor a degree of sartorial splendor so compelling—including "immaculate linen [and] large black scarf and a collar . . . so high . . ." he was forced to "hold his head erect"—that the awestruck patients of this romantic fellow even coined a popular phrase: *"Despues de Dios, Doctor Don Ricardo,"* or "After God, Doctor Richard."

"There was millions in medicine. Just millions!" exclaimed another male practitioner, an army physician in Prescott, Arizona, whose annual earnings of $1,181 in private practice in 1877 seemed distant from his exaggerated expectations, yet left him ever hopeful, still convinced that medicine, like the gold rush or the silver boom, would shower him with riches and turn the ordinary into the epic. Fees, like reputations, might vary wildly, yet few could boast of the gold and glitter earned by a very few male physicians—especially not women.

Yet fortune occasionally beckoned practitioners of both sexes, particularly during the early, boisterous frontier days when the lure of gold, grain, acreage, and autonomy sparked rampant hopes and an occasional surge of largesse. In the newly formed territories, money flowed freely, women's services were held at a premium, and some female doctors, such as Helen MacKnight Doyle, founded practices so lucrative as to "exceed a doctor's Arabian Nights dream." In 1883 Bethenia Owens-Adair earned the surprising sum of "fully $7,000"—an amount she never again achieved. Although surveys of doctors at specific times and different localities have suggested a wide range in earnings, such as one nineteenth-century Canadian physician who never billed more than $750 for medical services in any one year.

As medicine became more sophisticated

and more doctors entered the western market, the need to regulate fees and services grew. Medical societies were formed, with their members drawing up fee bills to establish minimum rates for service, printed and boldly displayed in offices to inform patients of the full range of services and charges. Prices usually increased with the advent of more sophisticated medical practices, although fees generally were lower in more remote settings. As noted by Margaret Coffin in *Death in Early America,* a medical society in upper New York State in 1810 assigned the following charges as medical guidelines:

> Fee for each visit 25¢
> Riding per mile 20¢
> Doctor in night 38¢
> Consultation $1.00
> Cathartics 13–25¢

According to the ledgers of Nebraska's Dr. Georgia Arbuckle Fix, prices hovered in the low range, from 50¢ to $4.00, for medicine or treatment. Yet many doctors had increased their fees by midcentury, with local records in 1846 from Waukesha County, Wisconsin, listing thigh, leg, or foot amputation at $50, finger or toe amputation at $5, vaginal surgery, $10, tonsillectomy, $10, and hip or shoulder joint amputation or expirating (blowing matter out of) an eye, $100. Some practices still remained a bargain. In 1849 the Western Medical Society of Wisconsin recommended bleeding at 50 cents, cupping (a form of bleeding) for a dollar, and house calls at $1 for a town visit and $2 for a rural call, or 50 cents

per mile. While the typical weekly average wage for a day laborer was $1, the typical monthly income of a beginning generalist hovered close to $20, including the value of goods and services received.

High or low, doctors' fees proved prohibitively expensive in most frontier households, where a median income of less than $300 a year was already stretched to cover grain, farm tools, kerosene, kitchen staples, and occasional clothing. Impoverished settlers who were mud-bound, drought-ridden, discouraged, and in debt would delay medical attention as long as possible, turning instead to domestic medical manuals, prayers, patent elixirs, and an endless stock of folk remedies, often imported from Europe and clumsily altered for the new diseases of the Americas. Ailments brought out the "ointment" doctors long before the medical professionals were called; health issues rested in the clumsy hands of untrained pitchmen, whose touted advertisements of "no cure, no pay" seemed attractive and who charged modestly for medication, not consultation. In a society with scant cash and a surfeit of self-reliance, formal medical treatment was often the last resort.

Susan Anderson hated the "nonsensical pride of poverty" that prevented families from seeking essential medical help—particularly during a woman's confinement—but recognized how threatening medical bills could be. To impoverished men and women, whose existence hung in the balance and whose fortunes were pinned to the ragged hope of avoiding crop failure, land loss, poverty, and even illness,

Henriette Martens, a homeopath,
one of the first doctors in south Florida, 1899. She had the first telephone
outside downtown Miami and a pineapple/vegetable farm
just south of Lemon City.

Florida State Archives

payment for a house call was a near impossibility. "How am I going to get 35 dollars to have a doctor?" wailed a farmer in Idaho in 1916. "He will not come for less and not unless we have the cash." "My babies come fast and where am I going to meet the Doctors bills?" wrote another in 1918. "The doctor I have been treated by ... intends to charge me $15.00 which I find ... quite hard to meet," complained a third, who deeply resented the physician's insistence on a traveling fee of $1.00 per mile. Conversely, doctors often saw their patients as ingrates: "When the bill comes in they shed their gratitude as naturally as a buck deer sheds his horns," stated a physician in Oregon. Wyoming doctor Bessie Efner wrote:

> *My fee for a confinement case was $25 and mileage, but often I was not able to collect that. It was not because the settlers were deadbeats or unwilling to meet an honest obligation, but because they had nothing to give. ... In some cases I had to take farm produce as payment for my services, such as potatoes and vegetables, butter and eggs, a slab of salt pork or a ham, a part of a beef or whatever they happened to have. I was glad to make such an exchange because I, too, had to make a living and support my little girls.*

Fees for distance traveled drove up the price of a home consultation far beyond general ability to pay, and only in the second half of the nineteenth century could doctors tend their patients in hospitals instead of making house calls. Assignment in a local hospital eliminated the physician's travel charges—although hospital care itself was far from inexpensive. Payment was also meted out according to the doctor's specialty and by referral—a frequent nineteenth-century practice in which the surgeon, or specialist, would give part of his patient's fee back to the referring doctor. "Many was the argument over fee splitting," recounted Claudia Potter.

In rural America income was tied to the turning seasons and illness. Payment for the treatment of illness was often simply postponed until the crops were in. "Nobody got sick, nobody needed a doctor, and there I sat waiting," wrote Iowa physician Bessie Efner, whose tenuous earnings hinged on, if not an orderly occurrence of illness, at least one that was predictable. Efner had borrowed money enough to pay the first month's rent on her office, but as days passed, she "felt like a spirited race horse champing at the bit," eager to begin her practice, anxious about her future, concerned for the well-being of her patients, and particularly gnawed by financial worry,

And no wonder. Rural townsfolk had found a second rationale to justify their general reluctance to pay, preferring the free outreach of altruism and charity to medicine-for-pay. Many recalled the benevolence of Catholic nuns such as the Sisters of Charity of Providence, the first order to arrive in the West. They were medical pioneers who brought hospital care to the Pacific Northwest as early as 1856, and whose vows of poverty compensated for years of humility, self-sacrifice, door-to-door begging, and working for pennies in private residences. Just as these selfless women embodied the ideal of Christian charity, so too were other women, including female doctors, associated with the same virtuous ideal, and the women doctors who best embodied this concept found themselves in the greatest demand. After all, it was expected that Christian women, particularly medical women, would minister from the spirit of human compassion, which came without charge.

More inclined to heal than to hound, less assertive physicians were particularly hard hit when it came to fee collection, often allowing unpaid bills to linger out of a sense of delicacy, even embarrassment. Besides, in the imbroglio of frontier economics, a debt was considered canceled by any number of inexplicable events—aborted attempts at repayment, not having change for a large bill but offering anyway, or the ubiquitous practice of payment in kind, in which a rooster, a cask of wheat, a jug of cider, or even manual labor was calculated as a medical honorarium. Even bounteous crops and a "good year" gave no assurance of a cash payment; more often, rural economics resulted in the homely bestowing of a Mason jar of cream, butter, a loaf of bread, or eggs in a wooden packing box accompanied by the promise of more soon, or at least when possible. Wrote Portia Lubchenco of her tiny community in Colorado:

It was hard to realize how quickly good times can turn to bad in the wake of nature's harshness. Folks were not able to pay their bills. Much as they wished to meet their obligations, they found themselves able to do so only in kind. We became the recipients of horses, cows, cattle and chickens. At one time Dr. Jim owned fifty-seven horses, which ran the plains.

Doctors who accepted products for services often found themselves backed into farming as a secondary occupation, as their burgeoning menagerie of donated livestock grew daily. "We tried to make our produce payments meet some of the expenses for us. . . . We started the Haxtun Dairy," wrote Portia Lubchenco, "[but] it costs money to run a dairy, too." Georgia Arbuckle Fix, given a plump yearling calf by a particularly grateful patient, acknowledged her dual role and eventually resigned herself to medicine–cum–cattle ownership. Utah physician Lena Schreier was paid in firewood and fresh eggs for her services, while two Virginia surgeons in the 1700s earned half a hogshead of tobacco for their deft skills. Nineteen hundred pounds of tobacco went to unlicensed doctor Katherine Hebden for performing "chirurgery upon the legg of Dr. John Greenwell," plus a successful postoperative treatment of "diet[ing]

> *I am always having financial chills regarding doctor's fees.*
>
> — DR. BERTHA VAN HOOSEN

People's Free Dispensary, Portland, Oregon.

National Library of Medicine

him for seven weeks or thereabouts." Helen MacKnight Doyle and her husband were paid with a "beautiful gold-lacquered, four-poster, metal bed, with bars running between the posts to support a canopy top . . . decorated with carved pineapples," hauled on muleback from Mexico to grace the humble adobe of a Mexican neighbor, Jesus, whom they had cured of a severe streptococcal infection of the arm. Even though amputation was called for, Jesus refused the surgery—if he couldn't ride his horse, proudly ensconced on his silver-trimmed Mexican saddle, what was life worth? Doyle agreed not to operate, and with patience and prayer his arm healed—there were no modern antibiotics to combat infection in the early 1900s. In gratitude, he gave the doctor the bed she had once "innocently admired." So routine was payment in kind that the goods received were often recorded on a physician's bill; one, dated June 16, 1799, listed "two quarts of corn" received in payment for "one portion of Pink Root, two Portions of Physic and calling to visit [the] child."

Others might pay a token amount, then gratefully interpret the doctor's silence as a clean reckoning, an invitation to begin afresh. Full payment in cash was a rare event, experienced by physician Mary Rowland only once in her career when a shining bounty of silver dollars was counted out, one by one, from the hat of a Korean man delighted with the doctor's handling of his wife's confinement. But more common were repayment schemes like that of a Minnesota patient who wrote to the U.S. Government Children's Bureau, praising the payment schedule devised by her rural physician: "Am washing for the Doctor now to pay for the bill."

According to Dr. Mary Rowland, it was "many years before [women doctors] began to be more diligent about collection." In early-nineteenth-century America, before the passage of the Married Women's Property Act, women were legally unable to bank or transfer money without the assistance of a male relative—the idea of collecting it was even more difficult. Women physicians, particularly those with more retiring personalities, were no match for matter-of-fact, musculative collection techniques. In fact, few practitioners of either gender could match the collection success of a rowdy male physician from the Owens Valley, whose legendary fiscal skills were based on a simple technique: He freely dispensed powders and pills to all who asked from a seemingly inexhaustible store carried in his pockets, and he never presented a bill. Yet when his funds ran short, he would suddenly collar some patient on the street and cry out, "I've got to have some money, and I want you to get it for me damn quick!"

Some might have questioned the business sense of more retiring women physicians; others simply hoped to take advantage. One young man, convinced that in the realm of "female medicine" less experienced meant less expensive, approached Margaret Stewart about assisting in his wife's confinement. "He had decided that since I was a woman doctor I wouldn't be likely to charge as much," wrote Stewart, who surprised him by naming a standard fee, without discount. Momentarily nonplussed, he finally replied: "Oh, well. I'll take you anyway, because you're a woman and probably need the money more than the men do."

His was not the popular point of view. Society dictated that a spinster living alone should not profit unduly from her medical calling, that "real" proceeds must go to male physicians, the sole supports of families. Women who charged should, by this standard, expect far less than a male breadwinner would earn. "I expect to call her of course, but I don't expect to pay her!" exclaimed a woman in Rawlins, Wyoming, regarding her appointment with the newly certified young female physician in town, Dr. Lillian Heath. Why should a woman be as well paid as a man, particularly for doing what any caring woman would "naturally" do?

So fixed was the idea of the nurturing woman, morally ordained to carry out society's humanitarian role, that confusion over payments invariably resulted. "Mama always took care of [the sick]," wrote Lillian Heath. "There was no one else to do it. . . . We never got a cent for the care or the feeding for any of them!" Women physicians who claimed the sisterhood of obligation and good works were assured that the steady inflow of needy sick would never dwindle, but still had to face the question: to bill or not? "I wasn't going to sit idle when I saw people suffering," said Hilla Sheriff, who routinely treated patients with little or no income and whose outreach eventually led her into public health practice. "The monetary rewards . . . are the least of the returns that await those who elect to follow in the footsteps of The Great Physician," wrote Dr. Nina Baierle, linking Christian duty, medicine, and economics.

Besides, weren't married women supported by their mates, and thus able to donate time as a community service? A truly virtuous woman should bind wounds, dose fevers, and deliver babies without concerns of profit, even dipping into her own pocket when necessary. Such was the spirit of psychiatrist and heiress Sarah Campbell Allan, of Charleston, South Carolina, who when "called upon . . . in psychiatric cases never sent a bill." As a woman of independent means, fees and salaries were of passing importance to her. Eventually she wound up a caseload of over five hundred patients, many referred by other Charleston M.D.'s.

Even for less wealthy female doctors, altruism was not uncommon. The poor and sick would always find a source of free powders, mixtures, cordial drops, purging potions, and "vomit doses" from Colorado doctor Susan Anderson, who routinely wrangled extra sample pills from pharmaceutical companies for free distribution. Although medical pioneer Dr. Hannah Longshore treated the "best families" in Philadelphia, she routinely gave service to the indigent. Physician Harriet Belcher, tending an elderly woman with a wounded eye, uttered a sigh as she voiced her future fiscal policy: "She can only pay me in gratitude." In the countryside, rural doctors

Unidentified office.

might travel for miles to reach a patient and find the household in distress, children running wild, a husband distraught, and the pantry empty. What to do? Treat the patient and forget the kitchen? Cook and keep house for the entire family, and if so, for how long? Susan La Flesche Picotte found that simple house calls were not enough. Arriving on a freezing night in midwinter to find a family hungry, without furniture, and the patient lying on a single bed or cot, she would return to her office and load a sled with milk, eggs, and meat to whisk together in a steaming hot meal.

Altruism prompted physician-surgeon Bertha Van Hoosen in her fledgling practice. She worried constantly about charging patients, and would often blush and tell them, "Just pay the usual fee," only to be given a dollar or two when the real monetary value of her services was many times more.

In my anxiety to succeed I put aside everything that might interfere with my career. I had seen how fond people were of money, what people would do to obtain money, and how even a great career might be crushed under the strain of money. Accordingly, I vowed that money should never keep me from reaching my goal. I never kept a book or sent a bill during the first ten years of my practice.

She seemed remarkably free of pessimism, always trusting that enough bills would be paid to sustain her from month to month.

I did not, like Amy McPherson, string up a clothes line on which grateful patients might pin money as a voluntary contribution for my skill, but every day I picked up enough cases laid on my desk so that I never had to draw on the three hundred dollars I had saved to start my career.

Mary Glassen of Phillipsburg, Kansas, known in medical circles as an excellent backwoods diagnostician and a woman driven by her compassionate nature, always welcomed impoverished patients, as well as the old and the infirm. Her delight in identifying a rare disease —in one case, the symptoms of pernicious anemia spotted in an elderly female patient—was quelled by the sad vision of the woman's condition as the "wife of a poor farmer, whose wheat crops had been wiped out . . . by violence of nature"—a desperate woman with no means to drive herself 240 miles to the nearest hospital. The "poor woman had no one else to bring her in." How could Glassen say no? Another physician, Corrine Chamberlin, was known in Gresham, Oregon, as "the doctor who could not say no," and who kept extraordinarily long office hours because of it. According to a newspaper report, physician Lena Schreier from Castle Dale, Utah, "helped many people" by her medical ability, "yet she has never sent a bill." Anna Broomall, one of the foremost surgeons and specialists in obstetrics in the nation, always charged "minimum fees on principle," and had, according to one of her students, "a great fear that medicine would become commercialized."

For physicians, the potential of collecting high fees in Texas was offset by the fact that the doctors themselves "almost invariably get sick while sickness is prevailing, and . . . they have not made much here in the past season having been themselves sick a considerable portion of the time."

Some miserly and calculating patients of Florida's Dr. Anna Darrow had their own gambit—to offer the obliging "Doc Anner" a $50 bill in payment, hoping that if she lacked change for the bill, the fact that the payment was attempted would be as good as the payment made. After several such encounters, Darrow took measures: she never left for a house call in her four-wheeled buggy without change. Despite the fact of her carrying cash being common knowledge, she was never attacked or robbed.

Married women doctors had to consider the spousal viewpoint. Dr. Mary Glassen found her charitable impulses questioned by her husband after a late-night house call that included skidding turns and near collisions along an icy road. She wasn't surprised at her husband's angry comments. The patient, he claimed, was not even hers! He was "on county relief." Why didn't she say no? Glassen wondered what upset her husband more, the near collision or the patient's charity status. "Let me remind you, Clarence," she wrote, "a poor man's belly can hurt just as much as a rich one's."

With a sympathetic flair for both humanity and commerce, women doctors cast an eye to alleviating "sin and suffering" first and profit last, a philosophy which often landed them on the brink of privation, victims of their own largesse. Wrote Harriet Belcher:

I'm mercenary as possible and growing no better fast. I am beginning to look at everyone with a single eye as to how much, in cash, they are good for. And the sick ones get well so disgustingly fast that I want to poison them mildly, just to keep them hanging on my hands. And the poor ones have such a hard time in the struggle for existence. I can't make it any harder so I charge them very little.

PART FIVE

Tools of the Trade

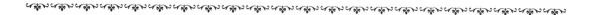

I Cure Women

OF FEMALE DISEASES AND PILES

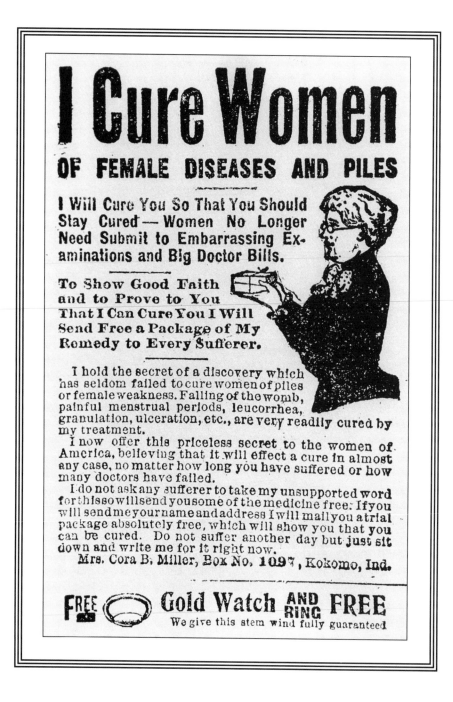

I Will Cure You So That You Should Stay Cured — Women No Longer Need Submit to Embarrassing Examinations and Big Doctor Bills.

To Show Good Faith and to Prove to You That I Can Cure You I Will Send Free a Package of My Remedy to Every Sufferer.

I hold the secret of a discovery which has seldom failed to cure women of piles or female weakness. Falling of the womb, painful menstrual periods, leucorrhea, granulation, ulceration, etc., are very readily cured by my treatment.

I now offer this priceless secret to the women of America, believing that it will effect a cure in almost any case, no matter how long you have suffered or how many doctors have failed.

I do not ask any sufferer to take my unsupported word for this so will send you some of the medicine free. If you will send me your name and address I will mail you a trial package absolutely free, which will show you that you can be cured. Do not suffer another day but just sit down and write me for it right now.

Mrs. Cora B. Miller, Box No. 1097, Kokomo, Ind.

FREE **Gold Watch AND RING FREE**
We give this stem wind fully guaranteed

Rural Remedies

The real payoff is not money but seeing
someone really ill return a few days later with sparkle
in his eyes and happiness in his face.

— LENA SCHREIER

HEN ILLNESS STRUCK ON THE FRONTIER, THOSE AFFLICTED—THE farmers, mule team drivers, homesteaders, cattlemen, or teachers at the country's farthest perimeters—often turned into eager consumers of medicine, ready to accept any solution from any source, as long as the regimen was prompt and thrifty. Yet, when the crisis was done, rules of self-sufficiency again applied and the freethinking frontiersman reverted back to a deep-rooted skepticism. To solicit medical advice was one thing, but to actually accept a doctor's instructions and follow them to the letter was quite another. "Many people refused to call the physician if it could be avoided, preferring to trust nature and domestic remedies, instead," said one rural physician, blaming it on the "terrible character" of medicine in the 1800s, with its "nauseant drugs . . . and the terrible thirst [from mercury]."

Who could ignore the painful results of a "blistering" session, in which hot coals seared welts into the skin in the hope that external heat would draw out internal inflammation? The actual

"I Cure Women" ad, ca. 1900.

National Library of Medicine

results were severe burns, scarring, and a pain so severe that, indeed, all memory of the inflammation vanished. Other home remedies were standards: ice baths to induce shaking, a bag of camphor to prevent infantile paralysis, and purgative drugs to clear the bowels. Calomel, a powerful cathartic, was a potentially toxic mercurial preparation that turned deadly if too great a dose was taken. Women particularly suffered from overdoses of chloride of mercury, which broke down into irritating and highly poisonous components in the intestine, causing convulsive reactions. Calomel was prescribed by unenlightened doctors well into the latter part of the nineteenth century. Even college-educated, female physicians resorted to a "good strong dose of calomel followed by Epsom salts" to cure many undefined ailments, noted Mary Rowland, who learned in medical school that this popular concoction would readily keep the "emunctories" clear— the bowels, kidneys, and skin. So popular was calomel that it was jokingly claimed by frontier families to "butter their bread." A cholera epidemic in St. Louis caused physicians to tote containers of calomel in their pockets and dose it out in teaspoonfuls. Yet these same physicians might be confounded by the later results of their efforts: loose, rotting teeth, exfoliated lower jawbones, and rotted-away parts of the

tongue and palate—evidence of mercury poisoning as well as the fact that medicine, as practiced by both men and women, was science-in-progress. Elizabeth Blackwell recalled the "suffering in the mouth from calomel" of an elderly woman who declared that "no physician ought to receive his diploma till he has been salivated, that he may know the torture [of calomel] he is inflicting on his patients." Nor were mercury, antimony, arsenic, or "fly-blister" any more forgiving.

Natural healing also called for a supply of leeches. In a typical bloodletting, about a pint of drawn blood was said to cure a myriad of complaints, from dog bite to bladder inflammation—even epilepsy, smallpox, or measles. The ancient technique of bloodletting enjoyed a nineteenth-century revival; it was used to cure fever, and in women it was considered a natural complement to the cycles of a woman's menstruation and birthing (anthropological theories suggest that bloodletting had symbolic value as a form of artificial menstruation). Since the body was believed to hold nearly twice the necessary amount of blood, why wait for the healing powers of Nature? Bleeding was practiced with a vengeance up until the 1870s—physicians might remove up to four fifths of the body's blood, either by cutting a vein with a lancet (venesection or phlebotomy) or by "cupping," to extract smaller amounts, by suction, into heated, inverted jars placed over the skin. This drew less blood than lancing, and was less traumatic—although one elderly man when cupped cried out "that he'd rather go to kingdom come" than continue the

For melancholy: *Bleed from a vein in the foot.*

For goiter: *Rub with the hand of a corpse.*

For cancer: *Anoint affected area several times a day with the juice of the friar's crown (a woolly thistle).*

For whooping cough: *Breathe into your lungs the breath of a fish.*

For tapeworms: *Take scrapings of pewter spoons, 20 grains mixed with sugar.*

For a headache: *Put a buckwheat cake on the head.*

For wrinkles: *Steep wool clippings in hot alcohol to precipitate yellow grease. Thus it has the effect of smoothing out the wrinkles produced by the attenuations of those tissues which come with age. An antiquated lady has nearly removed from her temples the unwelcome footprints of a thousand figurative crows, by six weeks use of it.*

—MRS. CORNELIUS,
THE YOUNG HOUSEKEEPER'S FRIEND
(BOSTON: BROWN, JAGGARD; CHASE, 1859)

process. In the West, a type of "cupping" for the release of blood was sometimes used, with a heated cup placed over a slit vein as a vacuum, the cure pronounced effective when the patient fainted. Male physicians, employing these so-called heroic and showy methods of healing, often bled a patient to the point of fainting, frequently taking the ever-more-feeble pulse. "Old Dr. Colby was in the habit of getting his lancet out and laying it upon the table before even removing his hat, or before ascertaining what the disease might be that he was called to see," wrote an early physician skeptical of the bleeding that routinely took place. Although bloodletting was eventually abandoned in the United States, some patients, such as the consumptive Deborah Fiske of New England, grew so practiced that she raised her own leeches, causing wry speculation. "You had better look out . . . for my wife," warned her husband, Professor Fiske.

Without X rays, wounds and unbroken flesh were often probed by a slender implement similar to a darning needle, sometimes with a small scoop for cleaning foreign matter from a wound. In response to the pain and suffering caused by rugged-looking steel bone gauges, more flexible probes of fine steel or whalebone were used later in the nineteenth century. Delicate or not, a medical search for infection using a probe was often excruciatingly painful, and often led to mortality. Similarly, the insertion of a catheter caused much discomfort, as they were designed with scant knowledge of the anatomy of the female urethra.

Bearing the memories of such harsh treatment, patients often tried to avoid allopathic medicine, turning to the popular "granny women" and herbalists who plied their trade in pills, nostrums, and snake-oil brews to palliate or blunt the suffering of the general population. From wrinkles to constipation, the condition in question called up an appropriate remedy in sugarcoated pills or effervescing salt, sold by traveling pill dispensers and herb doctors or through the newspapers. A typical ad read, "If you would like to have a safe yet certain Cough Remedy in the home, try Dr. Schoop's—at least once. It is thoroughly unlike any other Cough preparation. Its taste will be entirely new to you. . . . No opium, chloroform, or any other stupefying ingredients are used [, just] the tender leaves of a harmless, lung healing mountainous shrub." Remedies were rife. One man, torn between various prescriptions assigned by sundry healers, sighed: "I am forbidden and enjoined to take almost everything."

Although most traveling herbalists were men, one woman mentioned in the annals of the Daughters of the Utah Pioneers was described as slight, gray-haired, wrinkled and tanned, dressed in shabby clothes, driving a wagon festooned with withered and dangling herbs, its plank bed layered with roots, bark, and onions, all used for medicines. "We never found out the contents of a certain box she always carried," recollected Kate C. Snow, but this "witch doctor" of the early villages no doubt dispensed an array of folk remedies. Typical of this type of unofficial "healer" was Mormon Paulina Lyman of Parowan, Utah, who cured a young girl whose face had been burned so badly that the blistered skin hung in shreds. Lyman applied a mask of linseed oil to the afflicted flesh and covered the oil with varnish—an age-old remedy, often used and generally successful.

Until "new thought" and scientific research provided an alternative, many cures were rustic. Nature's supplies, scrounged for different purposes, included teas steeped from native plants, rhubarb bitters for indigestion, catnip tea to fight pleurisy, and sassafras tea to cleanse the blood. Every citizen knew that carrot scrapings reduced inflammation and that a tincture of false-unicorn root would fight infertility. As for snakebite, a popular remedy that appeared in the *Phoenix Herald* in 1899 recommended ingesting ammonia along with unnamed "stimulants," or else applying coal oil, turpentine, or slabs of freshly killed chicken directly to the bite. The most hardy were prepared to cut broken snake fangs out with a razor, heat an iron bolt in a campfire to cauterize the wound, swill gulps of ammonia to "neutralize" the poison, then bury the afflicted limb in wet sand to reduce the fever. Utah pioneer Ann Hafen, who had "in the old country" relied solely upon doctors, learned to accept lay advice: "Gradually we learned home remedies after much sad experience. I remember that Brigham Young recommended hot gopher sand to cure hand felons."

Rural infants were given catnip tea until the age of five or six weeks for the herb's opiate qualities; according to a rural Mississippi woman in 1916, "Mother gave it to her children & I am giving it to mine." Others of the early twentieth century relied almost exclusively upon the "soap stick," a soap-filled suppository for constipated youngsters, but it could be dangerous; a Michigan child who was "too worn out to cut his last two baby teeth" had died at the age of two and a half, due, his mother was convinced, to the "indiscriminate use of the soap stick . . . and lime water."

One common rural remedy was employed even by physicians—snow treatment for frozen appendages. One glance at ears that appeared blue and stiff, sticking awkwardly out from beneath a ten-gallon hat, revealed their condition. A stagecoach driver once peered inside the coach to find a passenger frozen, with ears so fragile that any quick movements might "shake 'em right off." Protesting, the man was dragged outside and his ears gently rubbed with snow until he felt a flash of heat. The treatment was finished with a length of flannel tied about his ears.

Folk medicine was used for mental and emotional problems as well, including spiderwebs in pill form for hysterics or phosphoric acid and sulfur for memory loss. Some remedies were applied externally, such as a bag of hop blossoms stored under a pillow to banish a headache or hot bran poultice to cure swelling, from inflamed eyes to affected glands. Dr. Jane Bruce Guignard promoted her own brand of lore, believing that "if the genitals be immersed in cold water for some time" a nosebleed would stop.

A young physician arriving at a rural site fresh from medical school counted among her supplies the latest drugs, including bromides for epilepsy, tartar emetic for meningitis, mustard plaster and bleeding for pneumonia, quinine and mercury to rout syphilis, opium and boiled milk for diarrhea, or simply quinine, administered in massive doses, to combat malaria and typhoid. Throat swabs of ferric chloride on cotton were commonly used for diphtheria, and in more advanced cases, nostrils were cauterized with silver nitrate and the nasopharynx rinsed with a spurt of warm water.

As supplies of quinine or opium dwindled, the bedridden and fevered turned to a panoply of rural remedies, often approved by a physician who realized that need dictated use, and that often what lay outside the medical bag determined a patient's fate far more than the contents inside. Straight whiskey was given for pulmonary tuberculosis, fresh foods to cure scurvy. The hope was strong that herbal medicines, once prescribed, would not cause further harm.

The West was the realm of the croup kettle, the mustard plaster, and the ubiquitous castor oil, and no doctor would set forth without at least passing knowledge of the art of turning pantry into pharmacy. Lacking her own pills and powders, she might use household items such as scorched flour for baby powder, catnip tea for a baby's colic, lime water and oil for burns, beefsteak for bruises, whiskey packs and egg whites for boils, baked onion juice, sugar, and glycerin for bronchitis, and wet tea leaves for inflamed eyes—even a stale-bread poultice or castile soap shavings

mixed with sugar for jaundice. Hops, celery seed, and Holland gin aided kidney troubles. Lettuce "milk" fought "coughs and irritability," while a dog oil massage routed gout and rheumatism. Bad colds called for sagebrush, grape root tea, and a full-body "greasing" with turpentine or kerosene, while mandrake root, or powdered podophyllum, was a strong cathartic—a so-called powerful physic that took up to eight hours to release its extreme emetic effect. For the same result, Colorado homesteader Norine Holland downed a teaspoon of coal oil "out of a can"—sweetened with sugar, but nonetheless the same variety that was put in a lamp to burn.

Most of rural America obeyed the mandate to "heal thyself" by grinding, juicing, and boiling flowers and herbs into extracts, infusions, liniments, lotions, oils, plasters, powders, syrups, tinctures, confections, and other decoctions. Plasters and poultices were sometimes infused with heat-producing irritants such as mustard or cantharides, a powder made of "Spanish flies" to blister the skin, creating a suction to lure the toxins outward, away from the vital organs.

Medicine was both science and lore, and the preparation of actual medicines was eventually to be defined by national standards set in 1876 and such local regulations as California's Pharmacy Regulation Act of 1872. Conscientious practitioners kept abreast of new drugs and treatments but were often forced to find remedies close at hand, easily available and without cost, perhaps herbs gathered along a streambed, such as rhubarb

Fleishman's Drugstore, ca. 1885.

Arizona Historical Society, Tucson

root and wild lettuce to mix with charcoal, an old southern remedy for colds. Falling upon her own resources, the doctor would travel the hills to collect raspberry, spearmint, and peppermint leaves and other roots and bark to mix into soothing potions.

Women physicians quickly grasped the intrinsic relationship between nature and healing, an affinity that was highly developed in Mormon practitioners in Utah, whose use of herbs was rooted in homeopathy. Priddy Meeks, a pioneer doctor of Utah, used lobelia for both diagnosis and cure. When "taken inwardly," she believed, it "acted like intelligence," spreading rapidly throughout the system to find the affliction, which it overcame by "relaxing the parts, and scattering the pain and misery, causing it to escape with perspiration and neutralizing the poison in the blood." She believed lobelia was the most powerful "diffusive stimulant known in medicine," and was equally useful for hydrophobia, to deliver a dead fetus speedily, and for preventing a threatened miscarriage if the child was alive. Further exploring the world of natural remedies, Dr. Meeks dispensed "female relief pills" concocted "wholly out of those wholesome herbs that the Lord said in the Word of Wisdom He had ordained for the constitution or nature and use of man." Not only were these marvelous pills "anti-poison" and "compounded as to act upon every organ of the whole system" but they would affect the system, "pleasant and slow," in "perfect harmony with any food that mankind ought to eat or drink." The ingredients were not mentioned.

Some physicians cannily used placebos, as did Jane Bruce Guignard, whose own kitchen concoction to ease the pain and anxieties of her older patients was dubbed "the pink medicine"—an all-around elixir prescribed regularly. Others healed by using "stimulating medicines and wine." Burnt brandy was a stimulus to speed up pulse and respiration, helping many shocked victims through the worst part of a crisis. Even vapor action was used as a stimulant to open the pores and "produce copious perspiration, and by that means dislodge the depositions which are dammed up between the two skins, namely, the exterior skin and the thinner one beneath it."

Old pharmacy records reveal the prescriptions given by female physicians. Adelaide Brown of San Francisco regularly used sodium salicylate, while Edna Fields believed that cuttlefish and oil of wintergreen were useful, although for undisclosed purposes. Marcia B. Cleveland, also of San Francisco, voiced concern for her patient's well-being in the use of sulfur suppositories. "Please make them as small as possible," she enjoined.

Physicians with an adequate medical supply kept a supply of emetics and cathartics on hand, used to cleanse the stomach and bowels. Emetics produced vomiting, and cathartics or purgatives acted as laxatives. "The action was cyclonic . . . equal to a regular oil-well gusher," wrote William Buchan in a popular layman's handbook. Favorites were calomel, ipecac, tartar emetic, or jalap, a purgative that induced violent vomiting, and a combination of opium, ipecac, and antimony, called Dover powder, to generate sweat. Wrote one physician in *Daniel's Texas Medical Journal* of 1887:

> *In beginning the malaria treatment, I give a hypodermic dose of morphine to quiet the patient, and relieve his distress. I immediately commence to give him calomel and antimony, until the secretory system is aroused, at the same time I use rubifacients and diuretics, such as Bitart Potash, Nitrate Potash, to keep up the action of the kidney, and avoid hemorrhage. . . . I have no use for astringents. . . . Keep the secretion flowing, and let it dissolve and carry the blood out of those organs. Spirits of turpentine in diuretic doses with spirits nitre is sometimes of great service. Strychnine should be administered every two hours to stimulate and sustain the nervous system.*

Quinine was used to combat fevers; iodine was an antiseptic or was taken as drops to prevent the growth of ugly goiters. Dr. Mattie Hughes Cannon recommended to a sick patient the "compound tincture of iodine . . . every *five* days—with *thorough syringing* with hot, not warm water, three times a day. . . . Mark my word." Opium, a narcotic extracted from the poppy, was commonly assigned for pain relief, cough control, sedation, and diarrhea control, but had to be watched carefully. If too much was given, the result could be stupor, erratic or impaired breathing, upset stomach, or constipation. Given to patients in great

pain and in need of being "narcotized," its analgesic powers also sustained women through painful postpartum complications.

The usual antidote for alcoholism was opium or morphine "by mouth or syringe together," or heroin and laudanum. In 1909 the Smoking Opium Exclusion Act banned all imports of the drug, except those given by hypodermic. But other powerful and dangerous drugs took its place. Wrote one physician in *Daniel's Texas Medical Journal*:

> *I recently had an opportunity of treating a severe case of gout in which there was extensive swelling of the big toe, with cocaine, locally. I used six percent solution, with the most gratifying results. The cyanotic appearance being diminished in a few hours and the pain subsiding in twenty minutes. The solution of cocaine was applied by means of soft C.H. pencil about every five minutes, on the painful member, until pain was relieved.*
>
> *It does look as if, in cocaine, we have found the greatest boon to suffering man. Its uses are innumerable.*

Physician Mary Canaga Rowland believed that narcotics laws were written too late to deter numbers of unstable physicians from drug addiction, as well as their patients. Intoxication was the result of administering large and frequent doses of opium. One physician, Dr. Rice, recounts a typical prescription to a woman about to have her teeth extracted: "Gave first

150 drops of laudanum. Twenty minutes later, gave 250 additional. Waited ten minutes and gave 100 drops more. Gave 200 drops more with intervals of five minutes. Whole amount given 500 drops in forty-five minutes."

Elizabeth Blackwell's first medical experience with narcotics occurred at her father's deathbed. In her diary, written in 1836, at the age of seventeen, she describes her father's slow demise:

> *When the physicians came early this morning they thought him if anything better. Oh how delightedly did we hail the gleam of hope, a dose of laudanum & brandy was administered to him & they all agreed that salivation was the only chance left so Mr. Browne rubbed his joints with mercurial ointment several times, I sponged him with a solution of muriatic acid and through the day we gave him his medicines & as much chicken broth & brandy as he could take. Dear, dear father he always took whatever I brought him though God only knows what an effort it must have cost him.*

Water cures provided the ill a chance to bathe and gulp down huge quantities of water —a poor man's version of the popular spas of Europe. Middle-class women would retire annually to local sulfur springs for a regimen of diet, exercise, and water.

The practice of colon irrigation was also used frequently by rural doctors in the early years of the twentieth century—part of an ongoing attempt to rid the body of impurities. Omaha Indian physician Susan La Flesche Picotte refers to the practice frequently in her notes: "baby sick . . . gave it a colon irrigation."

Sick babies were only part of an ongoing parade of disastrous disorders, seemingly designed to confound even the most cautious, often driving the dogged practitioner back to medical textbooks to compare symptoms for specific identification. What could be done with patients whose flulike symptoms included a 106-degree temperature, vomiting, and a distended gallbladder? Textbooks would note that the bile duct was walled with smooth muscle fibers, and the doctor would then know that a dose of atropine would provide relief.

Some patients found relief in surgery, undertaken at great risk. Anesthesia by ether was introduced for operations in 1846, and in 1847, chloroform for operations was introduced by James Simpson. Ether, discovered by an American dentist, was often used in childbirth, along with chloroform. Both were considered safe and effective—chloroform, particularly, was cheap and easy to transport, although its use produced some danger of cardiac arrest. Wrote surgeon Bertha Van Hoosen in 1915: "When I began the study of medicine, chloroform . . . was the popular anesthetic. But later [it] was found to produce changes in the liver, harmful to health . . . and to life."

In response, a new type of anesthesia was developed—scopolamine, which produced "twilight sleep." So enthused was Van Hoosen by its success, established in over five thousand operations, that she promoted its use in a book: "I am still thrilled at seeing a patient brought to the operating room, unconscious of removal from her room, the ride on the rumbling cart, and the disagreeable preparation for the operation," wrote Van Hoosen. Not all physicians were so enthused; although the drug produced long periods of unconsciousness, it also prompted erratic behavior, often thrashing about or screaming. During one home delivery, a patient who had received scopolamine spent hours getting out of bed and filling a tea kettle during contractions. Another expectant woman, stripped from the waist down, threatened attendants with an upheld chair. She was calmed only when Van Hoosen, who acted upon some inexplicable impulse, draped her own head mysteriously in a sheet, leaving only her eyes uncovered, and gazed mutely at the woman, carrying on her own belief that "twilight sleep makes great demands on nurses and interns as well as on obstetricians."

After 1870, ophthalmoscopes and laryngoscopes were in use; after 1874, improved plaster-of-Paris bandages freed fracture patients from long sieges of bed rest, while air pumps could aspirate body fluids at the site of an incision, thus reducing the possibility of infection. Bausch & Lomb three-piece microscopes became available in the late nineteenth century, while to cauterize hemorrhoids, benzine in a bottle with an atomizer bulb produced the necessary heat. Scalpels did not have removable blades—the early steel knives, often with black wooden handles,

were honed on a whetstone for an hour or more to develop a cutting edge. Those doctors hoping to keep up with the latest nineteenth-century developments might purchase a tracheal trochar and cannula, which cost less than five dollars and were last-ditch, emergency pieces of equipment for use in tracheotomies in diphtheria cases. If a patient's larynx was blocked to the point that he could not open his mouth and put out his tongue, then the instrument was inserted through the neck, from the outside, to create airflow. Some physicians might be advanced enough to use the sphygmomanometer to measure blood pressure—or, if truly innovative, a blood transfusion apparatus.

An early practitioner's black bag might contain a surgical saw and a finger or early skull saw; cupping instruments and a lancet for bleeding; folding scalpels; and syringes. Also a hypodermic syringe for the subcutaneous injection of morphia. Inside the bag might be found scissors, needles, and sutures; probes; obstetrical forceps; and a device or two for pulling teeth, along with surgical dressings and assorted drugs. The stethoscope was becoming common, while thermometers were used only rarely, usually on the East Coast.

Other contents of the ubiquitous bag might be scissors, needles, and sutures, along with surgical dressings and assorted drugs. Obstetrical needs were met by the contents of a "confinement case," along with the everyday assortment of plaster bandages and splints. After 1870, the use of the monaural stethoscope, or "tube," was common. Flexible stethoscopes allowed closer scrutiny, often leading to early diagnosis of tuberculosis. Lengthy chest examinations would reveal the difference between normal and abnormal sounds. A sensitive instrument would help identify pericarditis, for example, by the sounds of "crunching" or "grating."

Generally, the doctor's bag reeked of carbolic acid and iodoform, with which instruments were cleaned and walls and furniture washed down during operations. After 1870, Lister's antiseptic spray was used to combat contagion.

⸼⸜⸽

Often, the worst conditions sprang from rampant infection, which, from the Civil War until the end of the century, was viewed as an active and credible part of the healing process. Battle wounds were left to fester, either through inattention or as part of this belief, with little attempt to cleanse the wounds. Antiseptic practices were unheard of until rural doctors, who frequently handled gunshot victims, learned the danger of a penetrating wound and how a rapid and dirty infection could bring death within hours.

By the end of the nineteenth century, even the most remote rural practitioners had the skill and means to apply surgical dressings, although with deep wounds or open sores, the applications were "a nightmare," according to Helen MacKnight Doyle. Open sores bore inflammation and "corruption" into the system, often directly into the bone, and had to be packed with iodoform gauze. The dressings

had to be pried away several days later, then renewed, making sure "every time that the probe carried the gauze to the extreme depth of the cavity"—all without anesthesia.

The most dread of all diseases, typhoid, struck even the strongest, turning towering men into groaning, gaunt skeletons with swollen, parched tongues, sordes-covered teeth, fever, and swollen lips—misery that could be alleviated only by careful nursing, various pharmaceutical powders, dousing in cool water, and the constant administering of cool water or fresh milk, "one teaspoonful at a time," according to Helen MacKnight Doyle. A mine superintendent found nearly dead of typhoid was delivered to Doyle, who knew to lower his temperature with a long, cold bath and to give him plenty of cold milk. Few Americans bathed with any regularity at the time. There was a lack of indoor plumbing as well as the belief that baths were dangerous and caused illness. But Doyle drenched the patient in a rigged-up canvas bath and found a volunteer to ride miles for the milk, haul bathwater in barrels, split wood to keep the fire going for sterilization and laundry, and "dispose of excrement so it would not become a menace to the camp." A victim of typhoid fever might take to bed, fully clothed, covered with a sweater, "starved and doped until he got well or died, practically with his boots on," said Doyle. A rural doctor, whether an "irregular" doctor or one who was credentialed, had to learn to recognize typhoid's symptoms. A temperature of 105, tense neck muscles, and pinpoint pupils demanded quick evaluation;

vomiting and chills heralded the grim reality of typhoid fever—no matter who the physician was, death would soon follow unless the right remedies were applied. Georgia Arbuckle Fix once failed to recognize the symptoms of typhoid in a local teenage girl. A recent typhoid scare had produced a host of imagined victims in the area—the girl was apparently one of them. Thinking she was simply malingering, Arbuckle prescribed a "river water cure." When the girl's condition worsened, Arbuckle recognized typhoid and immediately dosed her with her special sage brew and wrapped her in a milk-dipped sheet. It took eighteen trips to the girl's bedside for the crisis to pass.

A case of "remittent fever" was a form of malaria that occurred frequently in the early Appalachian frontier and was held at bay by opening a vein in the arm and bleeding the patient until faint and sick, at which point, it was hoped, the wild delirium would fade and the sickness subside. After, opium was administered to "allay all irritability of the bowels and stomach." If these measures failed, there was always Peruvian bark, gentian, columbo, and quinine, although usually it was priced such "that Hoosiers could not afford to use it," at the royal sum of $30 per ounce.

Quinine was so popular it seemed to be in the hands of everyone, to be used "without stint or discrimination . . . a panacea for every evil." In fact, doctors were irked about the availability of quinine to the general population: "If a man is sick, he takes it to cure himself. If well, he takes it to prevent getting sick.

I may say, in some families it is almost an article of diet." Taken carelessly, it "paralyzes the vaso motor system of nerves, lowers arterial tension, and precipitates collapse and hemorrhage." In the 1850s quinine was the most commonly prescribed drug, in keeping with the prevalence of malaria, or ague. The illness would peak in the late summer and fall, but even in late winter fevers would reoccur. From the 1870s on quinine was used as a strengthening tonic, usually in conjunction with iron.

❧

The rural woman doc was forced to excel in the basics of "physical diagnosis," a critical yet instinctive analysis of symptoms. Early medical diagnosis seemed part imagination, part hopeful guessing, and only a little actual scientific knowledge, as witnessed, again and again, by fabulous misdiagnoses and subsequent deaths. Was the body skin "smooth and puffy with crepitation on pressure"? Then death was imminent. Sophia Presley, the first woman member of the Camden County, New Jersey, Medical Society in 1890, was an excellent diagnostician. When asked to describe some of her interesting cases, she identified a case of cholelithiasis, in which there was "no operation, but the patient passed, by rectum, eight large gallstones, the largest measuring $15/16$ of an inch at its shortest diameter and $1\frac{1}{16}$ at its longest diameter." Worse, she then had to face a case of constipation and catarrh of the bowels, in which the "lining of the colon and rectum was thrown off in large worm-like masses, handfuls at a time, white and tense." The patient recovered.

At American medical schools in the 1850s, diagnosis was not taught; the only skills acquired were a superficial knowledge of the science and art of surgery, *materia medica,* and therapeutics. The observant learned how to diagnose, but theories as to the cause of disease, and its subsequent treatment, usually relied upon enormous doses of opiates, mercurials and whiskey, or the infinitesimal dosages of homeopathy. Obscure cases with indefinite symptoms were labeled neurasthenia, whether the actual cause was a gallbladder problem or pregnancy. Tonics were prescribed whether disease was discovered or not.

Dr. Portia Lubchenco, trying to renew her skills for licensing in the United States after having spent years in Russia with her husband, was distracted from her nightly studies "under a trusty kerosene lamp" by a devastating flu epidemic.

The flu cases were depressing for the doctor because treatment was not known. We had to feel our way and learn from experience. Such learning must be quick, and it must be positive. Even the medical journals gave little help. It was from trial and, hopefully, not too much error, that we began to treat through stimulation rather than depressants. The severe infection in itself, we reasoned silently, depleted the patient.

She encountered more puzzling symptoms when her daughter developed a severe case of tularemia, or "rabbit fever," characterized by malaise and swollen lymph nodes. The girl had been practicing "her interest in surgery" by dissecting rabbits that had been killed on the plantation when she fell ill. Specialists could offer Lubchenco no help, advising her to contact the Department of Public Health in Washington and gloomily informing her that if her daughter lived for a week, she would no doubt develop an immunity.

Swelling and inflammation often ominously presaged dire conditions—even women physicians recoiled in shock from a condition vaguely called "cold in the breast" that often occurred after childbirth, in which the breast was large, inflamed, often suppurating. A "moderately generous" diet was often prescribed, to keep the "bowels soluble," as well as a "light bread poultice"; lancing was saved for the unhappy last. When swelling appeared in a foot or arm, the doctor looked for a splinter or some type of "foreign or extraneous substance" in the muscle. Often "laying open" the inflamed area with an implement such as the bistoury (a knife with a long cutting edge used for cutting internal organs) sufficed to reduce the edematous state, followed by baths in weak, hot lye and dressings of hot spirits of turpentine.

Dropsy was a conjectural term for nearly all types of bloating, and "dropsy of the uterus" might refer to any situation, from a miscarried fetus to uterine hemorrhage.

Spasms accompanied a myriad of ailments, from malaria to "sinking spells," and were invitation to a number of treatments, from lard poultices to bleeding. Just as the haruspex tried to tell fortunes through entrails, so the doctors tried to predict future health through the bowels—watching carefully for signs of indisposition, catharsis, or feverish, morbid secretions accumulated in the alimentary canal. The bowels should "commence running off" to ensure health—and this was achieved with syringe and enema.

The stomach was treated as a minor deity in the body, its goodwill bargained for, its irritable tossings and turnings viewed with alarm, its rumblings examined for signs of nausea or "gastric derangement," its entity dosed with any number of purgatives or powders in order to relieve distress. When malfunctioning, the stomach could cause patients to "sink into a stupor," a grave and somnolent situation induced by any number of toxins, from excess alcohol to sepsis. Patients who were generally "sunk down" must be excited out of their state, either with stimulating potions, starch injections, or tepid water baths.

Medicine, unlike law or the sciences, had to overcome—or incorporate—decades of lore, apocrypha, and home innovation, as well as the sense that its practitioners were suspect.

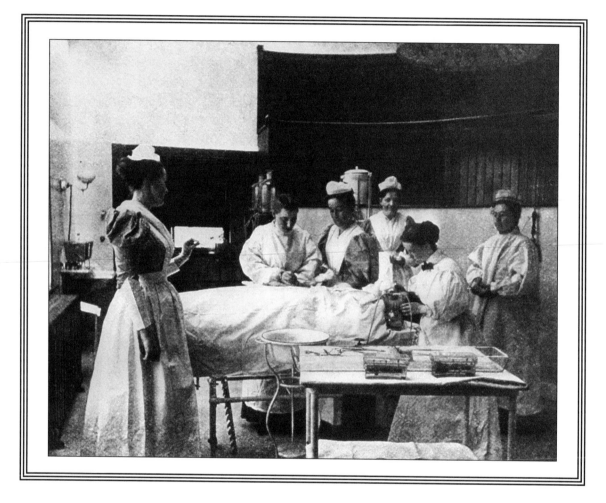

Operating theater.

National Library of Medicine

CHAPTER FOURTEEN

Kitchen Table Surgery

When I have learned to use the knife, the wounds to my
pride and sensibilities will soon heal.

— DR. BERTHA VAN HOOSEN

URGERY IN THE EARLY YEARS WAS CONSIDERED A "HEROIC" ENTER-
prise that could be performed by any person with a steady hand and unclouded mind
—"any man, unless . . . an idiot or an absolute fool," according to A. G. Goodlett, the author of the
1838 work *Family Physician*. Men performed surgery, since only a man's strength could restrain
the anguished and terrified unanesthetized patient bent on escape. "Cutting it off" was often the
quickest solution, even with accidents involving only fractures. Yet surgical results were often
fatal, simply listed as "death by complication." Given the use of primitive surgical techniques, the
lack of antiseptics and anesthesia, and the penchant for wartime amputations, it was a miracle that
patients recovered at all.

Even though early-nineteenth-century surgery was part of general medicine, and was performed, to some degree, by every practicing physician, doctors were skittish about unfamiliar procedures and would seek any alternative. Complicated operations, perhaps resections or artery

ligations, were in the realm of eastern specialists, who were usually male. Frontier surgery, conducted reluctantly and often without painkillers, occurred only after treatment with a brew called "shotgun mixture," in which twelve to thirty ingredients were prescribed for the wound, in hopes that one would help the recovery. One popular, nonsurgical remedy was described in an 1859 diary, in which a veteran medical man recommended for the treatment of frozen flesh "a poultice of Indian meal, moistened with young Hyson tea, softened with hot water and lard," to alleviate the pain.

Prior to anesthesia, patients bit bullets or quaffed whiskey to allay the pain. Before 1847, opium, and its derivative morphine, were widely used, despite the resulting side effects of nausea, constipation, and its darker consequence, addiction. But suffering was deemed "worthy," and conservative religious forces rejected the idea of altering predestined pain through the use of anesthesia. Linking the knife to pain had deep religious overtones—it was thought that even easing the pangs of childbirth through artificial means might deny women the necessary steps to character building. Women, it was believed, were inclined to an "idle life, abuses of civilization . . . dissipations and follies of fashion," and chemical assistance during childbirth would deny them an opportunity to gain such inner strength. Moral indictments of this kind were commonplace in Victorian America, coming even from female physicians such as Bertha Van Hoosen at Cook County Hospital, Chicago, who in 1915 published a paper that cited the pain of childbirth as a result of civilization, or at least the result of sexual organs used for pleasure first, reproduction last.

Dr. Ellis Shipp took pride in having excised a "fatty tumor upon the deltoid muscle," in which the patient refused any painkiller and chose to endure "excruciating pain" with only mental forbearance. "He fully sensed every stroke of the knife," Shipp recalled. "The most extreme pallor o'erspread his face but scarcely a groan was perceptible." Such strength of will caused Shipp to ponder her own frailty as well as that of mankind, and to wonder if she, too, could perform so well.

Emmeline Cleveland, dean of the Pennsylvania Women's Medical College, was in 1875 the first female physician to perform major surgery. Women who followed her lead were few, but those who did were well versed in the use of instruments and techniques and, after 1846, the use of anesthesia. With this development, many previously "incurable" conditions were remedied surgically. The informal code that once restricted women physicians to an all-female clientele ironically gained them purchase into a general practice that often included surgery. Since anesthesia and Joseph Lister's procedures for antiseptic surgery had been introduced by the mid-1800s, so-called painless surgery invited the participation of women—it was, simply, easier work, physically. And women were well suited to suturing, often having a nimbleness of finger that made difficult stitching simple. Even so, women practitioners, according to Victorian critic Samuel Gregory, were thought to be "of a more delicate nature." In fact, they were "Nature's Handmaidens," stalwart enough for cases that required "promptness of action . . . a hemorrhage, for instance," but lacking the physical prowess to restrain a patient. Most general practitioners—whether allopaths or homeopaths—deferred to surgeons in surgical matters, but women physicians were always expected to defer to men, both to maintain their professional security and to deflect criticism. Often, they tried to reassure male colleagues that they offered no real competition; sometimes this was a subterfuge, sometimes it was heartfelt. Although women physicians also subscribed to the notion of heroic surgical methods, some, such as anesthesiologist Dr. Sarah Bowen, were "least happy" if forced to operate. Isolated in the high reaches of the mountains of northern New Mexico, Bowen's obstetric and pediatric skills were legendary among her Hispanic patients, and included appendectomies, tonsillectomies, and simple trauma work. She resorted to major surgery only when necessary, and turned to outside help for major surgical "problems."

Dr. Agnes Harrison, who delivered over two thousand babies during her early career in Washington State, performed countless home surgeries with anesthesia: "It kept me mighty busy, and often I was soaked with perspiration when I was through. In desperate cases, it was terrifying to know I had no one to help me, no one to turn to. A life—sometimes more than one—depended on my next move. I've mixed prayers and chloroform many times."

But anesthetics, particularly ether, could be dangerous. In one case attended by Texas physician Claudia Potter, a table in an overcrowded room was sterilized and laid out for surgery, and the operation ensued, lit by the glow of the crackling fire. Although the flames were at least ten feet away, Potter was still anxious about its proximity to the anesthetic—explosion was always a concern. Since she "expected a flame to come up from the pillow any minute," she stocked large, wet towels on the table beside the patient's head, in case of fire. In another operation, also conducted "late at night . . . on [a] kitchen table by kerosene light," female neighbors held lamps as high above the ether as possible while the patient's uterus was delicately opened. Tired to exhaustion, one of the lantern-bearers fainted, her lantern bouncing to the floor, nearly splintering and causing a flurry of concern that the wooden floor and the volatile ether would ignite.

Another tool of the surgical trade was nitrous oxide, or "laughing gas," once used as entertainment at state fairs by couples "caged" for their own protection in special amusement booths, where they would inhale the gas until giddy, or enjoy home "euphoria" parties, where all would fall prone from the "funny" fumes.

The use of sulfuric ether, morphine, laudanum, or nitrous gas often affected the doctor-administrator and others as well. A paper presented before the Georgia State Medical Society in 1848 recounts how nitrous oxide gas was introduced in a company of young men assembled at night in the village of Jefferson, Georgia—a plantation village 140 miles from the closest railroad. The plantation families' sons were "anxious to witness the effects of nitrous oxide. After inhaling, all were so pleased with its effects that . . . the practice soon became quite fashionable in the county." Doctors enjoyed the "influence of ether" themselves, quite frequently, often finding bruises and scrapes produced in the etherized state but with no recollection of how they had occurred. In fact, getting drunk with nitrous oxide was a popular source of amusement, with countless "frolics" held in the physician's office in the state popularly called "suspended animation." As a medical anesthetic, it was spewed from the engine of a Gatch machine during surgery. After 1906, chloroform joined ethylene as a popular inhalant, with disastrous explosions often resulting from careless handling.

Records kept by licensed female M.D.'s reveal an adequate knowledge of the surgical implements available, as well as the various anesthesia. They had practiced various dissecting regimens late into the night, studying the sympathetic nervous system, and as medical students employed the same degree of chicanery and persuasion as men in order to wangle surgery hours. Bertha Van Hoosen, when enrolled as a student at the New England Hospital for Women and Children, was warned that staff surgeons often cheated beginning students of their "rightful opportunity" to perform one third of the scheduled operations. Instead, Van Hoosen found that

her female instructors, Dr. Mary Smith and Dr. Keeler, were overly generous with surgical hours and showed "perfect fairness" in every case. In response to each operation she was offered, Van Hoosen stayed up long after midnight studying the anatomy of the area, imprinting in vivid detail a mental map of the "intricately woven muscles and fascia" of each structure. While teaching at Northwestern University Women's Medical School, Van Hoosen had "handled and been responsible for the dissecting of over a hundred bodies"; she was competent to perform any surgery needed.

With the deepest gratitude and a fierce determination not to disappoint [Dr. Keeler] I . . . dug into the anatomy and surgery of the breast until the small hours of the morning. . . . Dr. Keeler was there to assist. I took off the breast, and started to remove the glands from under the arm when Dr. Keeler suggested leaving them.

I handed the knife over to her, admitting, "I will probably not do it so rapidly or so well as you, but," with sharp emphasis, "the glands must be removed."

She did not accept the knife, but directed, "Proceed!"

Harriet Belcher recounted a surgery at which she had assisted: "Five physicians, all women, opened the abdomen and removed two small ovarian tumors and one of another kind. . . . Then for three weeks, I remained

B/..152.   B/..158.

B/..170   B/..188.   B/..212.   B/..194 & 230.

CHLOROFORM AND ETHER INHALERS. — Continued.

B/. 152	**Schimmelbusch's**, complete anæsthetic set containing 1 mask, 1 bottle, 1 Heister's mouth gag, 1 Esmarch's tongue forceps, 1 piece of gauze and oilcloth, in telescopic metal case. ········	$ 8 50
B/. 158	**Schoenemann's Inhaler**, with double bulb, patented. ··········	8 50
*B/. 164	**Richardson's Spray**, for local anæsthesia. ····················	2 50
B/. 170	**Gutsch's Maxillary Support** during narcosis. ·················	2 00

BOTTLES FOR CARRYING CHLOROFORM AND ETHER.

B/. 188	**Chloroform Bottle**, with pointed dropper. ···················			0 75
B/. 194	"	**Drop Bottle**, with enameled label "Chloroform." ·····		1 50
*B/. 206	"	"	**Esmarch's** (see B/. 50). ·········	0 50
B/. 212	"	"	**Schimmelbusch's**, with stop-cock ·····	1 50
*B/. 218	**Ether**	"	" **"Philadelphia."** ···············	0 60
*B/. 224	"	"	" **Robert's.** ··················	0 90
B/. 230	"	"	" with enameled label "**Ether.**" ··········	1 50

ALL INSTRUMENTS BEARING THE K.-S. CO.'S ☙ TRADE MARK ARE SOLD UNDER GUARANTEE.

ANAESTHETIC.

Catalog page.

Kansas State Historical Society, Topeka

and took care of [the patient] night and day. . . . Success or failure was so much more to us professionally than it would have been to men."

⤮

Any encounter with the surgeon's knife outside a hospital or teaching university became a public event, held on dusty tables or makeshift operating platforms on a screened porch for better ventilation and light, surrounded by curious onlookers drawn to the spectacle of sawing and hacking. Or a kitchen might serve for impromptu surgery or dental emergencies, with rough-hewn kitchen chairs placed one in front of the other, train-fashion, to provide the doctor a better grip on the offending tooth as she stood behind the patient. For Dr. Claudia Potter, surgery on a Texas cotton picker with a ruptured appendix took place on a plank set on two wooden carpenter's horses in the front yard of his squalid shack, "with the sky for the ceiling above" and "God's hot sunshine to sterilize the air."

Early surgeons worked without masks, failed to scrub their hands, and would often merely wipe off bloodied knives and scalpels with a rag before returning them to the medical bag for another operation. In fact, careless handling seemed an early surgical metaphor, with sepsis, misdiagnosis, and confusion linked to the makeshift conditions, and inevitably taking a steep toll on rural patients. Country physicians had few opportunities to brush up on their surgical skills, and often were too poor to buy the needed instruments.

According to *The Journals of William A. Lindsay*, estate records of doctors in six Indiana counties reveal that less than half the doctors who practiced prior to 1840 owned any surgical equipment at all. The harrowing details of a typical operation were described by E. Harryman, 1894.

> [S]he had peritonitis . . . and Dr. Parker & Dr. Hyman came and put her under the influence of chloroform. Her womb was turned upside down and . . . they had to open her and take the ovaries [out]. They was one hour and a quarter doing the whole, then the third day they thought blood poison would set in. They had to take the stitches out so they could treat the incision. She had a nurse from the city for four weeks she charged $15 a week then they got a cheaper one.

The most common surgical procedure was lancing, in which a steely access lancet tapped into an abscess, relieving swelling and inflammation, or into an inflamed joint region, to release collected water or matter. Amputation of deeply lacerated limbs was routine, and if the operation was successful, the medic would never lack for future patients. Conditions were primitive and medical resources limited, although they were seldom as brutal as the conditions experienced by a snake-bitten emigrant traveling west in 1849. "Although every available remedy was tried upon the wound," wrote diarist Catherine Haun, "his limb had to be amputated with the aid of a common handsaw." Thanks to the ministrations of a "good brave wife," he was cheered back into "health and usefulness" by journey's end.

In amputating limbs, the surgeon used the flap method or the circular method. In the flap technique, large pieces of skin were left to fold over the stump, while the circular method would excise a more modest amount of diseased muscles, flesh, and bone from the limb. Arteries were tied off, healthy muscle taken from the amputated stump, and the remaining skin tied over and fastened with a bandage called the Malta cross. Amputations usually completed the trauma of a laceration of partial severing—many injuries took place on the threshing-room floor and demanded a quick response from the doctor—but a South Dakota resident recalled how the brusque, mannish Dr. Jennie Murphy had casually sewn back part of a finger he had cut off in a bicycle sprocket.

"No man can be a surgeon who does not have eyes in the ends of his fingers," a surgical instructor, Dr. McLean, pointed out to his young medical student, Helen MacKnight Doyle. Many cases called for quick diagnosis and surgical skill. An appendectomy demanded an incision more than an inch long—the skilled doctor would quickly insert an index finger in the opening and "run it around" until the appendix was located, then she would "flip" it out, tie it off, sterilize the aperture, and close the opening, all in about a minute, according to Dr. Claudia Potter. Equally innovative was Dr. Mary C. Rowland, who established her reputation in rural Oregon with her nimble surgical skills. One early case involved a seventeen-year-old invalid plagued by a purulent discharge and high fever. Rowland diagnosed an infected pelvis, removed the affected tissue, and saw almost immediate improvement.

Surgery was an elite specialty, and those women who aspired to the skill might spend an entire winter studying and preparing for a difficult operation. Intense study and a record of success turned impromptu operations into near routine for Lillian Heath, Wyoming's noted "First Lady of Medicine." Her vigor and lack of squeamishness was a constant surprise to resident cowhands, desperadoes, and ailing citizens of the tiny, windswept community of Rawlings. Her girlish, petite demeanor belied her skill; she seemed dwarfed by the voluminous leather satchel filled with medical paraphernalia, yet her tabletop emergency procedures were quick, precise, and successful. When a cowhand was shot by a local sheriff and lay sweating and suffering on a cot, stretched out in the big ballroom of the old courthouse, Heath scarcely hesitated. "Whiskey!" she demanded, ordering up the first component of any makeshift frontier operation. Strong drink, a flat surface, and a bystander strong enough to pinion the patient's jerking legs and flying fists were surgical necessities. Heath "expected the boy to make an awful commotion," but the twenty-five-year-old doctor, performing her first surgery, had yet to understand the strength of the universal western code: bravery in the face of nearly anything, including the probe of a sharp

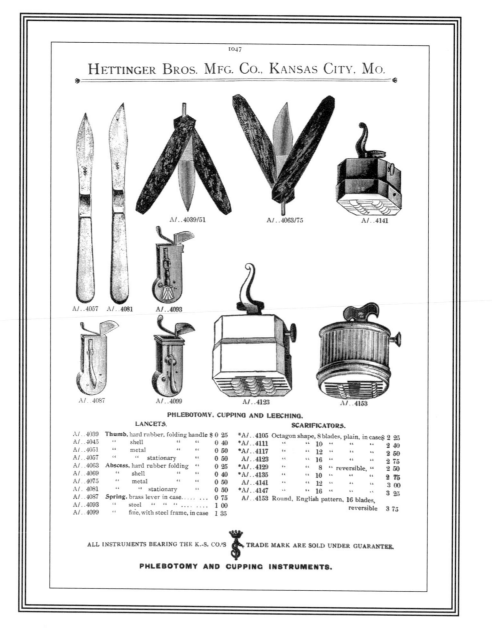

HETTINGER BROS. MFG. CO., KANSAS CITY, MO.

A/..4039/51   A/..4063/75   A/..4141

A/..4057   A/..4081   A/..4093

A/..4087   A/..4099   A/..4123   A/..4153

PHLEBOTOMY, CUPPING AND LEECHING.

LANCETS.   **SCARIFICATORS.**

A/..4039	**Thumb,** hard rubber, folding handle	$ 0 25	*A/..4105	Octagon shape, 8 blades, plain, in case	$ 2 25
A/..4045	" shell " "	0 40	*A/..4111	" " 10 " " "	2 40
A/..4051	" metal " "	0 50	*A/..4117	" " 12 " " "	2 50
A/..4057	" " stationary "	0 50	A/..4123	" " 16 " " "	2 75
A/..4063	**Abscess,** hard rubber folding "	0 25	*A/..4129	" " 8 " reversible, "	2 50
A/..4069	" shell " "	0 40	*A/..4135	" " 10 " " "	2 75
A/..4075	" metal " "	0 50	A/..4141	" " 12 " " "	3 00
A/..4081	" " stationary "	0 50	*A/..4147	" " 16 " " "	3 25
A/..4087	**Spring,** brass lever in case...... ...	0 75	A/..4153	Round, English pattern, 16 blades,	
A/..4093	" steel " " "	1 00		reversible	3 75
A/..4099	" fine, with steel frame, in case	1 35			

ALL INSTRUMENTS BEARING THE K.-S. CO.'S ☥ TRADE MARK ARE SOLD UNDER GUARANTEE.

PHLEBOTOMY AND CUPPING INSTRUMENTS.

Catalog page.

Kansas State Historical Society, Topeka

knife for a soft slug, no matter where it was buried. In the gunman's case, the bullet had rammed through the shoulder, pushing before it several layers of dirty undershirt. As Dr. Heath recounted to an interviewer years later, the young gunfighter was her first emergency —she clearly recalled the long incision, the quick twist of forceps to remove the bullet, followed by sterilization with anything at hand, namely, whiskey. Dr. Phoebe Flagler Hagenbuch, a practitioner in Pennsylvania and Ohio, often recalled her "table top operations," one of which was the successful amputation of the arm of a neighborhood man whose arm had been mangled by a corn shucker.

Surgery was often performed in the dental chair, and women as well as men were often called upon to extract teeth, even though the number of frontier dentists surpassed that of physicians. For dental surgery, the patient might be dosed with anesthetic, or not. "I had to extract many teeth," wrote Dr. Portia Lubchenco of her "colored" patients in South Carolina. "It fell my lot to perform for [them] the [services] my white patients were able to get from specialists."

When the Lubchenco family emigrated west, to Haxton, Colorado, the doctor found that dusty, mite-infested facilities threatened her surgical antisepsis. "We tried to avoid operations because of the danger from dirt," she wrote. "We operated very early in the morning. We protected patients as best we could, but cleanliness became impossible." She described dust-darkened afternoons so stormy that after every strong wind, in spite of wet sheets hung in front of the windows, the hospital floors would be coated with "at least two bucketfuls of fine dust." The patient's sheets had to be shaken out at intervals, releasing a slide of dun-colored sand.

One advantage held by urban practitioners over rural was the X ray, discovered in 1895 and put to use almost immediately by members of the scientific community, who were convinced that the magical rays were "capable of penetrating all woven fabrics as if they were mere vapor." Taken in context, the strides of nineteenth-century women physicians were defined, in great part, by their surgical success. Their "soul-satisfying" success led to increased dignity, recognition, and a lessening of the medical profession's "war against women."

Shack with patent medicine ad.

National Library of Medicine

CHAPTER FIFTEEN

Pink Pills and Innovations

The experiment was a success and it was soon noised
about that old Doc Anna was a fine doctor, so every-
thing that lived and breathed became a patient.

— ANNA DARROW

THE EARLY PRACTICE OF MEDICINE WAS PART INTUITION, PART APPRE-
ciable skill, part occasional prayer and a unilateral ability to improvise on the spot,
with or without the suitable tools. Frontier remedies ran the gamut, including the homespun innovation of a man who battled biliousness by reclining on a board on the ground, layering another
board on top and remaining in the position for at least twenty-four hours. Iowan Sarah Gillespie
wrapped her legs with towels to the shoe tops to relieve chilblains while two men had to come up
with a quick solution when faced with a wolf-bitten man who had turned rabid and was found
"raving, snarling, and attempting to bite everybody or thing that came his way." Without a physician to intervene, they applied the only remedy possible: he was finally smothered between two
feather beds.

Frontier health hung delicately in the balance, somewhere between myth and medicine and
sheep fat lotion. Rural medics turned to folk remedies when pharmaceutical supplies ran out,

knowing that they would cause most dramatic and visible signs of healing, thus justifying the expense of becoming a "paying" patient. Besides, nondomestic drugs such as quinine, Peruvian bark, gingerroot, opium, and gum Arabic were in scarce supply in pre–Civil War America, as they were imported from England and usually en route, or sold out. When supplies ran short, imagination took charge.

For some, innovation struck early, even before a medical career had begun. Elizabeth Blackwell, as a young girl writing home to her mother in 1845, cited her "first professional cure" as taking place when she mesmerized away a severe headache that afflicted "Miss O'Heara, a kind-hearted, child-like, black-haired little old maid" who had just recovered from an unnamed illness. Both illness and headache were cured by the young girl's mild power of suggestion.

Childbirth offered the rural medic ample opportunity for invention, with procedures that ranged from breech births to the treatment of puerperal fever. To assist in delivery, a physician might employ "pulling" cloths tied to the end of the bed or specialized birthing devices such as forceps. One, a handmade leather harness with large leather cuffs to encircle the thighs, held the legs wide apart while an adjustable metal bar pressed the knees to the chest and a strap looped up over the shoulders. Despite its look of medieval menace, the constraint actually helped a trembling and unstable mother maintain what was thought to be the best birthing posture.

Such precautions were particularly useful to women physicians, since delivering mothers, even when numbed with such tranquilizers as scopolamine, were unexpectedly strong and unruly. Bertha Van Hoosen finally lost patience with laboring patients who ripped away their sterile sheets and tried to fling themselves out of bed. In response, she devised a homemade birthing tool to "strap the patient's knees into knee crutches" that extended out from the delivery stirrups. Dr. Ellis Shipp rushed to the aid of a woman thought to be dying at the end of an exhausting three-day labor. The mother lay listlessly in the heat and dust of a Mexican town, miles by wagon from the bordertown of Juarez. A uterine obstruction blocked the child's delivery, leaving the mother almost too weak to struggle. Ellis's first response was prayer; her second was the skillful insertion of a catheter, and in a "half hour, the woman and babe [were] safe and well." Equally innovative was Mary Canaga Rowland, who realized that the doctor assisting her in a breech delivery was unable to pull the baby's head from the birth passage. "I instructed him to let the baby's legs straddle his arm and to slip his finger into the baby's mouth," she wrote. Thus prompted, the baby flexed its chin onto its chest and slipped right out, a healthy, living child.

The carelessness of others might have dictated the exacting standards of cleanliness employed by Bertha Van Hoosen, who was shocked into action when she saw nurses using unclean sponges to pack wounds. Before her next operation, she sterilized all the hospital paraphernalia in a small laboratory she assembled at home.

> I purchased cheap containers called "telescopes," large enough to hold gowns, sheets, sponges, etc., and a fish kettle for instruments. Everything that was to be used in the operating room I sterilized, packed, and took in the buggy with me to the hospital. . . . Long before . . . the operation, I . . . wiped all the furniture with lysol solution, unpacked and set up the operating room. We allowed no nurse in the room.

Inspiration guided the surgical hand and influenced many split-second decisions. On an instinct, Dr. Lillian Heath of Rawlins, Wyoming, speeded up the operation of a female patient by temporarily "removing one of her eyes," which, oddly enough, she had injured by "falling against a chair." Earlier, Heath had assisted a local physician in one of the most sensitive and difficult tasks of plastic surgery ever conducted in a rural setting, performed long before the field of cosmetic surgery even had a name. A despondent sheepherder had tried to shoot himself by placing a rifle muzzle under his chin and firing. "Apparently," she recalled, "the force of the blast snapped his head backward so that the bullet didn't go into his skull." Instead, it ripped away most of his countenance from the chin up. In the process of refitting the muscles and tendons of his terribly disfigured face,

Heath and Dr. Maghee had to perform thirty or more operations.

> His eyes weren't damaged, but the lower part of his face . . . was just completely gone. We fed him with a tube for weeks, meanwhile doing a little patching at each successive operation. Finally, after we had sewn up the flesh in the lower jaw, it began to heal. We didn't have to perform a bone graft. The jawbone grew back — by itself — filling out the round and all. It healed by first intention without any infection. . . .
>
> Eventually, he had some teeth made but before that we had to make a nose for him. We used silver tubes for nostrils and took a keystone of skin from up high on the forehead, twisted the skin and sewed it to his face in the shape of a nose. The tip of the keystone was, of course, left attached at the top to continue blood circulation.
>
> The man's nose took shape with little puckering on one side and none on the other. Completely healed, the man's face showed no scars. But when he had recovered sufficiently to pay attention to himself, his chief occupation was jerking hairs out of the middle section of his nose.

Innovation teamed with an icy calm allowed women physicians to master their environment. How else to perform an emergency tracheotomy on a suffocating child than by slashing the windpipe and inserting a breathing tube—the hollow quill of a feather? How else to initiate skull surgery, marshaling enough physical strength to actually remove bone from the skull? Nearly fainting, Dr. Mary C. Rowland of Kansas bravely reached into a head wound in which the temporal artery was spurting blood, determined to stop the flow. "I put my finger on the artery just in front of the ear and bore down," she recalled; this successfully stopped the bleeding. In another case, surgery proceeded without a knife, from a cut made by pulling the skin taut from two ends and snipping with scissors. Equally innovative was Colorado's Susan Anderson, often called the best diagnostician west of the Rockies, who healed with whatever was at hand, once using a woman's corset to truss a lumberjack's broken ribs and a patient's own hair to "suture" closed a scalp laceration, saving the expense and pain of stitches. None could have been more prepared for delicate handwork than Doc Susie, whose girlhood had been spent nimbly embroidering—hence the skill to thread tiny hairs together into a tight, stitchlike weave. Likewise, Texas physician Claudia Potter had to hand-fashion her own surgical supplies, and "this did not mean just folding sponges." She had to "take raw catgut, wind it into small coils about a yard in length," then store it in liquid alboline after it was sterilized. An entire day would pass in the process, and if the room temperature was too high, the catgut would turn brittle and break. "Many a tear was shed over this failure," she admitted. "But we would just try again."

Conscientious physicians tried to keep up with new medical techniques; they read medical journals, acquired new instruments when they could, and experimented with different ointments and unctions for rashes, scalds, and burns. One doctor might apply soothing liniment or at other times simply keep the burned skin moist, while another might shock the flesh with electric currents in a water bath, which was powerful enough to contract the muscles violently and relieve the pain of the burn. Dr. Rowland had read about an innovative French method that caught her imagination—a combination of paraffin and resins that would soothe the damaged skin: "We melted it over a spirit lamp and rolled it on with a cotton swab. The paraffin kept the air away and protected the new skin that begin to form." Dr. Rowland was quick to understand the advantages of this brand-new product manufactured by Johnson & Johnson; whenever it was used, she boasted, scars were avoided.

Europe had been the seat of medical innovation, tempting American physicians with new implements and methods advertised in medical journals, whether pure iodine as a cure for scrofula or the "science" of phrenology as a way of judging intellect and personality by the bumps in the head. Staying skillful often meant trying the untried, perhaps the use of such an innovation as the clinical record chart, which had never been used in San Francisco hospitals until introduced by Dr. Emma Sutro Merritt, who knew that the recorded temperature, pulse, and respiration

rate of patients would provide valuable conti-
nuity among rotating physicians. She launched
into the project with great enthusiasm, but
found that the printer had never seen a degree
symbol before and decided to add them wher-
ever he thought appropriate.

Imagination also prevailed when it came
to diagnosis, as Dr. Rowland, who had
recently moved to Lebanon, Oregon, discovered. A surprising number of rural dwellers
were stricken with scurvy, yet failed to recognize its symptoms, including the local physician who was treating a local infant. There
was no progress, and the distraught family
brought their child to Rowland, who studied
her medical books all night and finally decided that the symptoms could be reversed by
a teaspoonful of orange juice twice a day. Her
remedy was immediately successful, and
Rowland's reputation in the town was established. Said Dr. Rowland: "That mother
thought I could raise the dead."

Given the degree of public ignorance concerning health, particularly sexual hygiene, it
was little wonder that the supposed cancer
causing a "foul escape" from the vagina of a
patient was not a disease at all, but an "embedded rubber-covered spring pessary" that had
"buried itself in the vaginal walls" and worked
its way into the rectum—to be discovered by
New York physician Dr. Elizabeth Cushier in
1882. Cushier removed the pessary but faced a
delicate operation of threading balky silver
wire sutures through the rectum and delicately manipulating them to close the wound.
This was her first operation and "it proved to

be the most difficult piece of work I had ever
done," she wrote.

Such significant "first" occasions were the
essence of innovation, and for many women
doctors, they occurred as the physicians were
trying to develop a clientele in a new setting.
How to win patients? How to convey an
impression of trustworthiness as well as scientific acumen? Often the breakthrough moment came when they were called upon to
treat not humans but animals. After all, they
had healing skills, so why not put them to use?
As Anna Darrow recounted:

> One night I heard a rap at the kitchen
> door. Being a light sleeper I hopped out
> of bed and hurried to the window and
> called, "Who is there?" A man's voice
> answered, "Doc, my shoat is having
> convulsions." Here I was stumped. I did
> not know what a shoat was but thought
> it was the name of his child.... So I
> said, "How old is the child?" "Oh doc,
> it's my three weeks old pig that has
> drank so much cane skimmings he is
> having convulsions." Then I ran back to
> Dr. C.R. [her husband] and told
> him.... Dr. C.R. answered back,
> "What does he think I am, a vet?" I
> realized that our reputation might be at
> stake so I hurried back and asked him if
> he could tell me how much the shoat
> weighed. I figured out quickly that it
> would come to the 12 pound weight of
> an infant....
>
> Now here was a challenge to my

ingenuity. A 12-pound shoat with con-
vulsions. I hastened to the chart, figured
out what was indicated and gave the
pellets to Will and told him to give one
every two hours with water from a
small bottle. If the piggie acted cold to
cover it up. The experiment was a suc-
cess and it was soon noised about that
old Doc Anna was a fine doctor, so
everything that lived and breathed
became a patient.

Another physician to win the acceptance of a skittish and critical frontier population in Wyoming—none of whom cared to consult her professionally—was Dr. Bessie Efner, who felt herself to be a complete outsider until one day she was begged to attend an ailing horse, a "very urgent case." Innocent of all things veterinarian, she nevertheless pondered the symptoms until a vague idea grew: The horse might be suffering from colic, thus might respond to a human medicine. She brewed up a concoction that was four times the human dosage and healed the animal, deciding that the offered payment of 75 cents for the animal's successful recovery was acceptable, considering the actual reward of increased business. "[The horse] was my friend ever after and my best publicity agent."

An intuitive flash of inspiration also served Susan Anderson well when she was trying to establish herself in a tiny, mud-spattered mining town in the Colorado Rockies. Rumor and suspicion had long followed her, fed by a pervasive gender distrust that generally kept patients away from any woman doctor. Without patients, Anderson whiled away her days on snowshoes, trudging back and forth from her cabin to the general store, where she "helped out" as a clerk for lack of better pursuits. Thus when an anxious cowhand begged her to tend to a horse that had tangled itself in barbed wire, she leaped at the opportunity to practice her skills. Out turned the crowds—rowdy, jostling, and irreverent locals drawn to a show that no resident of Fraser, Colorado, would miss. The doctor assembled freshly boiled water, a sewing kit with "big carpet needles and some tough canvas thread," and her instrument kit filled with gleaming tools before facing down the snorting stallion; its owner must "twitch" the horse, she demanded, by tightening a strip of rawhide around its nose and mouth to prevent movement. Anderson spent hours cleaning each of the animal's lacerations with carbolic acid, then she reached up under the horse's hide, into the gaping wounds, to reconnect the severed muscles first, followed by the sinews and blood vessels, drawing it all together until each cut was drawn tight. In the single procedure she overturned the prevailing wisdom that women "weren't meant to be doctors—it wasn't natural." A lady doc able to confront a horse and spend hours in the hot sun helping to heal its wounds had transcended gender stereotypes; "Doc Susie" had arrived.

When anesthesiologist Claudia Potter was told about a patient with a "very large ventral hernia" and was asked to bring a larger-than-usual quantity of ether, she wasn't surprised to find that the patient was a "four footed fine registered sow" worth $1,500. As an anesthesiologist, Potter had gently maneuvered every size patient "off into dreamland," but never a hog:

I started out rather slowly, but even at that she objected—[she] just did not like any of the procedure. I dropped ether a little faster; with that she brought her front foot up and all but knocked my mask out of my hand.

I said, "Someone hold her hands, please."

Doctor Curtis said, "Front hands or hind hands?"

Anyway, feet or hands, they were controlled. I finally got her to third plane anesthesia. Preparation of the abdomen was done by our best technique and Dr. Brindley repaired the hernia and she was returned to her bed in a nice floored pen and made an uneventful recovery. I think she farrowed a litter of pigs in about fifteen months.

Women physicians turned enthusiastically to the latest in technology and drugs, depending on budget. Dr. Portia Lubchenco's new X-ray machine "was costly, over two grand," in addition to $15 for electricity. Yet, she wrote, "no body can operate [it at] present."

They also sought the latest drugs, relieved that more scientific means were available after decades of questionable elixirs, powders, pills, and essences. "I was the first doctor in our county in Kansas to use newly introduced antitoxin," wrote Mary Rowland, securing the patronage of the entire Swedish settlement of Herndon, Kansas, when two Swedish children with diphtheria "made a quick recovery" with shots of her antitoxin. Colorado's Dr. Lida B. Russell promoted a "milk diet" for tuberculosis.

Other female discoveries: Eliza Mosher, M.D., one of the founders of the American Posture League, was noted for designing an enteroptosis belt and a kindergarten chair, while in 1900, Dr. Margaret Vaupel-Clark's method of measuring the mental and physical well-being of children was so effective it was used at the Iowa State Fair, drawing such crowds that a women's and children's building was erected on the state fairgrounds. Dr. Alma Lautzenheiser Rowe championed freedom for babies from the confines of fashionable, overlong baby clothes. Such freedom began with the mother's body, which, she believed, should conform to its own natural lines rather than be pushed and contorted by tight corsets. As a practicing physician before 1900, her freewheeling outlook was an offshoot of frontier bloomerism.

Ethel Kirkland and class.

National Library of Medicine

CHAPTER SIXTEEN

Breaching the Bulwarks

Birth Control

In time of stress a woman turns to a woman.

—DR. STEWARD TO RUTH BARNARD

NSEXED!" WAS THE FAMILIAR CRY THAT ACCOMPANIED THE PATH OF the woman doctor through her territory—an accusation deeply resented by stalwart medical women who were often married, frequently had families, and whose reserves of science *and* femininity were constantly tapped as they combined sisterly advice with *materia medica*. One such area had to do with birth control. Women physicians generally had fewer children than other women, since they were familiar with birth control techniques. In fact, one female doctor referred obliquely to a "Malthusian appliance" she bought on a trip to London—probably a diaphragm available in London in the 1890s but not in the United States until the 1920s.

As the gold boom veered into the Roaring Twenties, more women turned to prostitution, syphilis was rampant, and out-of-wedlock births were endemic—there was no lack of vulnerable female patients. Prohibitory Victorian ideals had precluded premarital sex, and a strong religious grounding defined the moral bulwarks. For young girls to make a personal choice in sexual matters was anathema in most rural communities, and any transgression invoked religious ire, moral campaigns, and community criticism. Yet often the allure of a moonlit night proved too great. "I did not need to ask an embarrassing question," wrote Oregon physician Mary C. Rowland regarding one of her patients. "I knew [the young girl] was pregnant." The distraught teenager insisted that she would jump in the river, but the doctor persuaded her to confess to her mother, who suggested a solution: the girl's older, married daughter was infertile and wanted a child, which the younger daughter willingly offered. Unspoken among them was an even darker aspect to the imbroglio—that the girl's father had been her partner, and the child to be raised by family members would bear the family's darkest genetic secrets. Birth control methods were needed, but the achievement of this took on various complexities.

Cynicism and religion surrounded this female issue. And, with a prescientific population still eager to dose itself with rusty nail water, flaxseed injections, or the ingestion of gunpowder, the idea of going to a medical doctor because one didn't want to become pregnant seemed extreme.

In fact, homespun methods abounded, and many were common knowledge as early as the late 1800s. Between 1820 and 1873 newspapers and pamphlets advertised contraceptives and abortifacients, and tracts, pamphlets, and circulars touted prudent methods of family limitation. According to estimates, by 1860 one in six pregnancies had been ended by abortion, although the question arises: How were these results obtained?

Ignorance, for the most part, prevailed. Dr. Mary Canaga Rowland enjoyed telling the story of the rural girl who insisted she could not be pregnant as she had "only tried it once and then just for a moment." Rowland's dilemma was whether or not to inform her of the nearly thirty different chemical abortifacients readily available, some advertised and sold through the newspapers with euphemistic descriptions such as a "cure for interrupted menstruation," which was sufficiently vague to satisfy Victorian scruples while making available what was so desperately needed.

Yet when actually faced with the serious question of family planning, most seemed confused or referred to folk wisdom as a solution. In 1850 the average married couple had nearly six children, hardly a recommendation for the folk approach.

Women routinely prolonged breastfeeding and refrained from sex while nursing, or turned to bloodletting, herbal remedies, pes-

> *You know we women can talk heart to heart more freely with each other than we can explain to any man.*
> — MRS. F.D., QUEBEC, DEC. 18, 1921, FROM FILES AT THE CHILDREN'S BUREAU

saries, or pennyroyal tea as an abortifacient. In the most desperate cases, there was infanticide. Women were "in the soup" all too often, prompting such statements as the one Rose Williams made to Allettie Mosher on September 27, 1885: "You want to know of a sure preventative? Well plague take it. The best way is for you to sleep in one bed and your Man in another." If abstinence proved unworkable, there was the "pessary" of wood, cotton, or sponge, which was a lightweight, expandable device used inside the vagina. The tiny pessaries designed by Dr. Marie Stopes in 1920 and fitted for indigent urban women were not routinely available in rural sites. Those too shy to request what was popularly called the "pisser" could blurt out the words "female preventative," which cost one dollar. Douching with a syringe filled with alum or sulphates of zinc or iron was common, as was the use of crude sponges. Women turned to Native American abortifacients as a last resort, using ergot, a black fungus growth that sprouted in brittle grains on rye grass, to stimulate the uterus into delivery. Recommended was a formula of one to two teaspoons, taken six times a day. Countless unnamed women must have sickened and died from the ingestion of such toxins, their stories unknown because few rural physicians recorded their experiences with herbal abortifacients.

The era of modern birth control was ushered in by Margaret Sanger around 1914. But the general sermonizing, medical denouncement, and even media condemnation accompanying her efforts clearly equated the idea of reproductive freedom with immorality. By 1921 Sanger had organized the first American Birth Control Conference in New York City, trying to tie the issue of women's reproductive rights to child relief rather than female freedom.

The doctor who acted as counselor, minister, healer, and friend could also count among her patients young women distraught over the inability to bear children, which haunted and cursed many. What advice could be offered? Rural physician Amelia Dann encountered a married couple unhappily embroiled in just such a problem. One day in 1879 Dann found a "stylishly dressed young woman" in her waiting room. High-heeled and tightly corseted, the anxious woman was fidgety and red-faced from poor circulation and she was also distraught because her husband would come home drunk, "punishing her because she had not become pregnant" with an ugly assortment of slaps and beatings, followed by "pull[ing] her breasts and bit[ing] her nipples until they bled." Was this normal for men? she wondered. When her corset was unlaced, Dann was shocked to see the woman's true girth, and she also noted the misshapen condition of the woman's feet, long confined to narrow shoes. Under such painful restriction, no wonder she failed to conceive! Dunn's advice to the woman was sisterly and scientific. The woman must allow her stomach and internal organs to remain unfettered and revise her wardrobe accordingly; she must speak openly with her mate—even bringing him in for a conference. Dann had great empathy for women, including the prostitutes she treated on a regular basis. The bawdy houses were filled with young girls ignorant of both disease and reproduction. One thirteen-year-old believed the speckled rash she bore was chicken pox, not syphilis. Dann knew prostitution well because of its disease-ridden aftermath; in sympathy, she set up a counseling center in an empty basement of the opera house, where the girls could visit her secretly and "learn more about themselves."

Young girls who were pregnant out of wedlock turned to women practitioners rather than men, calling women abortionists "female physicians" despite their lack of a degree. Few women physicians would participate in abortions, but were often called in at the last minute to patch up the results of a "killing job." A typical abortionist, described by physician Elizabeth Blackwell, was known as a "female physician" and "made a large fortune, drove a fine carriage, had a pew in a fashionable church," and, although "always arrested, was always bailed out by her patrons." "Female physician" was a euphemism for the unscrupulous, back-alley operator who, armed with hooks, prods, and knives but little science, might perforate the womb. An exception to the usual profile of the abortion doctor was Portland's Ruth Barnard, whose license in naturopathy allowed her the title of doctor. "To do this minor surgery I must have the proper credentials," wrote Barnard, who studied anatomy, physiology, histology, and chemistry for twenty-seven months to obtain a degree. Her early inspiration had been Dr. Maude Van Alstyne, a prominent physician, surgeon, and abortionist who had graduated

from the University of Oregon Medical School in 1902. Another was Dr. Griff, one of the earliest women physicians in the Northwest, specializing in women's ailments. Described as powerful and vivacious, Griff attracted young Ruth Barnard as a student, prompting a career that would make Barnard one of the most notorious abortionists in the West. Barnard was completely swayed by Dr. Griff, who "handled herself with charm and confidence." Not only did Dr. Griff take Barnard along to Good Samaritan Hospital to visit the maternity wards, but she allowed the young girl to watch her perform appendectomies, hysterectomies, and cesareans. Dr. Griff's eyes seemed to reveal, to the younger woman, a world of female authority and promise. To Barnard, "they were the first cold brown eyes I had ever seen."

And no wonder. In her maternity practice, Griff had encountered hundreds of tearful requests to provide abortions. So profuse were these pleas that she began to specialize, allowing her impressionable young acolyte, Barnard, to assist her. To the young student, "it seemed . . . the most wonderful work in the world," and she decided to enter the field. Barnard's second mentor was Portland's first abortionist, Dr. Albert Littlefield, whose practice began in a rustic room above a hardware store in 1890 and who instructed Barnard "in the painstaking details of his technique." Once she became familiar with his array of custom-made, solid bronze instruments, and his habit of never using a dilator, she was ready to open a practice of her own. As a naturopath, Barnard could perform surgery as long as the entry was made through a natural body opening. Dr. Barnard's own abortion as a young girl had convinced her of the necessity of freedom of choice, and the practice she began in the 1920s continued for fifty years. "I do not honestly know how many abortions I have performed in the half century I have made this work my profession," wrote Barnard, but estimated it to be nearly forty thousand abortions since 1918. "I have a light touch and have never perforated a uterus," she claimed. "I was unwilling to perceive any crime in what I . . . had done. . . . I still cannot see the wrong in abortion."

> *Madam, do not*
> *be impatient.*
> *The Lord is performing*
> *a hysterectomy on you.*
>
> — DR. BERTHA
> VAN HOOSEN,
> QUOTING DR. WATKINS
> TO HER PATIENT

Although abortion was largely accepted by society in the early part of the nineteenth century, women physicians, particularly, had to guard their fragile position in the community by staying well within the law. Abortion was considered an unethical practice, criminalized by many state laws. Between 1860 and 1890, forty states enacted antiabortion statutes. Through the American Medical Association, doctors unilaterally convinced state legislators that there was no place for abortion in modern health care.

Many women physicians had a difficult choice: to follow conscience, or the law. In the early 1870s Dr. Mary Colander of Boulder, Colorado, was convicted of manslaughter in an abortion-related maternal death and was the first woman sentenced to the state penitentiary. Many felt she was the victim of prejudice. Washington State physician Dr. Mayme MacLafferty was denied membership in the King County Medical Society because of her willingness to provide safe, aseptic abortions. So touchy was the issue that even adoptions seemed dangerous. Dr. Mary Rowland grew careful when an infertile female patient begged her to help find a baby. The subterfuge would be that the girl simply "went away for a while," then returned with an adopted baby, telling her husband she had given birth to it. Rowland advised her that it would be against the law to "perpetuate such a fraud." If the husband ever found out, it would be grounds for litigation; he could divorce his wife and sue the doctor. In fact, Rowland's work with teenage mothers raised the ire of religious women from the Portland rescue home, who accused her of selling babies through facilitated adoptions. When a police matron arrived to investigate, she could only agree with Rowland that the baby's fate was at risk. Wouldn't the adoption by two prosperous parents, as well as the emotional release of the terrified young mother, make sense? "Of course, I was not in the business of selling babies," Rowland assured the police matron. "I'm sure I did the baby a good turn and the girl too." After all, wouldn't the child be "less

impaired?" Since the girl had made the transfer herself, Rowland had done nothing illegal.

Young girls who finally sought abortions encountered female physicians who had already been faced with, and made, the difficult choice of whether or not to provide the service. Most women physicians avoided abortions because of the risk to their hard-won status. "I think some of us [women physicians] do try to prevent abortions," wrote Colorado's Dr. Minnie Love, while Alice B. Stockham, M.D., writing in the late 1800s, advised against the

practice: "The woman who produces abortion, or allows it to be produced, risks her own health and life in the act, and commits the highest crime in the calendar." Although set against bringing "sin-cursed, diseased children into the world," she believed that men should temper their passion, denying themselves gratification at the expense of conjugal happiness and unwelcome children. Failing all else, a woman seeking natural, induced abortion might try the opposite of Stockham's cautions against "lifting, straining, a fall, a jar, a blow, a violent cold, or an acute attack of disease, sudden mental emotions, etc." In her book, the *People's Home Medical Book,* a more specific method was "a preparation of arsenic, iron and nux vomica," taken in tablet form, four a day. Nux vomica, made from the poisonous seed of an Asian tree, is also the source of strychnine. Like most women physicians, Dr. Stockham took a strong antiabortion stance. After all, in her "thirty years [in] the practice of medicine," she had "seen a great deal of trouble and sorrow caused by the production of abortion." Many, however, began by performing occasional abortions for humanitarian reasons, then found their practice increasing.

Emotional evidence indicates that women physicians might sympathize with women's abortion woes—but the subject is seldom discussed in historical sources. Most references come from patients, not their physicians, but those descriptions are telling nonetheless and reveal the loneliness of women when facing the despair of too many children. "I have resorted to drugs, trying to prevent [conception] or bring about a slip. I believe I and others have caused bad health to ourselves and our children," wrote one English woman. Mary Kincaid wrote to her cousin in 1896, troubled that she had not taken "George Willard's receipt" (possibly for an abortion) and left the "nasty thing" alone. "Next time you bet I will not have any more if I live through this time," she wrote. A popular explanation for sickly, ailing children was that they had been damaged in the womb by the mother's attempt at

drug-induced abortion, or a "slip." However, judging by the entries in *Daniel's Texas Medical Journal* of 1888, male practitioners were fully versed in this taboo area.

There is a prevalent idea that if abortion occurs once, it is more apt to do so again. That a habit may be established. As to prevention . . . some years ago "black haw" was much in vogue, and was thought to possess almost specific properties. Rest in bed, and hips elevated, as suggested in Dr. Gregg's paper, are the safest means. . . .

And Dr. Q. C. Smith wrote in 1887:

Doctors as a rule are pretty well up in the treatment of abortion; but it requires nice judgement to determine just where to cease efforts to prevent and to conduct the case to a thorough and complete evacuation.

Few know how difficult it is to get into the womb, with the tedious means of dilation generally at hand. Is opposed to tamponing; it is possible to thus conceal a dangerous hemorrhage. Prefers Barnes dilator; but there is a little invention, a century old, perhaps, which has been lately revived, that he resorts to most generally, where dilation is necessary and difficult.

Ergot gives tonicity to the womb. Thirty to forty drops of ergot injected into the rectum, is better than any quantity by the mouth.

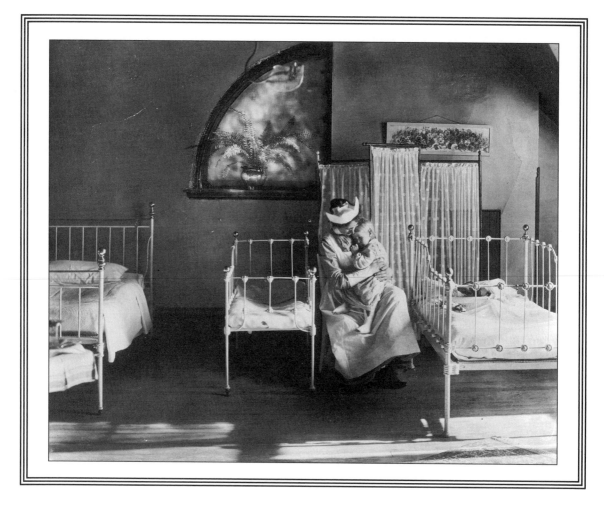

Children's Ward, Northwestern Hospital for Women and Children,
Minneapolis, ca. 1900.

Minnesota Historical Society

CHAPTER SEVENTEEN

"Lying-In" and Childbirth

To me it seemed that nature was bent on killing every

mother and baby that came to confinement, and the duty of

a woman doctor was to defeat this object at all costs.

—DR. KATE MEAD

ONFINEMENT AND DELIVERY TOOK PLACE WITH THE SAME UNENDING regularity as the seasons. Along with lambing, planting, and harvesting came the birthing cycle—maternity was not without predictability. Rural doctors knew that summer would yield a bumper crop of confinements, the results of long, chilly nights in high-country terrain, where housebound couples acted upon instinct.

Beneath starry skies or in howling windstorms, obscured by snow or burned by sun, rural women continued to bear children, assisted by midwife, friend, family, physician, or, if left to their own resources, alone. Such fecundity often loosed rounds of illness, death, and female melancholia. "O . . . I wish there was no such thing as having babies!" cried expectant mother Mary Kincaid in 1896, fearing the host of woes that often befell expectant mothers, including dropsy, urinary distress, hemorrhoids, and nausea. Women spent most of their adult lives bearing and raising children, beginning as young as fifteen and enduring well into their forties. Births were usually fifteen to twenty months apart, depending upon the length of nursing, though some extended the period up to two years or even more.

Confinement, often mentioned briefly in women's journals and diaries as "the time" or "lying-in," invited a round of female-centered activities and invoked a tradition of midwives, female neighbors, and eventually, female physicians. Before 1760, childbirth had been strictly a women's affair, functioning within the realm of women's domestic culture. Physicians, needless to say, were strongly concerned about the use of midwives.

Most midwives were strongly rooted in folk medicine, potions, and nostrums, but in a pinch, anyone with a medicine chest might do. Although there was some prejudice against "Indian doctors," or those who used native remedies, women physicians freely prescribed herbs, tinctures, and concoctions made from blue cohosh, or squaw root, to ease a woman through the travails of a slow and painful delivery. Listed in the U.S. pharmacopeia from 1882 until 1905 as a labor inducer, it was also given before pregnancy to prepare the uterus for childbirth.

Anna Darrow of Florida described some of her obstetrical experiences:

[Mrs. K. was] a fine looking middle-aged woman with black hair, flashing black eyes and a faultless complexion, straight as a ramrod, the mother of five grown up children and about to . . . see a child born for the first time. Her daughter . . . was suddenly in the throes of labor. I was sent for in a hurry. There was no extra bedroom or bed. My patient was lying on an old Army cot in the middle of the room alongside a rough homemade table with a kerosene lamp on it. Of course, there was nothing prepared for this emergency so I had to think quickly to calm the situation. I had told her to please heat water . . . to boil up my instruments. Anything to keep her busy and calm her nerves.

The patient had one of those resting spells . . . and the mother got very excited thinking that something had gone wrong. In order to be doing something myself I turned the patient over on her side and massaged her back and told her she was doing fine. All of a sudden the ordeal was over so I delivered, on her side, a fine six pound girl. Grandma was delighted.

A short time after that I got a call one night . . . Dr. Alsobrook wanted me to help him on a confinement case, said he did not like to put on forceps. I got dressed and hurried down to our drugstore where Dr. Alsobrook was waiting for me. We hurried through the woods and prairie and as we sped on I noticed we passed Mrs. K's place, then on into a hammock where there was another old tin shack. Just as we stopped . . . and got out our instruments, out came Mrs. K. dressed in a dark house dress with a white apron frantically waving it up and down screaming at the top of her

T o o l s   o f   t h e   T r a d e

voice, "Oh my God I have done it — oh my God I have done it. I turned her over on her side just like Dr. Anna did my daughter and here comes the baby! . . . my God I have done it." We stopped in to take a look at the situation. Here was a bouncing 12 pound baby and a badly lacerated mother. Dr. Alsobrook took one look and said, "Doc sew her up!" and hopped into his tin lizzie and sped for home.

When Mary Canaga Rowland found that the residents of Herndon, Kansas, preferred the local midwife to any physician, male or female, she adopted a tolerant approach: "I could have stopped her from operating," wrote Rowland, "but I thought she needed the money." Stopping a midwife was one thing, but preventing the involvement of the rural population proved to be quite another. Dr. Helen MacKnight Doyle found that "if a woman is 'expecting,' every good wife knows just when, can tell how long her 'morning sickness' lasted, and will venture an opinion on the sex of the child by the way the mother is 'carrying it.' When a woman is known to be in labor a kind of tenseness settles over the whole community until word is passed about that it is all over. Then the length of labor, the sex and weight of the child, whether 'they' wanted a boy or a girl, and other important factors connected with the case are reviewed in detail."

Folk remedies passed from mother to daughter, much as in the spirit of pioneer Nettie Fowler McCormick, who wrote to her pregnant daughter in 1890, "Dearie, I wish I were there to thoroughly rub olive oil upon your hips, your groin muscles, your abdominal muscles all throughout—in short all the muscles that are to be called upon to yield, and be elastic at the proper time." For her, the "strong hand of mother" along with olive oil, "freely applied," was all the medicine needed.

Folk wisdom and experience occasionally broke down—in one case, a patient had been in labor three days without delivering, and the midwife was unable to tell how the baby was presenting. It was time for Mary Rowland to step in: "On examination, I discovered that it was normal, but that the sac holding the baby had not ruptured. . . . I separated the blades of my scissors and inserted one blade alongside my finger. When I came to the membrane, I ran the blade through the sac and out came more than a gallon of fluid. . . . In thirty minutes the baby was born. Those people sang my praises from then on."

Midwifery, and its common touch, created a disdain for obstetrics among many women physicians. They resisted the shadow of maternity and "female" issues, fearing that they would be associated with midwifery. Bertha Van Hoosen, an anatomy instructor at a woman's college and a surgeon and generalist in private practice, found that obstetrical clinics were subject to "notorious disapprobation and disesteem," and often closed without warning. Although Van Hoosen "loved obstetrics," she was also "keenly aware of its unpopularity." "Because I was a woman," she

worried, "to specialize in obstetrics would brand me as a midwife, a Cinderella step-sister of the usurping 'man-midwife.'" She finally decided it would "be wiser" to gain recognition in surgery in order to "enter obstetrics through a surgical door." Only then could she work in the birth room "with skill and distinction."

In 1910 there was only one doctor per 609 people in the country, prompting the idea that *lack* of medical care caused the "alarming" statistics of maternal mortality. Yet some believed it was just the opposite, and that particularly at risk were those who were attended by male doctors,

Navajo delivery.

National Library of Medicine

and could recount gruesome instances of a physician's bungling that were whispered throughout rural communities. Samuel Gregory's *Man-Midwife Exposed* includes the story of a Doctor Septimus Hunter, of New York, who was sentenced to a year in the penitentiary for causing the death of a woman at childbirth. Although he had practiced for over eight years, he still mistakenly tore away the uterus instead of removing the placenta—a common practice among men who learned female anatomy with a leather doll and a makeshift uterus instead of an actual, human model. "Who ever heard of a midwife making such stupid and shocking blunders?" blustered Gregory. Since male physicians generally disliked treating confinement patients, particularly those from indigent or working-class families, "fetching the doctor" was often an exercise in futility, as the doctor seemed always to "want his rest," might refuse to attend, or, being inebriated, would send a midwife in his place.

Medical school was often inadequate when it came to women's issues—even young female doctors were innocent of all but the most obvious knowledge. One young doctor recalled her instructor standing with "arms dripping with carbolic solution" as she demonstrated the course of labor on an "old rubber phantom and flabby doll that served as examples of natural as well as abnormal labor." "She stared at us," she recalled, "while we tried to manipulate that slippery doll through the dripping phantom."

Indiana physician William A. Lindsay always found the removal of the placenta a "difficult & unpleasant operation under the most favorable circumstances." Besides, it was considered most indelicate to uncover a woman's genitals except at the end of the labor, when it was requisite to support the perineum. A student who could not pass a catheter by touch, "without seeing the urethra," was considered very awkward. Though a male physician might boast that he had overcome the "indelicacy" problem by always

delivering women under their bedclothes and never uncovering them for a gynecological exam, often the necessary, painstaking examinations were ineptly performed by men with limited knowledge or interest. Extremely modest women might avoid medical consultation entirely due to fear and suppressed sexual anxiety. One of the first duties of the doctor was a hands-on examination to ascertain which part of the child "presented," and whether this "presentation" was natural or not, and because of this, critic Samuel Gregory feared for the virtue of all birthing women, likening "depraved" doctors to bank clerks who devalued the money handled daily.

Lingering suspicion of males in the delivery room was noted in Oregon in 1912 by Dr. Mary Rowland, who worked one night with a male anesthesiologist. "No monkey business," the woman's husband shouted at the doctor, and Rowland, recognizing potential trouble, gave the jealous husband the task of pouring the sterile water while she worked. "I made up my mind that if he tried to interfere with me while I was working I would stab him with my scissors, but he caused no further trouble and she made a recovery."

Fear of male medical attention lingered, turning up even as late as the 1920s. "I need advise," wrote a mother of nine to the U.S. Children's Bureau. "Does it make a Mother unvirtuous for a man physician to wait on her during confinement? There isn't any midwives near us now. I am not friendless but going to you for advise too keep down gossip."

Men were equally concerned about the

use of male physicians. To many, it was a source of "sad regret and great affliction" to have a "gentleman attendant" for their pregnant wives. "The humane husband possessed of a correct and delicate regard for his wife would find a doctress," exhorted a minister from Maine in 1850. "The husband's hands alone are to have access to his sacred wife," wrote George Gregory, author of a treatise titled *Medical Morals,* who feared that even "modest-looking doctors" were inflamed with thoughts of the women they delivered and were, according to Gregory, "driven to adultery and madness" by their charges.

Far-fetched, perhaps, but a salient argument to some, considering the many examples that existed of a woman's labor ceasing the moment a male accoucheur entered a room and remaining stalled for hours or days. Indeed, it was a recognized phenomenon that a male presence in the sick chamber could have a retarding influence; many male physicians concluded that, because of such debilitating modesty, absence might be the best of prescriptions. The sheer number of cases in which this occurred, Gregory believed, proved that "a woman, when left to herself, may often be delivered naturally, [rather than suffering] the greatest agony at the hands of her medical attendants." "In gynecological and obstetrical examinations [when] patients were wide awake," wrote Dr. Esther Lovejoy, "with the modesty of the early nineties they resisted the exposure of their persons above the ankles and protested against being 'gaped at and pawed over' by strange young men."

Male physicians often showed a lack of empathy, notably one Columbus Pemberton, of Hmer Hamilton, Iowa, who was oddly unsentimental about a woman's delivery: "Mrs [Caroline] Porterfield went to work the other morning to produce an abortion and along in the evening sometime she squeezed out a little plug about the size of a fat oyster." Adding a moral appraisal, he was also sure that the "wickedness of the patient was being visited upon the head of the child."

Male insensitivity to women's suffering had social precedent. In nineteenth-century thought women primarily fulfilled a childbearing role, and this duty took precedence over concerns for her own health. Consumption, for example, normally would be a contraindication to pregnancy. But all too often, a woman's male physician would ignore the complaints and symptoms and allow her to proceed with the pregnancy—a ranking of values that placed pregnancy over health, and even life.

Women physicians, on the other hand, would counsel prudence instead of pregnancy, which was code for abortion. As professionals, they could see beyond the maternal role, perhaps advising the woman that a long life could be lived in some fashion other than childbearing.

Often, the birthing mother's fear-based instincts against male physicians were sound, since male-centric, "heroic" measures too often resulted in death or disfigurement. Men insisted on "scientific" delivery implements, including ergot, inhalers, bottles of ether, and, that most terrible of all implements, the forceps. Many turned to the new skill of embry-otomy (removing an embryo surgically), in which perfectly normal cases often ended in "atrocious butchery." "Beware of rash and hasty resorts to mechanical aid," cautioned professors of midwifery, who felt that so long as a man was "posted at bed-side" then "instruments *must* be used." A callous attitude often dictated harsh, even unnecessary surgery. Mary Dixon-Jones held out against a male sur-gical consensus during a long and "tedious" labor she attended in 1894. The men urged a craniotomy, in which the child's head would be drilled in order for it to be removed from the womb. But the doctor "spoke as a woman," insisting upon a live delivery. She responded not only to immediate medical dictates, but to the intuited needs of the mother. "The child must not be destroyed," said Dixon. "All the long eight years this woman has had no baby; this will be her comfort, her happiness; it may be her last; we must save it. I insist . . . that it not be destroyed." Terrified women knew they could be destroyed by the unnatural devices used to assist the "natural" powers. "One of the most fearful perineal lacerations I ever saw," said Dr. Belle Carver in the *Woman's Medical Journal* of July 1895 was that inflicted upon a "retiring and sensitive" woman who was so terrified of an operation that she refused all medical assis-tance in the hopes of not being irreparably wounded. Often so blatant was the butchery that men and women pleaded *against* having a doctor attend. On March 10, 1845, after his patient's forty-hour labor, one sorry physician determined that she lacked strength, her uterus lacked resolve, and he must extri-cate the child piecemeal with a jackknife—even retiring to the barn to sharpen the blade. He "made a sudden plunge . . . gave the knife a rotary movement, and withdrew it to think what was next best." Nature intervened, the uterus gathered its strength, and the child was born, wounded in the right temporal region. Of such obstetric practitioners, Gregory exhorted, "Practice butchery rather than midwifery, for in that case they could sell what they slay!" "For baby cases women generally preferred a lady doctor to a man," wrote Wyoming's Bessie Efner, "for these cases gave me an opportunity to gain the confidence of people for other cases."

A famous male physician of the early 1900s suggested that every mother be deliv-ered of her first baby by a method dubbed "prophylactic forceps," to be used after "the opening to the vagina has been cut." The method was adopted by specialists only, and freely administered, along with cesarean sec-tions, to mothers at the slightest provocation. Not all invasive birth techniques were male-

> *Behold the miracle of childbirth, again and again easing the pain of passing from this world.*
>
> — MARY CANAGA ROWLAND, M.D.

inspired, but the preponderance of men in medicine lent a crisis-based interpretation to even the simplest events. On the other hand, older midwives, women physicians, and thoughtful obstetricians "made an art" of slow, careful delivery of a baby's head without injury to the muscles of the perineum—a delicate, natural, and time-consuming process destroyed by the technological invasion of forceps, cesarean section, and episiotomy.

Could men, it was wondered in the darker medical years before the end of the nineteenth century, even learn the art of producing a "natural and quiet birth"? Injured women inevitably blamed the doctor for their condition. "Few know how difficult it is to get into the womb, with the tedious means of dilation generally at hand," wrote male practitioner Dr. Q. C. Smith of Texas in 1888. In the late part of the century there were many deformed children who had been materially injured by such operations and women who could no longer bear children again because of severe cases of prolapsed uterus caused by poor medical care.

Who were these unqualified doctors? Often they were drunk or otherwise undependable. In addition, many were addicted to narcotics, and their slack and repugnant personal habits often incurred the wrath of the community. When Mary Canaga Rowland was forced to use a male doctor to assist her in deliveries, she shuddered at his personal habits, which included a severe morphine addiction. Even worse, she wrote, he "used no antiseptic [and] looked so dirty I hated to have him do

anything. . . . I really thought my patient that day might die from infection because the doctor was so dirty." Rowland practiced impeccable hygiene, seeing to it in every case that "everything was as clean as possible." When the baby was born, she never left any part of the placenta or membrane, knowing it would cause an infection. "A doctor deals with human life," she maintained. "And if [she] is careless [she] loses the most precious thing an individual has." In this, female rural doctors often felt bound to their obstetric patients by virtue of their shared biological experience, as well as the "ideology of domesticity and nurturance, which women as well as men in society accepted as the proper order of things," as described by historian Judith Leavitt.

Commonly, however, expectant frontier mothers had difficulty actually finding a doctor, particularly one who would make house calls. "The two Doctors in our county were both out, miles away when we wanted them," wrote a rural Minnesota woman as late as 1921. "Neither one got back to the office until our Babe was several hours old." Her final conclusion? That without him, they "got along fine."

Women physicians, whether from empathy or a stronger sense of duty, were more involved. As a matter of course, Helen MacKnight Doyle "let down the gates in barbed-wire fences to reach women in confinement, babies with pneumonia, and those afflicted with all the diseases and injuries that make up the practice of the country doctor." "I can easily number my home-delivered babies at more than a hundred," mused Dr. Portia

Lubchenco McKnight. Obstetrics gradually become the purview of women, and the talents of the nineteenth-century female accoucheur were widely advertised in treatises and broadsides. A typical offering was taken from an early *Boston Post*:

CONSULT
DOCTOR WALLER
(ACCOUCHEUR)
On All Diseases
Particularly
Midwifery And Diseases
of Women and Children

Fevers And Agues
Diseases of the Skin
Bone Setting, Sore Legs
Tooth Drawing
Squinting Cured

A doctor's skill was part practice, part education, and only an experienced practitioner knew if a baby was coming too fast, or how to ease a child from the birth canal to avoid tearing. "The uterus has the strongest muscle in the body and it contracted in my hand like a vise," wrote physician Mary Canaga Rowland, marveling at the emerging welter of feet, legs, and tiny body. "My hand and arm were so paralyzed that I let the other doctor finish delivering the baby." No wonder it was so difficult. In the birth process the birth canal had to stretch to a size to admit a baby's head, the stretching accomplished by sporadically contracting the womb muscles, which pushed the baby's head against a tiny opening. Fifteen to thirty contractions per hour would "mold the baby's head from the shape of a ball to that of a sausage" while the mother's tissues became "soft and jellylike."

A female doctor, perhaps a mother herself, could grasp the emotional idiom of childbearing, as could the midwife. Katherine Gibson Fougera, riding with Custer's cavalry, described the expertise of a Mexican midwife. "Few births occurred without her expert help. She was a careful midwife, no less an embryo trained nurse, and she handled those babies not only with efficiency but with marked tenderness as well." The fact that she turned out to be a female impersonator, an ex-soldier who preferred to live and work as a woman, did not seem to interfere with her work.

Within such limited choices, no wonder some women preferred to deliver alone, or with the assistance of friends or family. Martha Morrison Minto, who had married at fifteen, was matter-of-fact about childbirth: "When my second child was born my husband and I were alone, three miles from any woman or doctor; my oldest child [was] 18 months old." Her only discomfort stemmed from the fact that her husband had to attend her at this private moment and perform women's work, such as the washing of the family clothes and also the birth cloths.

Physicians who understood and believed the germ theory would sterilize everything thoroughly. Typical was Dr. Bertha Van Hoosen:

In the big dishpan I had ready: boiled forceps, a linen cord, a few needles and some silk sutures. I had chloroform and ergot, sterilized cotton and gauze, a bedpan, towels, a baby bathtub, and a solution of permanganate of potassium. This solution would be applied to my hands and arms until they were a dark mahogany color which was removed by scrubbing in a solution of oxalic acid. . . . I was confident I could conduct a delivery free from infection.

Their greatest fear: that contamination would bring on childbed fever, often fatal. Not until 1843 did Oliver Wendell Holmes link childbed fever to contagion; in 1847 the Viennese scientist Ignaz Philipp Semmelweis recommended washing the hands in chlorine water before delivering babies, and in the 1870s Lister applied the germ theory to childbirth. "I aired, scrubbed, boiled and soaked in bichloride of mercury solution the sheets, mattresses, beds, walls, floors and the patients and doctors gowns," wrote Dr. Bertha Van Hoosen. "I did this not once, but day after day." She was haunted at night by dreams of "four tall coffins" looming over the foot of her bed. Patients were also haunted. The rural female population, as late as the 1920s, seemed woefully uninformed about conception and the birth process. Even as late as 1915 prenatal care was unheard of—the female doctor often saw many of her patients for the first time when she went to their homes to deliver their infants. Dr. Amelia Dann could only shake her head when one rural farm wife complained of pains, headaches, weak legs, and exhaustion. With six children, she was terrified of another pregnancy—and with good reason. Weekly the woman dreaded "Nail Day," the one day during the week when she cut all the finger- and toenails of six children, plus those of her husband and herself. An unkempt litter of one hundred and sixty dirty nails! Had she known of such a thing before marriage, she sobbed, she would still be single.

Rapid emigration had separated women from supportive female family members; in their isolated settings, without recourse to friends, medical advice, or often, extended family, many women in the 1920s wrote to the government asking about parturition, nursing, birth control, and even mental health, and always begging for a personal visit from a government-assigned female physician. The idea of the Children's Bureau had emerged from a conference held in 1909 by President Theodore Roosevelt, the first of a series of White House conferences on the health of children. The bureau was immensely influential and was staffed, for the most part, by civic-minded and energetic women, many of whom were physicians. One letter received by the bureau reveals the bleakness of life in the rural West. Mrs. A.P. wrote to an unnamed Dr. H. from Wyoming in the early 1900s. She lived sixty-five miles from a doctor and was "filled with perfect horror" that she would be *very* badly torn . . . through the rectum" during delivery, as had occurred with her two other children. "If there is *anything* that I can do to escape being torn again wont you let me know," she pleaded. The female Dr. H. evidently ministered in such a way as to calm the woman's fears and touch a deep chord of sisterly compassion.

When medicines failed, forceps, or "instruments," were viewed as the last resort by patients and doctors alike—used only when the baby was breech, and might be shifted from the transverse position in the pelvis into a cephalic presentation. A doctor must know, instinctively, how to reach in and turn a baby in the womb, and had to understand the "malposition, malformations, and emergencies" that stood between the birthing mother and the delivery of a healthy child into the world—skills that were often learned with no more than a "worn leather pelvis and a shabby leather baby" demonstrated quickly to predominantly male medical students.

Where science failed, good sense often prevailed: Dr. Lillian Heath, of Rawlins, Wyoming, mingled midwifery, medicine, and common sense in treating one of her first births out of medical school, where the mother, a "great big healthy girl," was "lazy" and afraid she would be in pain. It was her first baby, wrote Heath, and

she refused to "work on the delivery—just laid there hour after hour. Finally I just rolled her over and swatted her backside good three or four times. The delivery started soon after and she gave normal birth to a big healthy boy without any trouble!"

In a ten-year period Mary Glassen delivered "nearly 1,000 babies, mostly in homes." According to all reports, her "luck was good—she never lost a mother." Nor did she have a case of puerperal fever. Not so fortunate was Dr. Elizabeth Cushier, whose first year of residency in 1873 was met by an epidemic of puerperal fever. It was the first time she had been in close contact with illness and suffering, and she found the days "busy and anxious." Although her patients recovered, it was more luck than science, she decided, looking back upon a time of limited knowledge of antisepsis. "I wonder that they did not all die."

> *Certainly the suffering is indescribable and I guess not to be comprehended by those who have not passed through it.*
>
> —MARTHA SLAYTON

I had been with laboring women from the first annoying discomfort to their final catastrophic release, so sudden that the long strain and tension gave way to chattering teeth and shaking limbs. . . . I had admired their determination to be brave, and willingness to pay the price of motherhood though it might be great. . . .

The intense suffering had shocked

me when women in labor cast aside all conventionalities, and grasped anything or anyone, with the ferocity of birds of prey, crying out and begging piteously for help, "Give me something, anything! Give me poison! I cannot live! I cannot stand another pain! . . . I am dying — I am gone." Over and over, repeating these appealing words until, exhausted, they lapsed into unconsciousness.

Changes in the attitude toward childbearing determined the medical course taken by women physicians. In the late 1800s anthropologists believed that primitive people had far fewer parturition-related complications than white women, whose "idle life, abuses of civilization . . . dissipations and follies of fashion" made them incapable of withstanding the stress of labor. Such weakness invited the use of intervention: anesthesia, analgesia, and instruments, even for the most normal of labors.

Maternity cases were frequent, success varied, and the despairing loss of either mother or child a brooding, ever-present reality. For the young Claudia Potter, death came mysteriously after a normal delivery in Little River, a remote Texas setting. "I felt her pulse in a few minutes after delivery and it was more rapid than before. I then raised the sheet to see if she were having any hemorrhage. Not a bit—the pad was not even stained. I went back to the head and she looked even paler and pulse had less volume. . . . the patient was going into shock [as with] a postpartum hemorrhage but there was not a bit of

blood coming from the vagina."

Proximity to more sophisticated care would have saved her; Potter had to run to the nearest store, use the only telephone in town to call a nearby physician to "get an intravenous ready"—she would be up as quickly as her old Ford could make it. They returned over ditches and rough roads, but half a mile from the patient's house they were stopped by the husband's distraught screaming. "My God, doctor, what did you let her die for?" No amount of training, empathy, or obduracy would protect a doctor from the sorrow of that loss.

Mary Rowland described a typical visit to an outlying patient in Oregon in 1916, when the roads were nearly impassable.

A man came for me to go out into the country seven or eight miles to confine his wife. He took me in an old Model T Ford and every time he came to a mud puddle he stooped, got out, and took off the chains. He repeated the stopping several times on the way there. They lived in an old prune drier in the middle of a plum orchard. I had to wade in mud to my shoe tops to get into their dwelling where they had hung quilts, rag rugs, and whatever else they could to petition off living quarters. . . . There was only one room for living, cooking and sleeping. Nothing looked clean. I had never seen the woman before and she had no prenatal care. Thirty minutes after the baby was born she went into convulsions. I

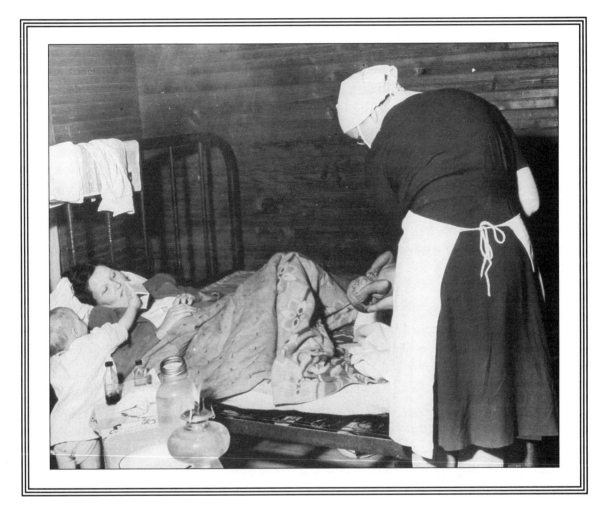

Nurse-midwife Rose Clark assists with home delivery.

National Library of Medicine

gave her two hypodermics, one of mor-
phine to control the convulsions and one
of pilocarpine to open the pores of the
skin. Then I wrapped her in a blanket
wrung out of hot water. . . . Then I gave
her Epsom salts every thirty minutes.

The woman recovered from her childbed experience, but not, it can be assumed, from the long-term effects of her impoverished life.

Childbirth was particularly riveting; Dr. Helen MacKnight Doyle recalled "a kind of tenseness" that settled over the remote Nevada mining community during a childbirth; after delivery, the length, sex, weight, quality of labor, and emotional orientation of the parents was intensely discussed—case review by word of mouth.

Typically, a woman would pour heart and soul into the delivery, unwilling to accept death as the reward for such intense labor. When Dr. Bertha Van Hoosen's sister, Alice, delivered a stillborn child, Bertha refused to leave the corpse. "I held the baby by the feet, head down-ward. . . . Seated on the floor, with my mouth pressed against the baby's, I sucked out the air, and then blew my own breath into those deli-cate lungs." Thirty-five minutes passed with-out a sign of life; five minutes later, a tiny flutter alerted her to life. Then she saw a "faint pink flush" followed by a heartbeat. Unable to give up, she had breathed life into her niece. "I wondered if God felt as I did?" she thought.

Typical of a midnight delivery was that undertaken by Dr. Portia Lubchenco in the hills of South Carolina:

The kerosene lamp began to flicker in the
midst of the delivery, and little light came
from the low fire on the hearth. I advised
the prospective father to fill the lamp
quickly. He went to the kitchen and
returned with an empty jug. My impa-
tience hurried him on his way across the
branch to borrow from neighbors.

The pangs of birth did not wait for a
dilatory dad. I put a newspaper on the
hearth for light. As if to take advantage of
the quick light, a fine baby boy was born.
He was cared for by the light of another
newspaper . . . suddenly, and with no
warning, a twin brother put in his
appearance! When the father arrived,
casually carrying a jug by its string han-
dle, I was almost angry with him. Anger
faded quickly, however, in the miracle of
birth, and we rejoiced together. . . . This
is the nearest I ever came to delivering a
baby in the dark.

Bertha Van Hoosen wrote: "In 1892 . . . home deliveries were the vogue." There was a marked difference between the obstetric atti-tude in the nineteenth century, when all deliv-eries were adjudged normal, and in the twentieth century, when any delivery may suddenly be considered abnormal.

Gender, however, was not an automatic vote of confidence, as revealed in the memoirs of Utah pioneer Hulda Smith, describing her own delivery by a female doctor. The physi-cian was first deemed "very nice," "very capa-ble," and possessing a diploma from the

University of Stockholm, Sweden, bearing the signature of the king. Smith began her travail with every confidence, eventually tumbling into pain and disillusionment before a final regaining of confidence. Wrote Smith:

I had a very hard, lingering labor, and I fully believe it was one calling for instrumental assistance, which [the doctor] understood, but at that time [we] were so prejudiced against doctors that even men doctors were very much criticized who dared to use instruments, and she, being a woman, was under far greater restraint; Few [women] had ventured far from the old and well-beaten path of woman's true sphere as to step into a professional career. She had, I believe, saved the lives of several people and gained quite a reputation as an M.D., and also aroused considerable prejudice and unfavorable criticism. When she found my case a difficult one, she tried the old methods of accomplishing the delivery. . . .

Oh! it had been a terrible ordeal. . . .

I thought that I had lost enough blood, also I had lost confidence in her and wouldn't allow her to touch me. [The doctor] went into the next room wringing her hands and saying that I was dying, and she dared not insist on anything for my life might go out with the least excitement, and I would not let her touch me. She came back to me and said, "Just let me put my hand on your stomach. I won't hurt or do anything to you."

I finally allowed her to place her hand on me. Shortly, her warm hand and a little pressure on the uterus began to give me a little relief. Then, as she moved to give a little attention to anything else, I feared she would leave me.

My doctor stayed with me all night and watched over me. She never even laid down. She continued to stay with me for three days.

Once Bessie Efner spent two weeks without changing her clothes or sleeping in her own bed: "I became so exhausted from loss of sleep that I was unable to go on . . . but I had to get some sleep, so I wrapped myself in my heavy fur coat, used my instrument bag as a pillow and lay down on the floor in one corner of the kitchen and went to sleep. The people continued to do their work as usual, walked all around me and even stepped over me. . . . I never heard a sound.

In addition to the night-and-day duty was also the boredom "of the long and tedious waiting for the arrival of the baby" as well as bedbugs, "man's worst enemies." Wrote Efner: "As I look back to those years of my practice on the frontier and recall . . . the hardships, the professional handicaps, the hazardous drives, the long and tedious vigils in the crowded homesteaders' shacks and the meager financial rewards . . . I wonder now how I had the courage to go on."

Bibliography

❧❧❧❧❧

1. FRONTIER MEDICINE

1790 to 1840 physicians statistics: Elizabeth Blackwell, *Pioneer Work in Opening the Medical Profession to Women: Autobiographical Sketches.* Kate B. Carter, *Heart Throbs of the West,* vol. 7 (Salt Lake City: Daughters of the Utah Pioneers, 1946) (New York: Shocken Books, 1977).

Childbirth: Richard W. Wertz, *Lying In* (New Haven: Yale University Press, 1986), 49. Judith Leavitt, *Brought to Bed: Childbearing in America, 1750 to 1950* (New York: Oxford University Press, 1986), 113. Sally G. McMillen, *Motherhood in the Old South* (Baton Rouge and London: Louisiana State University Press, 1990).

Dorothea Dix: Beatrice Levin, *Women and Medicine* (Lincoln: Media Publishing, 1988).

Doctors' exclusionary practices: Frances R. Packard, *History of Medicine in the United States,* vols. I and II (New York: Paul B. Hoeber, Inc., 1931).

Duden's Observations: Gottfried Duden, *Report on a Journey to the Western States of North America* (Columbia: The State Historical Society of Missouri and University of Missouri Press, 1980).

Bessie Efner: Alfred M. Rehwinkel, *Dr. Bessie: The Life Story and Romance of a Pioneer Lady Doctor* (St. Louis: Concordia Publishing House, 1963).

Galvanism: David Armstrong and Elizabeth Armstrong, *The Great American Medicine Show* (New York: Prentice-Hall, 1991).

Carter and Charlotte Hawk: *Green River Star* (Wyoming), August 26, 1891. Documents from the Wyoming Historical Society, including an article written by Hawk's niece, Marian Hodgkinson, "Wyoming Wasn't 'equal' for Dr. Charlotte."

The Drs. Hawks: Esther Hill Hawks, "War Reminiscences—1861" (unpublished journals).

Harriet Hunt: Beatrice Levin, *Women and Medicine* (Lincoln: Media Publishing, 1988).

Judith Leavitt: Judith Leavitt, *Brought to Bed: Childbearing in America, 1750 to 1950* (New York: Oxford University Press, 1986).

Logan's observations: Robert F. Karolevitz, *Doctors of the Old West: A Pictorial History of Medicine on the Frontier* (Seattle: Superior Publishing Company, 1967).

Florence Nightingale: Beatrice Levin, *Women and Medicine* (Lincoln, Nebraska: Media Publishing, 1988).

Nostrums: Phyllis M. Japp, "Pioneer Medicines: Doctors, Nostrums, and Folk Cures," *Journal of the West* (34:5), August 1987. William G. Rothstein, *American*

Physicians in the Nineteenth Century: From Sects to Science (Baltimore and London: The Johns Hopkins University Press, 1971). Ronald L. Numbers and Judith Walzer Leavitt, *Wisconsin Medicine: Historical Perspectives* (Madison: The University of Wisconsin Press, 1981).

Rebirthing: *Maternity Letters from Working Women,* collected by the Women's Cooperative Guild (London: G. Bell and Sons, Ltd., 1916).

Schoop's Cough Remedy and health coffee: *Whapeton Times* (North Dakota, 1911), cited in *Daniel's Texas Medical Journal: A Monthly Journal of Medicine and Surgery,* vol. 111 (Austin, Texas: July 1887 to June 1888).

M. Strong's book: Moses M. Strong, *History of the Territory of Wisconsin* (Madison: Democratic Printing Company, 1885).

Victorian society: Mary Patricia Ryan, *American Society and the Cult of Domesticity, 1830–1860,* dissertation (University of California, Santa Barbara, 1971). Ann Douglas, *The Feminization of American Culture* (New York: Avon, 1977).

Inez Whalin: Mollie Ladd Taylor, *Raising a Baby the Government Way: Mothers' Letters to the Children's Bureau 1915–1932* (New Brunswick, New Jersey, and London: Rutgers University Press, 1942).

Brigham Young: Susan Evans McCloud, *Not in Vain* (Salt Lake City: Bookcraft, 1984).

2. MEDICINE BY DEGREE

James Miranda Barry: Beatrice Levin, *Women and Medicine* (Lincoln, Nebraska: Media Publishing, 1988).

Elizabeth Blackwell: Elizabeth Blackwell, *Pioneer Work in Opening the Medical Profession to Women: Autobiographical Sketches* (New York: Shocken Books, 1977). Beatrice Levin, *Women and Medicine* (Lincoln: Media Publishing, 1988). Mary Roth Walsh, *"Doctors Wanted: No Women Need Apply": Sexual Barriers in the Medical Profession, 1835–1975* (New Haven and London: Yale University Press, 1977). Carol Lopate, *Women in Medicine* (Baltimore: Johns Hopkins Press, 1982).

Helen MacKnight Doyle: Dr. Helen MacKnight, *A Child Went Forth: The Autobiography of Dr. Helen MacKnight Doyle* (New York: Gotham House, 1934).

European medical schools: Rosalie Slaughter Morton, *A Woman Surgeon* (New York: Frederick A. Stokes Co., 1937).

Harriet Hunt: Beatrice Levin, *Women and Medicine* (Lincoln: Media Publishing, 1988).

Dr. Lavinder and Dr. Adams: Katherine W. Wright, "History of Women in Medicine, a Symposium: Nineteenth Century or Transitional Period," *Bulletin of the Medical Library Association,* vol. 44, no. 1 (January 1956).

Portia Lubchenco McKnight: Anna C. Petteys. *Dr. Portia: Her First Fifty Years in Medicine* (Denver: Golden Bell Press, 1964).

Kate Mead: Kate Campbell Hurd-Mead, M.D. *History of Women in Medicine* (Boston: Milford House, 1973).

Medical education in the nineteenth century: Mary Roth Walsh, *"Doctors Wanted: No Women Need Apply": Sexual Barriers in the Medical Profession, 1835–1975* (New Haven and London: Yale University Press, 1977). Katherine W. Wright, "History of Women in Medicine, a Symposium: Nineteenth Century or Transitional

Period," *Bulletin of the Medical Library Association,* vol. 44, no. 1 (January 1956). Ruth J. Abram, *Send Us a Lady Physician* (New York: W. W. Norton & Co., 1985). Kate Campbell Hurd-Mead, M.D. *History of Women in Medicine* (Boston: Milford House, 1973). *Medical Women of America* (New York: Froben Press, 1933).

Mary Canaga Rowland: Elizabeth Smith, *A Woman with a Purpose: The Diaries of Elizabeth Smith, 1872–1884* (Toronto: University of Toronto Press, 1980).

Hilla Sheriff: *Journal of the South Carolina Medical Association,* vol. 89, no. 1 (January 1993).

Rosalie Slaughter: Rosalie Slaughter Morton, *A Woman Surgeon* (New York: Frederick A. Stokes Co., 1937).

Elizabeth Smith: Elizabeth Smith, *A Woman with a Purpose: The Diaries of Elizabeth Smith, 1872–1884* (Toronto: University of Toronto Press, 1980).

Statistics on page 27: Judith Mandlebaum-Schmid, M.D., "Women & Medicine: An Unequal Past, A Common Future" (May 1992) and "The Indian Health Service" (January 1993).

Helen Taussig: Katherine W. Wright, "History of Women in Medicine, a Symposium: Nineteenth Century or Transitional Period," *Bulletin of the Medical Library Association,* vol. 44, no. 1 (January 1956).

Carol Lopate, *Women in Medicine* (Baltimore: The Johns Hopkins Press, 1982).

Bertha Van Hoosen: Bertha Van Hoosen, *Petticoat Surgeon* (Chicago: Pellegrini & Cudahy, 1947).

Women's Medical College of Pennsylvania incident: Gulielma Fell, *The Lady of the Grove: History of the Woman's College.* (Philadelphia, Penn.: J.B. Lippincott Co., 1850).

Women's medical schools and hospitals: Heins, Marilyn, "Women in Medicine: A Historical Perspective," *The Internist* (March 1986). Harriet Hunt, *Glances and Glimpses* (Boston: John P. Jewett and Co., 1856). Ruth J. Abram, *Send Us a Lady Physician* (New York: W. W. Norton & Co.,1985).

Chester Worthington: "Letters," mss. (Arizona State University, Tempe).

3 . W O M E N S C O R N E D

Susan Anderson: Virginia Cornell, *Doc Susie* (New York: Ivy Books, 1991).

Elizabeth Blackwell: Margo Horn, *Pioneer Work in Opening the Medical Profession to Women: Autobiographical Sketches* (New York: Shocken Books, 1977).

Anna Darrow: William M. Straight, M.D., "The Lady Doctor of the Grove," *Journal of the Florida Medical Association,* vol. 55, no. 8 (August 1968).

Helen MacKnight Doyle: Dr. Helen MacKnight, *A Child Went Forth: The Autobiography of Dr. Helen MacKnight Doyle* (New York: Gotham House, 1934).

Bessie Efner: Alfred M. Rehwinkel, *Dr. Bessie: The Life Story and Romance of a Pioneer Lady Doctor* (St. Louis: Concordia Publishing House, 1963).

Georgia Arbuckle Fix: Judy Alter, "Women Who Made the West," *Pioneer Doctor* (St. Louis: Concordia Publishing, 1983).

Evelyn Frisbie: Jake Spidel, Jr., *Doctors of Medicine in New Mexico: A History of Health and Medical Practice, 1886–1986.* (Albuquerque: The University of New Mexico Press, 1986).

Sarah Grimké: Kate Campbell Mead, "Medical Women of America," *Medical Review of Reviews* (March 1933).

Jane Bruce Guignard: "Jane Bruce Guignard, M.D.: 1876–1963," *Journal of the South Carolina Medical Association* (January, 1993). H. H. DuBose, *Jane Bruce Guignard, M.D.,* unpublished manuscript.

Charlotte and Jacob Hawk: Carter and Charlotte Hawk, *Green River Star* (Wyoming), August 26, 1891. Documents from the Wyoming Historical Society, including an article written by Hawk's niece, Marian Hodgkinson, "Wyoming Wasn't 'Equal' for Dr. Charlotte."

Mary Hays: Bernice Larson Webb, *Lady Doctor on a Homestead: The Thomas County Years, 1879–1890, of Mary Amelia Hay* (Colby, Kansas: Western Plains Heritage Publications, 1987).

Lillian Heath: Lillian Heath as told to Neal E. Miller, *The History of 111 West Lincoln Way,* 1954 manuscript 296A (Laramie: Wyoming Historical Society).

Sophie Herzog: Cindi Myers, "Daring Dr. Sophie," *True West,* vol. 41, no. 7 (July 1994).

Eleanor Lawney: Robert H. Shikes M.D., *Rocky Mountain Medicine: Doctors, Drugs and Disease in Early Colorado* (Boulder: Johnson Books, 1986).

Florence Sabin: Beatrice Levin, *Women and Medicine* (Lincoln: Media Publishing, 1988).

Elizabeth Smith: *A Woman with a Purpose: The Diaries of Elizabeth Smith, 1872–1884* (Toronto: University of Toronto Press, 1980).

Statistics on number of women M.D.'s in 1900: Gloria Moldow, *Women Doctors in Gilded-Age Washington: Race, Gender and Professionalization* (Urbana and Chicago: University of Illinois Press, 1987).

Bertha Van Hoosen: Bertha Van Hoosen, *Petticoat Surgeon* (Chicago: Pellegrini & Cudahy, 1947).

Caroline Van Horne: Alice Lake, *Journal of the American Medical Women's Association,* vol. 22, no. 6.

Women in the AMA: Geoffrey Marks and William K. Beatty, *Women in White* (New York: Charles Scribner's Sons, 1987). Regina Markell-Sanchez, *Sympathy and Science: Women Physicians in American Medicine* (New York: Oxford University Press, 1985). Carol Lopate, *Women in Medicine* (Baltimore: The Johns Hopkins Press, 1982). "Women in Medicine," *Journal of the American Medical Women Association,* vol. 1, no. 3 (1946).

4. WHO WILL BE A DOCTOR?

Elizabeth Blackwell: Elizabeth Blackwell, *Pioneer Work in Opening the Medical Profession to Women: Autobiographical Sketches* (New York: Shocken Books, 1977).

Mattie Hughes Cannon: John Sillito and Constance L. Lieber, eds. *Letters from Exile: The Correspondence of Martha Hughes Cannon and Angus M. Cannon* (Salt Lake City: Signature Books in Association with Smith Research Associates, 1989).

Aurora Leigh: Edward Fitzgerald, "Chronomoros."

Hannah E. Longshore: Beatrice Levin, *Women and Medicine* (Lincoln: Media Publishing, 1988), 29. Kate Campbell Mead, M.D., "Medical Women of America," *Medical Review of Reviews* (March 1933).

Sophie McClelland: Personal narrative of Alice Hamburg (Berkeley, Calif.).

Claudia Potter: Dr. Claudia Potter, *Recollections of Anesthesia Practice (1906–1948),* manuscript (Park Ridge, Ill.: Museum of Anesthesiology, 1992).

Hiram Rutherford: Willene Hendrick and George Hendrick, eds., "Dr. Hiram Rutherford 1840–1848," *On the Illinois Frontier* (Carbondale: Southern Illinois University Press, 1981).

Amelia Dann: Helen Dann Stringer, *Millie M.D. The Story of a Nineteenth Century Woman, 1846–1927* (Utica: North Country Books, 1992).

Isabel Davenport: Isabel M. Davenport, M.D., "Garden Work for Women in Public Institutions," *Illinois Medical Journal* (1918).

Georgia Arbuckle Fix: J. Grassick, M.D., *North Dakota Medical Sketches and Abstracts* (Bismarck: North Dakota Medical Association, 1926).

Mary Glassen: Vera Chance Ward, *How to Sleep on a Windy Night* (Phillipsburg, Kansas: Clar-Mar Press, 1970).

Jane Bruce Guignard: Jane Guignard Curry, "Jane Bruce Guignard, M.D.: 1876–1963," *Journal of the South Carolina Medical Association,* vol. 89, no. 1 (January 1993). H. H. DuBose, *Jane Bruce Guignard, M.D.,* unpublished manuscript.

Lucinda Hall: Frederick C. Waite, "Dr. Lucinda Susannah (Capen) Hall: The First Woman to Receive a Medical Degree from a New England Institution," *New England Journal of Medicine* (March 22, 1934).

Lillian Heath: Lillian Heath as told to Neal E. Miller, *The History of 111 West Lincoln Way,* 1954 manuscript 296A (Laramie: Wyoming Historical Society).

Sophie Herzog: Cindi Myers, "Daring Dr. Sophie," *True West,* vol. 41, no. 7 (July 1994).

Dr. Mary Lavinder and Dr. Adams: Katherine W. Wright, "History of Women in Medicine, a Symposium: Nineteenth Century or Transitional Period," *Bulletin of the Medical Library Association,* vol. 44, no. 1 (January 1956).

Hannah Longshore: Collection of the Longshore Family Papers (1819–1902), p. 75.

Gloria Moldow: Gloria Moldow, *Women Doctors in Gilded-Age Washington: Race, Gender and Professionalization* (Urbana and Chicago: University of Illinois Press, 1987).

Jane Myers: Kate Campbell Mead, "Medical Women of America," *Medical Review of Reviews* (March 1933).

Bethenia Owens-Adair: *Dr. Owens-Adair: Some of Her Life Experiences* (Portland, Oregon, 1905), quoted from Cathy Luchetti, *Women of the West* (New York: Orion, 1982).

Mary Canaga Rowland: Mary Canaga Rowland, *The Memoirs of a Frontier Woman Doctor* (Seattle: Storm Peak Press, 1994).

Lena Schreier: "Utah's Oldest Doctor is a Lady," *Utah Medical Bulletin* (March 1971).

Hilla Sheriff: Henry Heins, M.D., and Donna H. Bryan, "Hilla Sheriff, M.D., 1903–1988: First Lady of Public Health," *Journal of the South Carolina Medical Association,* vol. 89, no. 1 (January 1993).

Ellis Shipp: Susan Evans McCloud, *Not in Vain* (Salt Lake City: Bookcraft, 1992).

Rosalie Slaughter: Rosalie Slaughter Morton, *A Woman Surgeon* (New York: Frederick A. Stokes Co., 1937).

Elizabeth Smith: *A Woman with a Purpose: The Diaries of Elizabeth Smith, 1872–1884* (Toronto: University of Toronto Press, 1980).

Ellen Smith: Ruth J. Abram, *Send Us a Lady Physician* (New York: W. W. Norton & Co., 1985).

Bertha Van Hoosen: *Petticoat Surgeon* (Chicago: Pellegrini & Cudahy, 1947).

Mary Walker: Beatrice Levin, *Women and Medicine: Autobiographical Sketches* (Lincoln: Media Publishing, 1988).

Lillian Welsh: *Reminiscences of Thirty Years in Baltimore* (Baltimore: Norman, Remington Co., 1925).

5. Early Inspirations

Sarah Campbell Allan: W. Curtis Worthington, M.D., "Psychiatrist and Humanitarian Sarah Campbell Allan (1861–1954): South Carolina's First Licensed Woman Physician," *Journal of the South Carolina Medical Association,* vol. 89, no. 1 (January 1993). *Allan, SC. Diary for Jan. 1, 1900– May 16, 1900,* manuscript #640 (Charleston, South Carolina: Waring Historical Library, Medical University of South Carolina).

Sarah Armstrong: Katherine W. Wright, "History of Women in Medicine, a Symposium: Nineteenth Century or Transitional Period," *Bulletin of the Medical Library Association,* vol. 44, no. 1.

Anne Austin: James G. Ward, Jr., M.D., "That Crazy Anne Austin: Anne Austin Young, M.D. 1892–1989," *Journal of South Carolina Medical Society,* vol. 89, no. 1 (January 1993).

Emily Dunning Barringer: Emily Dunning Barringer, *Bowery to Bellevue* (New York: W. W. Norton, 1950).

Elizabeth Blackwell: Margo Horn, *Pioneer Work in Opening the Medical Profession to Women: Autobiographical Sketches* (New York: Shocken Books, 1977).

Esther Clayson: Esther Lovejoy, 1890–1894, *Oregon Historical Quarterly,* vol. 75, no. 1 (March 1974; Portland: Oregon Historical Society).

Elizabeth Cushier: Elizabeth B. Thelberg, M.D., ed., "Autobiography of Dr. Elizabeth Cushier," *Medical Review of Reviews* (March 1933).

Amelia Dann: Helen Dann Stringer, *Millie M.D., The Story of a Nineteenth Century Woman, 1846–1927* (Utica: North Country Books, 1992).

Anna Darrow: William M. Straight. M.D., "The Lady Doctor of the Grove," *Journal of the Florida Medical Association,* vol. 55, no. 8 (August 1968).

Helen MacKnight Doyle: *A Child Went Forth: The Autobiography of Dr. Helen MacKnight Doyle* (New York: Gotham House, 1934).

Emily Dunning: Geoffrey Marks and William K. Beatty, *Women in White* (New York: Charles Scribner's Sons, 1987).

Bessie Efner: Alfred M. Rehwinkel, *Dr. Bessie: The Life Story and Romance of a Pioneer Lady Doctor* (St. Louis: Concordia Publishing House, 1963).

Georgia Arbuckle Fix: Judy Alter, "Women Who Made the West," *Pioneer Doctor* (St. Louis: Concordia Publishing, 1983).

Mary Glassen: Vera Chance Ward, *How to Sleep on a Windy Night* (Phillipsburg, Kansas: Clar-Mar Press, 1970).

Jane Bruce Guignard: Jane Guignard Curry, "Jane Bruce Guignard, M.D.: 1876–1963," *Journal of the South Carolina Medical Association,* vol. 89, no. 1 (January 1993). H. H.

DuBose, *Jane Bruice Guignard, M.D.,* unpublished manuscript.

Elizabeth Hampsten: *Read This Only to Yourself: The Private Writings of Midwestern Women, 1880–1910* (Bloomington: Indiana University Press, 1982).

Esther Hill Hawks: *The Daily American* (Manchester, New Hampshire: Grebe, August 27, 1861).

Lillian Heath: Lillian Heath as told to Neal E. Miller, *The History of 111 West Lincoln Way,* 1954 manuscript 296A (Laramie: Wyoming State Museum).

Sophie Herzog: Cindi Myers, "Daring Dr. Sophie," *True West,* vol. 41, no. 7 (July 1994).

Harriet Hunt: Beatrice Levin, *Women and Medicine* (Lincoln: Media Publishing, 1988).

Hannah Myers Longshore: Beatrice Levin, *Women and Medicine* (Lincoln: Media Publishing, 1988). Kate Campbell Mead, M.D., "Medical Women of America," *Medical Review of Reviews* (March 1933).

Louise Abigail Mayo: Robert F. Karolevitz, *Doctors of the Old West: A Pictorial History of Medicine on the Frontier* (Seattle: Superior Publishing Company, 1967).

Florence Nightingale: Beatrice Levin, *Women and Medicine* (Lincoln: Media Publishing, 1988). Katherine W. Wright, "History of Women in Medicine, a Symposium: Nineteenth Century or Transitional Period," *Bulletin of the Medical Library Association,* vol. 44, no. 1 (January 1956).

Bethenia Owens-Adair: *Dr. Owens-Adair: Some of Her Life Experiences* (Portland, Oregon: Mann & Beach, 1905), quoted from Cathy Luchetti, *Women of the West* (New York: Orion, 1982).

Claudia Potter: Dr. Claudia Potter, *Recollections of Anesthesia Practice (1906–1948),* manuscript (Museum of Anesthesiology).

Fannie Quain: *Read This Only to Yourself: The Private Writings of Midwestern Women, 1880–1910* (Bloomington: Indiana University Press, 1982).

Hilla Sheriff: Henry Heins, M.D., and Donna H. Bryan, "Hilla Sheriff, M.D. 1903–1988: First Lady of Public Health," *Journal of the South Carolina Medical Association,* vol. 89, no. 1 (January 1993).

Ellis Shipp: Susan Evans McCloud, *Not in Vain* (Salt Lake City: Bookcraft, 1992).

Rosalie Slaughter: Beatrice Levin, *Women and Medicine* (Lincoln: Media Publishing, 1988).

Mrs. L. C. Smith: Robert F. Karolevitz, *Doctors of the Old West: A Pictorial History of Medicine on the Frontier* (Seattle: Superior Publishing Company, 1967).

Mary Harris Thompson: Ruth J. Abram, *Send Us a Lady Physician* (New York: W. W. Norton & Co., 1985).

Martha Spalding Thurston: Robert F. Karolevitz, *Doctors of the Old West: A Pictorial History of Medicine on the Frontier* (Seattle: Superior Publishing Company, 1967).

Bertha Van Hoosen: Bertha Van Hoosen, *Petticoat Surgeon* (Chicago: Pellegrini & Cudahy, 1947).

Mary Walker: Beatrice Levin, *Women and Medicine* (Lincoln: Media Publishing, 1988).

Mary Walker: Walker manuscript, affidavit of L. J. Woeden at Utica, March 21, 1866 (Syracuse, New York: Syracuse University).

Rhoda Waters: Summers (Kilgore) Chester Worthington, "Letters," manuscript (Tempe: Arizona State University).

Charlotte Wray: Margaret Coffin, *Death in Early America* (New York: Nelson, 1989).

6. FIRST LOVE

Susan Anderson: Virginia Cornell, *Doc Susie* (New York: Ivy Books, 1991).

Nina Baierle: Shirley P. Wheeler, *Dr. Nina and the Panther* (New York: Dodd, Mead & Co., 1976).

Elizabeth Blackwell: Katherine W. Wright. "History of Women in Medicine, a Symposium: Nineteenth Century or Transitional Period," *Bulletin of the Medical Library Association,* vol. 44, no. 1 (January 1956).

Martha Hughes Cannon: John Sillito and Constance L. Lieber, eds. *Letters from Exile: The Correspondence of Martha Hughes Cannon and Angus M. Cannon* (Salt Lake City: Signature Books in Association with Smith Research Associates, 1989).

Denver Medical Times quotes: Robert H. Shikes, M.D., *Rocky Mountain Medicine: Doctors, Drugs and Disease in Early Colorado* (Boulder: Johnson Books, 1986).

Helen MacKnight Doyle: Helen MacKnight Doyle, *A Child Went Forth: The Autobiography of Dr. Helen MacKnight Doyle* (New York: Gotham House, 1934).

Bessie Efner: Alfred M. Rehwinkel, *Dr. Bessie: The Life Story and Romance of a Pioneer Lady Doctor* (St. Louis: Concordia Publishing House, 1963).

Anne Ellis: Anne Ellis, *The Life of an Ordinary Woman* (Boston: Houghton Mifflin, 1990).

Georgia Arbuckle Fix: Judy Alter, "Women Who Made the West," *Pioneer Doctor* (St. Louis: Concordia Publishing, 1983).

Eleanor Galt: William M. Straight, M.D., "The Lady Doctor of the Grove," *Journal of the Florida Medical Association,* vol. 55, no. 8 (August 1968).

Mary Glassen: Vera Chance Ward, *How to Sleep on a Windy Night* (Phillipsburg, Kansas: Clar-Mar Press, 1970).

Mary McKibben Harper: "Medical Women of America," *Medical Review of Reviews* (March 1933).

Hawks: Esther Hill Hawks, "Army Doctor" *The Daily American* (Manchester, New Hampshire), August 27, 1868.

Lillian Heath: Lillian Heath as told to Neal E. Miller, *The History of 111 West Lincoln Way,* 1954 manuscript 296A (Laramie: Wyoming Historical Society).

Harriot Hunt: Beatrice Levin, *Women and Medicine* (Lincoln: Media Publishing, 1988). Katherine W. Wright, "History of Women in Medicine, a Symposium: Nineteenth Century or Transitional Period," *Bulletin of the Medical Library Association,* vol. 44, no. 1 (January 1956).

Bethenia Owens-Adair: Bethenia Owens-Adair, *Dr. Owens-Adair: Some of Her Life Experiences* (Portland, Oregon, 1905), quoted in Cathy Luchetti, *Women of the West* (New York: Orion, 1982).

Romania Bunnell Pratt: Claudia L. Bushman, *Mormon Sisters: Women in Early Utah* (Salt Lake City: Olympus Publishing Co.). Kate B. Carter, *Heart Throbs of the West,* vol. 7 (Salt Lake City: Daughters of the Utah Pioneers, 1946).

Mary Putnam: Katherine W. Wright, "History of Women in Medicine, a Symposium: Nineteenth Century or Transitional

Period," *Bulletin of the Medical Library Association,* vol. 44, no. 1 (January 1956).

Mary Canaga Rowland: Mary Canaga Rowland, *The Memoirs of a Frontier Woman Doctor* (Seattle: Storm Peak Press, 1994).

Lena Schreier: "Utah's Oldest Doctor Is a Lady," *Utah Medical Bulletin* (March 1971).

Statistics about married women physicians: Gloria Moldow, *Women Doctors in Gilded-Age Washington: Race, Gender and Professionalization* (Urbana and Chicago: University of Illinois Press, 1987).

Mabel Ulrich: Mabel Ulrich, "Life in the United States: Extracts from the Diary of an Apostate Woman Physician," *Scribner's Magazine* (June 1933).

Mary Walker: Walker manuscript, affidavit of L. J. Woeden at Utica, March 21, 1866, (Syracuse, New York: Syracuse University).

Lucy Weaver: Ruth J. Abram, *Send Us a Lady Physician* (New York: W. W. Norton & Co., 1985).

7. Dangers Faced, Hardships Borne

Charles Baldwin's diary quotes: Margaret Coffin, *Death in Early America* (New York: Nelson, 1989).

J. J. Best: Enid Bern, "Our Hettinger County Heritage," typescript ms. (Bismarck: North Dakota Heritage Center).

Julia M. Carpenter: Julia Carpenter, "My Journal," unpublished manuscript (Berkeley: University of California Bancroft Library).

Martha Dunn Corey: Ruth J. Abram, *Send Us a Lady Physician* (New York: W. W. Norton & Co., 1985).

Anna Darrow: William M. Straight, M.D., "The Lady Doctor of the Grove," *Journal of the Florida Medical Association,* vol. 55, no. 8 (August 1968).

Helen MacKnight Doyle: Helen Macknight Doyle, *A Child Went Forth: The Autobiography of Dr. Helen MacKnight Doyle* (New York: Gotham House, 1934).

Bessie Efner: Alfred M. Rehwinkel, *Dr. Bessie: The Life Story and Romance of a Pioneer Lady Doctor* (St. Louis: Concordia Publishing House, 1963).

Georgia Arbuckle Fix. Judy Alter, "Women Who Made the West," *Pioneer Doctor* (St. Louis: Concordia Publishing, 1983).

Eleanor Galt: William M. Straight, M.D., "The Lady Doctor of the Grove," *Journal of the Florida Medical Association,* vol. 55, no. 8 (August 1968).

Charlotte Hawk: *Green River Star* (Wyoming), August 26, 1891. Documents from the Wyoming Historical Society, including an article written by Hawk's niece, Marian Hodgkinson, "Wyoming Wasn't 'Equal' for Dr. Charlotte."

Lillian Heath: Lillian Heath as told to Neal E. Miller, *The History of 111 West Lincoln Way,* 1954 manuscript 296A (Laramie: Wyoming Historical Society).

Sophie Herzog: Cindi Myers, "Daring Dr. Sophie," *True West,* vol. 41, no. 7 (July 1994).

Mary Jane McGahan: Louise Shadduck, *Doctors with Buggies, Snowshoes and Planes* (Boise, Idaho:Tamarack Books, 1993).

Portia Lubchenco McKnight: Anna C. Petteys, *Dr. Portia: Her First Fifty Years in Medicine* (Denver: Golden Bell Press, 1964).

Mary Babcock Moore: John A. Forssen, *Petticoat and Stethosocpe: A Montana Legend* (published privately, Mabel Euscherer, 1978).

Jennie C. Murphy: J. Grassick, M.D., *North Dakota Medical Sketches and Abstracts* (Bismarck: North Dakota Medical Association).

Claudia Potter: Dr. Claudia Potter, *Recollections of Anesthesia Practice (1906–1948),* manuscript (Park Ridge, Ill.: Museum of Anesthesiology, 1992).

Mary Canaga Rowland: Mary Canaga Rowland, *The Memoirs of a Frontier Woman Doctor* (Seattle: Storm Peak Press, 1994).

Bertha Van Hoosen: Bertha Van Hoosen, *Petticoat Surgeon* (Chicago: Pellegrini & Cudahy, 1947).

Mary Walker: Walker manuscript, affidavit of L. J. Woeden at Utica, March 21, 1866 (Syracuse, New York: Syracuse University).

Susan Anderson: Virginia Cornell, *Doc Susie* (New York: Ivy Books, 1991).

Os Chase: *The Devil's Lake Journal,* April 1, 1912 (Ramden, North Dakota).

Margaret Coffin's citation of a doctor's diary: Margaret Coffin, *Death in Early America* (New York: Nelson, 1989).

Miriam Colt: Cathy Luchetti, *Women of the West* (New York: Orion Books, 1992).

Anna Darrow: William M. Straight, M.D., "The Lady Doctor of the Grove," *Journal of the Florida Medical Association,* vol. 55, no. 8 (August 1968).

Helen MacKnight Doyle: Helen MacKnight Doyle, *A Child Went Forth: The Autobiography of Dr. Helen MacKnight Doyle* (New York: Gotham House, 1934).

Health and disease concepts in the U.S.A.: Francis R. Packard, *History of Medicine in the United States,* vols. I and II (New York: Paul B. Hoeber, Inc., 1931).

Martha Heywood: Juanita Brooks, ed., *Not by Bread Alone: The Journal of Martha Spence Heywood, 1850–1856* (Salt Lake City: Utah State Historical Society, 1978).

"Illinois country doctor": Willene and George Hendrick, eds., *On the Illinois Frontier, 1840–1848* (Carbondale and Edwardsville: Southern Illinois University Press, 1981).

Lockjaw quote: Kate B. Carter, *Heart Throbs of the West,* vol. 7 (Salt Lake City: Daughters of the Utah Pioneers, 1946).

Esther Lovejoy: Tuberculosis in America: Esther C. P. Lovejoy, "My Medical School, 1890–1894," *Oregon Historical Quarterly,* vol. 75, no. 1 (Portland: Oregon Historical Society), March 1974.

Malaria in the U.S.A.: Willene and George Hendrick, eds., *On the Illinois Frontier, 1840–1848* (Carbondale and Edwardsville: Southern Illinois University Press, 1981). Ronald L. Numbers and Judith Walzer Leavitt, *Wisconsin Medicine: Historical Perspectives* (Madison: University of Wisconsin Press, 1981). Frances E. Quebbeman, *Medicine in Territorial Arizona* (Phoenix: Arizona Historical Foundation, 1966). Margaret Coffin, *Death in Early America* (New York: Nelson, 1989).

Rebecca: Juanita Brooks, ed., *Not by Bread Alone: The Journal of Martha Spence Heywood, 1850–1856* (Salt Lake City: Utah State Historical Society, 1978).

Agnes Reid: Judith Leavitt, *Brought to Bed: Childbearing in America, 1750 to 1950* (New York: Oxford University Press, 1986).

Hiram and Lucinda Rutherford: Willene and George Hendrick, eds., *On the Illinois Frontier, 1840–1848* (Carbondale and Edwardsville: Southern Illinois University Press, 1981).

Eleanor Galt Simmons: William M. Straight, M.D., "The Lady Doctor of the Grove," *Journal of the Florida Medical Association,* vol. 55, no. 8 (August 1968).

Tuberculosis in America: Esther C. P. Lovejoy, "My Medical School, 1890–1894," *Oregon Historical Quarterly,* vol. 75, no. 1 (Portland: Oregon Historical Society), March 1974.

9 · MEDICS IN THE MILITARY

Elizabeth Cushier: Elizabeth Cushier, *Medical Review* (New York: Parthier Publishing, 1901).

John Lauderdale incident: Daniel Barkowitz and Elizabeth Young Newsom, "Portrait of a Woman Doctor," *Journal of the South Carolina Medical Association,* vol. 89, no. 1 (January 1993).

Nursing during the Civil War: Beatrice Levin, *Women and Medicine* (Lincoln: Media Publishing, 1988). Roberts Bartholow, "Women in the Military," *New York Medical Journal,* vol. 5, no. 2 (May 1868). Nancy Woloch, *Women and the American Experience* (New York: Alfred A. Knopf, 1984). Stephen L. McDonough, *The Golden Ounce* (Grand Forks, North Dakota: University Printing Center, 1989). Susie King Taylor, *Reminiscences of My Life in Camp With the 33rd United States Colored Troops 1st S.C. Volunteers* (Boston: Published by the author, 1902). Richard Harrison Skyrock, "A Medical Perspective on the Civil War," *Medicine in America: Historical Essays* (Baltimore: Johns Hopkins Press, 1966).

Mary Walker: Walker manuscript, affidavit of L. J. Woeden at Utica, March 21, 1866 (Syracuse, New York: Syracuse University).

Anne Austin Young: James G. Ward, Jr., M.D., "That Crazy Anne Austin: Anne Austin Young, M.D., 1892–1989," *Journal of South Carolina Medical Association,* vol. 89, no. 1 (January 1993).

10. ETHNIC OUTREACH

African Americans in medicine: Gloria Moldow, *Women Doctors in Gilded-Age Washington: Race, Gender and Professionalization* (Urbana and Chicago: University of Illinois Press, 1987). Dr. Lucy Hughes Brown, "A Pioneer African-American Physician," *Journal of the South Carolina Medical Association,* vol. 89, no. 1 (January 1933). Maxine Martin, "Dr. Lucy Hughes Brown: Pioneer African-American Physician," *Journal of the South Carolina Medical Association,* vol. 89, no. 1 (January 1993). Thomas Wentsworth Higginson, *Army Life in a Black Regiment* (Boston: Beacon Press, 1962 [originally published in 1869]).

Lucy Brown: Dr. Lucy Hughes Brown, "A Pioneer African-American Physician," *Journal of the South Carolina Medical Association,* vol. 89, no. 1 (January 1933). Maxine Martin, "Dr. Lucy Hughes Brown: Pioneer African-American Physician," *Journal of the South Carolina Medical Association,* vol. 89, no. 1 (January 1993).

Rebecca Cole: Ruth J. Abram, *Send Us a Lady Physician* (New York: W. W. Norton & Co., 1985).

Anna Darrow: William M. Straight, M.D., "The Lady Doctor of the Grove," *Journal of the Florida Medical Association,* vol. 55, no. 8 (August 1968).

Bessie Efner: Alfred M. Rehwinkel, *Dr. Bessie: The Life Story and Romance of a Pioneer Lady Doctor* (St. Louis: Concordia Publishing House, 1963).

Matilda Evans: *Journal of the South Carolina Medical Association,* vol. 89, no. 1 (January 1993).

zona (Phoenix: Arizona Historical Foundation, 1966).

Susan La Flesche Picotte: La Flesche family papers, manuscript (Lincoln: Nebraska Historical Society, State Archives, Box 202b).

Doc Nellie: Helen MacKnight Doyle, *A Child Went Forth: The Autobiography of Dr. Helen MacKnight Doyle* (New York: Gotham House, 1934).

Bertha Van Hoosen: Bertha Van Hoosen, *Petticoat Surgeon* (Chicago: Pellegrini & Cudahy, 1947).

11. THE DOC IS IN

Nina Baierle: Shirley P. Wheeler, *Dr. Nina and the Panther* (New York: Dodd, Mead & Co., 1976).

Harriet Belcher: Ruth J. Abram, *Send Us a Lady Physician,* Harriet Belcher to Eliza Johnson, July 13, 1879 (New York: W. W. Norton & Co.).

Amelia Dann: Helen Dann Stringer, *Millie M.D., The Story of a Nineteenth Century Woman, 1846–1927* (Utica: North Country Books, 1992).

Bessie Efner: Alfred M. Rehwinkel, *Dr. Bessie: The Life Story and Romance of a Pioneer Lady Doctor* (St. Louis: Concordia Publishing House, 1963).

Federal law and Salt Lake City Ordinance: Kate B. Carter, *Heart Throbs of the West,* vol. 7 (Salt Lake City: Daughters of the Utah Pioneers, 1946). James O. Breedeen, ed., *Medicine in the West* (Manhattan, Kansas: Sunflower University Press, 1982).

Georgia Arbuckle Fix: Judy Alter, "Women Who Made the West," *Pioneer Doctor* (St. Louis: Concordia Publishing, 1983).

Rebecca Lee: Ruth J. Abram, *Send Us a Lady Physician* (New York: W. W. Norton & Co., 1985).

Lille Rosa Minika: La Flesche family papers, manuscript (Lincoln: Nebraska Historical Society, State Archives, Box 202b).

Gloria Moldow's book: Gloria Moldow, *Women Doctors in Gilded-Age Washington: Race, Gender and Professionalization* (Urbana and Chicago: University of Illinois Press, 1987).

Native American medicine: Kate B. Carter, *Heart Throbs of the West,* vols. 1 and 7 (Salt Lake City: Daughters of the Utah Pioneers, 1946). Virginia Bergman Peters, *Women of the Earth Lodges: Tribal Life on the Plains* (New York: Archon Books, 1995). Jack Weatherford, *Native Roots: How the Indians Enriched America* (New York: Fawcett Columbine, 1993). Frances E. Quebbeman, *Medicine in Territorial Ari-*

Margaret Ethel Fraser: Anne Byrd Kennon, "Dr. Martha Ethel V. Fraser," unpublished article (Denver: Denver Public Library Archives).

Mary Glassen: Vera Chance Ward, *How to Sleep on a Windy Night* (Phillipsburg, Kansas: Clar-Mar Press, 1970).

Jane Bruce Guignard: Jane Guignard Curry, "Jane Bruce Guignard, M.D.: 1876–1963" *Journal of the South Carolina Medical Association,* vol. 89, no. 1 (January 1993). H. H. DuBose, *Jane Bruice Guignard, M.D.,* unpublished manuscript.

Esther Hill Hawk: *The Daily American* (Manchester, New Hampshire), August 27, 1861.

Lillian Heath: Lillian Heath as told to Neal E. Miller, *The History of 111 West Lincoln Way,* 1954 manuscript 296A (Laramie: Wyoming Historical Society).

Sophie Herzog: Cindi Myers, "Daring Dr. Sophie," *True West,* vol. 41, no. 7 (July 1994).

Mary Putnam Jacobi: Mary Walsh, *Doctors Wanted: No Women Need Apply* (New Haven, Connecticut: Yale University Press, 1985). Ruth J. Abram, *Send Us a Lady Physician* (New York: W. W. Norton & Co., 1985).

Margaret Long: Kate B. Carter, *Heart Throbs of the West,* vol. 7 (Salt Lake City, Utah: Daughters of the Utah Pioneers, 1946).

Hannah E. Longshore: Beatrice Levin, *Women and Medicine* (Lincoln: Media Publishing, 1988). Kate Campbell Mead, M.D., "Medical Women of America," *Medical Review of Reviews* (March 1933).

Portia Lubchenco McKnight: Anna C. Petteys, *Dr. Portia: Her First Fifty Years in Medicine* (Denver: Golden Bell Press, 1964).

Elsie Pratt: Robert H. Shikes, M.D., *Rocky Mountain Medicine: Doctors, Drugs and Disease in Early Colorado* (Boulder: Johnson Books, 1986).

Doc Nellie: Helen MacKnight Doyle, *A Child Went Forth: The Autobiography of Dr. Helen MacKnight Doyle* (New York: Gotham House, 1934).

Mary Canaga Rowland: Mary Canaga Rowland, *The Memoirs of a Frontier Woman Doctor* (Seattle: Storm Peak Press, 1994).

Eleanor Galt Simmons: William M. Straight, M.D., "The Lady Doctor of the Grove," *Journal of the Florida Medical Association,* vol. 55, no. 8 (August 1968).

Margaret Stewart: Judith Leavitt, *Brought to Bed: Childbearing in America, 1750 to 1950* (New York: Oxford University Press, 1986).

Bertha Van Hoosen: Bertha Van Hoosen, *Petticoat Surgeon* (Chicago: Pellegrini & Cudahy, 1947).

12. FEES, BILLS, AND PAYMENT IN KIND

Ability to support: Francis R. Packard, *History of Medicine in the United States,* vols. I and II (New York: Paul B. Hoeber, Inc., 1931).

Sarah Campbell Allan: W. Curtis Worthington, M.D., "Psychiatrist and Humanitarian Sarah Campbell Allan (1861–1954): South Carolina's First Licensed Woman Physician" *Journal of the South Carolina Medical Association,* vol. 89, no. 1 (January 1993).

Susan Anderson: Virginia Cornell, *Doc Susie* (New York: Ivy Books, 1991).

Nina Baierle: Shirley P. Wheeler, *Dr. Nina and the Panther* (New York: Dodd, Mead & Co., 1976).

Harriet Belcher: Letter of Harriet Belcher to Eliza Johnson, Nov. 16, 1879, Archives and Special Collections on Women in Medicine (Medical College of Pennsylvania).

Elizabeth Blackwell: Elizabeth Blackwell, *Pioneer Work in Opening the Medical Profession to Women: Autobiographical Sketches* (New York: Shocken Books, 1977).

Jessie Laird Brodie: Gerald Weiggmanns, M.D., "Memo" (October 1991).

Anna Broomall: Beatrice Levin, *Women and Medicine* (Lincoln: Media Publishing, 1988).

Canadian physician: Jacalyn Duffin Langstaff, *A Nineteenth-Century Medical Life* (Toronto: University of Toronto Press, 1993).

Corrinne Chamberlin: W. R. Chilton, ed., *Gresham: Stories of Our Past* (Gresham, Oregon: Gresham Historical Society/ Davis and Fox Printing, Inc., 1993).

Anna Darrow: William M. Straight, M.D., "The Lady Doctor of the Grove," *Journal of the Florida Medical Association,* vol. 55, no. 8 (August 1968).

Richard Somerset Den: Rosa Newmark, "A Letter," *Western States Jewish Historical Quarterly,* vol. 5, no. 1 (1972).

Helen MacKnight Doyle: Helen MacKnight Doyle, *A Child Went Forth: The Autobiography of Dr. Helen MacKnight Doyle* (New York: Gotham House, 1934).

Bessie Efner: Alfred M. Rehwinkel, *Dr. Bessie: The Life Story and Romance of a Pioneer Lady Doctor* (St. Louis: Concordia Publishing House, 1963).

Georgia Arbuckle Fix: Judy Alter, "Women Who Made the West," *Pioneer Doctor* (St. Louis: Concordia Publishing, 1983).

Charles Forbes: Elizabeth Hampsten, *Read This Only to Yourself: The Private Writings of Midwestern Women, 1880–1910* (Bloomington: Indiana University Press, 1982).

Mary Glassen: Vera Chance Ward, *How to Sleep on a Windy Night* (Phillipsburg, Kansas: Clar-Mar Press, 1970).

Lillian Heath: Lillian Heath as told to Neal E. Miller, *The History of 111 West Lincoln Way,* 1954 manuscript 296A (Laramie: Wyoming Historical Society).

Idaho farmers' complaints: Molly Ladd Taylor, *Raising a Baby the Government Way: Mothers' Letters to the Children's Bureau, 1915–1932* (New Brunswick and London: Rutgers University Press, 1942).

Hannah Longshore: Beatrice Levin, *Women and Medicine* (Lincoln: Media Publishing, 1988).

Male physician in the Owens valley: Helen MacKnight Doyle, *A Child Went Forth: The Autobiography of Dr. Helen MacKnight Doyle* (New York: Gotham House, 1934).

Married Women's Act: Marilyn Ferris Motz, *True Sisterhood* (Albany: State University of New York Press, 1988).

Portia Lubchenco McKnight: Anna C. Petteys, *Dr. Portia: Her First Fifty Years in Medicine* (Denver: Golden Bell Press, 1964).

Medical society charges: Margaret Coffin, *Death in Early America* (New York: Nelson, 1989).

Minnesota patient's letter: Molly Ladd Taylor, *Raising a Baby the Government Way: Mothers' Letters to the Children's Bureau, 1915–1932* (New Brunswick and London: Rutgers University Press, 1942).

Bethenia Owens-Adair: *Dr. Owens-Adair: Some of Her Life Experiences* (Portland, Oregon: Mann & Beach, 1905), quoted from Cathy Luchetti, *Women of the West* (New York: Orion, 1982).

Physician's bill: Kate Campbell Hurd-Mead, M.D., *History of Women in Medicine* (Boston: Milford House, 1973).

Claudia Potter: Dr. Claudia Potter, *Recollections of Anesthesia Practice (1906–1948),* manuscript (Park Ridge, Ill.: Museum of Anesthesiology, 1992).

James Rutherford: Willene and George Hendrick, eds., Dr. Hiram Rutherford, *On the Illinois Frontier, 1840–1848* (Carbondale and Edwardsville: Southern Illinois University Press, 1981).

Lena Schreier: Lena Schreier, "Utah's Oldest Doctor Is a Lady," *Utah Medical Bulletin* (March 1971).

Hilla Sheriff: *Journal of the South Carolina Medical Association,* vol. 89, no. 1 (January 1993).

Sisters of Charity: Robert F. Karolevitz, *Doctors of the Old West: A Pictorial History of Medicine on the Frontier* (Seattle: Superior Publishing Company, 1967).

Margaret Stewart: Judith Leavitt, *Brought to Bed: Childbearing in America, 1750 to 1950* (New York: Oxford University Press, 1986).

Bertha Van Hoosen: Bertha Van Hoosen, *Petticoat Surgeon* (Chicago: Pellegrini & Cudahy, 1947).

Waukesha County fees: Ronald L. Numbers and Judith Walzer Leavitt, *Wisconsin Medicine: Historical Perspectives* (Madison: University of Wisconsin Press, 1981).

Western Medical Society fees: Urling C. Coe, M.D., *Frontier Doctor* (New York: Macmillan, 1939).

13. RURAL REMEDIES

Elizabeth Blackwell: Elizabeth Blackwell, *Pioneer Work in Opening the Medical Profession to Women: Autobiographical Sketches* (New York: Shocken Books, 1977).

Daughters of Utah Pioneers account: Kate B. Carter, *Heart Throbs of the West,* vol. 7 (Salt Lake City: Daughters of the Utah Pioneers, 1946).

Georgia Arbuckle Fix: Judy Alter, "Women Who Made the West," *Pioneer Doctor* (St. Louis: Concordia Publishing, 1983).

Paulina Lyman: Claudia L. Bushman, *Mormon Sisters: Women in Early Utah* (Salt Lake City: Olympus Publishing Co, 1976).

Portia Lubchenco McKnight: Anna C. Petteys, *Dr. Portia: Her First Fifty Years in Medicine* (Denver: Golden Bell Press, 1964).

Sophia Presley: "Sophia Presley, Camden County," *New Jersey Medicine: The Journal of the Medical Society of New Jersey,* vol. 87, no. 3 (March 1990).

Mary Canaga Rowland: Mary Canaga Rowland, *The Memoirs of a Frontier Woman Doctor* (Seattle: Storm Peak Press, 1994).

Kate Snow: Claire Wilcox Noall, "Utah's Pioneer Women Doctors," *Improvement Era,* vol. XLII (January 1939).

Treatments cited throughout the chapter: Elizabeth Bennion, *Antique Medical Instruments* (Berkeley and Los Angeles: University of California Press, 1979). Lee Anderson, *Iowa Pharmacy, 1880–1905: An Experiment in Professionalism* (Iowa City: University of Iowa Press, 1989). F. E. Daniel, M.D., *Daniel's Texas Medical Journal: A Monthly Journal of Medicine and Surgery,* vol. III (July 1887–June 1888). M. W. Harrison, M.D., "Tuberculosis," *Illinois Medical Journal,* vol. 32, no. 2. William P. DeWees, *Physical and Medical Treatment of Children* (Philadelphia: Lea & Blanchard, 1847). "Pioneer Medicines," *Heart Throbs of the West,* vol. 7 (Salt Lake City: Daughters of the Utah Pioneers, 1939). Frances E. Quebbeman, *Medicine in Territorial Arizona* (Phoenix: Arizona Historical Foundation, 1966).

Bertha Van Hoosen: Bertha Van Hoosen, *Petticoat Surgeon* (Chicago: Pellegrini & Cudahy, 1947).

14. KITCHEN TABLE SURGERY

Harriet Belcher: Ruth J. Abram, *Send Us a Lady Physician* (New York: W. W. Norton & Co., 1985).

Sarah Bowen: Jake Spidel, Jr., *Doctors of Medicine in New Mexico: A History of Health and Medical Practice, 1886–1986*

(Albuquerque: University of New Mexico Press, 1986).

Emmeline Cleveland: Regina Markell Morantz-Sanchez, *Sympathy and Science* (New York: Oxford University Press, 1985).

Samuel Gregory: Samuel Gregory, *Letter to Ladies in Favor of Female Physicians* (Boston: American Medical Education Society, 1850).

E. Harryman: Alfred M. Rehwinkel, *Dr. Bessie: The Life Story and Romance of a Pioneer Lady Doctor* (St. Louis: Concordia Publishing House, 1963).

William A. Lindsay: Katherine Mandusic McDonnell, eds., *The Journals of William A. Lindsay: An Ordinary Nineteenth-Century Physician's Surgical Cases* (Indianapolis: Indiana Historical Society, 1989).

Portia Lubchenco McKnight: Anna C. Petteys, *Dr. Portia: Her First Fifty Years in Medicine* (Denver: Golden Bell Press, 1964).

Claudia Potter: Dr. Claudia Potter, *Recollections of Anesthesia Practice (1906–1948),* manuscript (Park Ridge, Ill.: Museum of Anesthesiology, 1992).

Ellis Shipp: Blanche E. Rose, "Early Utah Medical Practice," *Utah Historical Quarterly,* vol. 21, no. 31 (1953).

Surgery: Frances R. Packard, *History of Medicine in the United States,* vol. I and II (New York: Paul B. Hoeber, Inc., 1931).

Bertha Van Hoosen: Bertha Van Hoosen, *Petticoat Surgeon* (Chicago: Pellegrini & Cudahy, 1947).

15. PINK PILLS AND INNOVATIONS

Susan Anderson: Virginia Cornell, *Doc Susie* (New York: Ivy Books, 1991).

Elizabeth Blackwell: Elizabeth Blackwell, *Pioneer Work in Opening the Medical Profession to Women: Autobiographical Sketches* (New York: Shocken Books, 1977).

Childbirth procedures: Catherine M. Scholten, *Childbearing in American Society, 1650–1850* (New York: New York University Press, 1985). Irvine Loudon, *Death in Childbirth: An International Study of Maternal Care and Maternal Mortality, 1800–1950* (Oxford: Clarendon Press, 1992).

Elizabeth Cushier: Elizabeth B. Thelberg, M.D., ed., "Autobiography of Dr. Elizabeth Cushier," *Medical Review of Reviews* (March 1933).

Amelia Dann: Helen Dann Stringer, *Millie M.D., The Story of a Nineteenth Century Woman* (Utica: North Country Books, 1992).

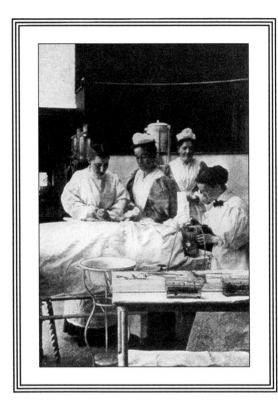

Anna Darrow: William M. Straight, M.D., "The Lady Doctor of the Grove," *Journal of the Florida Medical Association,* vol. 55, no. 8 (August 1968).

Bessie Efner: Alfred M. Rehwinkel, *Dr. Bessie: The Life Story and Romance of a Pioneer Lady Doctor* (St. Louis: Concordia Publishing House, 1963).

Sarah Gillespie: Suzanne L. Bunkers, *All Will Yet Be Well: The Diary of Sarah Gillespie Huftalen, 1873–1952* (Iowa City: University of Iowa Press, 1993).

Lillian Heath: Lillian Heath as told to Neal E. Miller, *The History of 111 West Lincoln Way,* 1954 manuscript 296A (Laramie: Wyoming Historical Society).

Herbal remedies: Jim Long, "Herbal Medicines in the Civil War," *The Herb Quarterly* (Fall 1992).

Portia Lubchenco McKnight: Anna C. Petteys, *Dr. Portia: Her First Fifty Years in Medicine* (Denver: Golden Bell Press, 1964).

Emma Sutro Merritt: Helen MacKnight Doyle, *A Child Went Forth: The Autobiography of Dr. Helen MacKnight Doyle* (New York: Gotham House, 1934).

Claudia Potter: Dr. Claudia Potter, *Recollections of Anesthesia Practice (1906–1948),* manuscript (Park Ridge, Ill.: Museum of Anesthesiology, 1992).

Mary Canaga Rowland: Mary Canaga Rowland, *The Memoirs of a Frontier Woman Doctor* (Seattle: Storm Peak Press, 1994).

Ellis Shipp: Ellis Shipp Musser, ed., *The Early Autobiography and Diary of Ellis Reynolds Shipp* (Salt Lake City: Deseret News Press, 1962).

Bertha Van Hoosen: Bertha Van Hoosen, *Petticoat Surgeon* (Chicago: Pellegrini & Cudahy, 1947).

16. BREACHING THE BULWARKS

Abortion in the United States: Rickie Solinger, *The Abortionist* (Berkeley: University of California Press, 1994).

Ruth Barnard: Rickie Solinger, *The Abortionist* (Berkeley: University of California Press, 1994).

Birth control: Gloria Moldow, *Women Doctors in Gilded-Age Washington: Race, Gender and Professionalization* (Urbana and Chicago: University of Illinois Press, 1987). Margaret Sanger, Diary 1869, manuscript (Washington, D.C.: Library of Congress). William G. Rothstein, *American Physicians in the Nineteenth Century: From Sects to Science* (Baltimore and London: Johns Hopkins University Press, 1971).

Elizabeth Blackwell: Elizabeth Blackwell, *Pioneer Work in Opening the Medical Profession to Women: Autobiographical Sketches* (New York: Shocken Books, 1977).

Mary Colander: Robert H. Shikes, M.D., *Rocky Mountain Medicine: Doctors, Drugs and Disease in Early Colorado* (Boulder: Johnson Books, 1986).

Daniel's Medical Journal: F. E. Daniel, M.D., *Daniel's Texas Medical Journal: A Monthly Journal of Medicine and Surgery,* vol. III (July 1887 to June 1888).

Doc Millie: Helen Dann Stringer, *Millie M.D., The Story of a Nineteenth Century Woman, 1846–1927* (Utica: North Country Books, 1992).

The People's Home Medical Companion: Alice B. Stockham, *The People's Home Medical Companion* (Chicago: Alice B. Stockham & Co., 1890).

Mary Canaga Rowland: Mary Canaga Rowland, *The Memoirs of a Frontier Woman Doctor* (Seattle: Storm Peak Press, 1994).

Margaret Sanger: Nancy Woloch, *Women and the American Experience* (New York: Alfred A. Knopf, 1984).

Alice B. Stockham: Alice B. Stockham, M.D., *Tokology: A Book for Every Woman* (Chicago: Alice B. Stockham & Co., 1890).

Rose Williams: Elizabeth Hampsten, *Read This Only to Yourself: The Private Writings of Midwestern Women, 1880–1910* (Bloomington: Indiana University Press, 1982).

17. "Lying-in" and Childbirth

Children's Bureau letter: Molly Ladd Taylor, *Raising a Baby the Government Way: Mothers' Letters to the Children's Bureau, 1915–1932* (New Brunswick and London: Rutgers University Press, 1942).

Elizabeth Cushier: Elizabeth B. Thelberg, M.D., ed., "Autobiography of Dr. Elizabeth Cushier," *Medical Review of Reviews* (March 1933).

Amelia Dann: Helen Dann Stringer, *Millie M.D., The Story of a Nineteenth Century Woman, 1846–1927* (Utica: North Country Books, 1992).

Anna Darrow: William M. Straight, M.D., "The Lady Doctor of the Grove," *Journal of the Florida Medical Association,* vol. 55, no. 8 (August 1968).

Mary Dixon-Jones: Judith Leavitt, *Brought to Bed: Childbearing in America, 1750 to 1950* (New York: Oxford University Press, 1986).

Doctors in 1910: Irving Loudon, *Death in Childbirth: An International Study of Maternal Care* (Oxford: Clarendon Press, 1992).

Helen MacKnight Doyle: Helen MacKnight Doyle, *A Child Went Forth: The Autobiography of Dr. Helen MacKnight Doyle* (New York: Gotham House, 1934).

Bessie Efner: Alfred M. Rehwinkel, *Dr. Bessie: The Life Story and Romance of a Pioneer Lady Doctor* (St. Louis: Concordia Publishing House, 1963).

Katherine Gibson Fougera: Katherine Gibson Fougera, *With Custer's Cavalry* (Lincoln: University of Nebraska Press, 1986).

Mary Glassen: Vera Chance Ward, *How to Sleep on a Windy Night* (Phillipsburg, Kansas: Clar-Mar Press, 1970).

Jane Bruce Guignard: "Jane Bruce Guignard, M.D.: 1876–1963," *Journal of the South Carolina Medical Association* (January 1993).

Lillian Heath: Lillian Heath as told to Neal E. Miller, *The History of 111 West Lincoln Way,* 1954 manuscript 296A (Laramie: Wyoming Historical Society).

William Lindsay: Katherine Mandusic McDonnell, ed., *The Journals of William A. Lindsay; An Ordinary Nineteenth-Century Physician's Surgical Cases* (Indianapolis: Indiana Historical Society, 1989).

Esther Lovejoy: Irving Loudon, *Death in Childbirth: An International Study of Maternal Care* (Oxford: Clarendon Press, 1992).

Maine minister: George Gregory, *Medical Morals* (New York: published by the author, 1853).

Male physician: George Gregory, *Medical Morals* (New York: published by the author, 1853).

Nettie Fowler McCormick: Judith Leavitt, *Brought to Bed: Childbearing in America, 1750 to 1950* (New York: Oxford University Press, 1986).

Portia Lubchenco McKnight: Anna C. Petteys, *Dr. Portia: Her First Fifty Years in Medicine* (Denver: Golden Bell Press, 1964).

Minnesota woman: Mary Canaga Rowland, *The Memoirs of a Frontier Woman Doctor* (Seattle: Storm Peak Press, 1994).

Columbus Pemberton: John Kent Folmar, ed., *This State of Wonders, The Letters of an Iowa Farm Family, 1858–1861* (Iowa City: University of Iowa Press, 1986).

Claudia Potter: Dr. Claudia Potter, *Recollections of Anesthesia Practice (1906–1948),* manuscript (Park Ridge, Ill.: Museum of Anesthesiology, 1992).

Mary Canaga Rowland: Mary Canaga Rowland, *The Memoirs of a Frontier Woman Doctor* (Seattle: Storm Peak Press, 1994).

Hulda Smith: Kate B. Carter, *Heart Throbs of the West,* vol. 7 (Salt Lake City: Daughters of the Utah Pioneers, 1946).

Dr. Q. C. Smith: F. E. Daniel, M.D., *Daniel's Texas Medical Journal: A Monthly Journal of Medicine and Surgery,* vol. III (July 1887 to June 1888).

Bertha Van Hoosen: Bertha Van Hoosen, *Petticoat Surgeon* (Chicago: Pellegrini & Cudahy, 1947).

Young doctors: Judith Leavitt, *Brought to Bed: Childbearing in America, 1750 to 1950* (New York: Oxford University Press, 1986).

Index

❧❧❧❧